D1251002

Shifting Loyalties

The University of North Carolina Press   Chapel Hill

Shifting Loyalties

The Union Occupation of Eastern North Carolina

JUDKIN BROWNING

McDowell County Public Library
90 West Court Street
Marion, NC 28752

© 2011 The University of North Carolina Press
All rights reserved. Designed by Courtney Leigh Baker and set
in Garamond Premier Pro by Tseng Information Systems, Inc.
Manufactured in the United States of America. The paper in this
book meets the guidelines for permanence and durability of the
Committee on Production Guidelines for Book Longevity of the
Council on Library Resources. The University of North Carolina
Press has been a member of the Green Press Initiative since 2003.

Library of Congress Cataloging-in-Publication Data
Browning, Judkin.
Shifting loyalties : the union occupation of eastern North Carolina /
Judkin Browning. — 1st ed.
p. cm.
Includes bibliographical references and index.
ISBN 978-0-8078-3468-8 (cloth : alk. paper)
1. Beaufort Region (N.C.) — History, Military — 19th century.
2. New Bern Region (N.C.) — History, Military — 19th century.
3. Beaufort Region (N.C.) — Social conditions — 19th century.
4. New Bern Region (N.C.) — Social conditions — 19th century.
5. North Carolina — History — Civil War, 1861–1865 — Social aspects.
6. Military occupation — Social aspects — North Carolina — Atlantic
Coast — History — 19th century. 7. Civil-military relations — North
Carolina — Atlantic Coast — History — 19th century. 8. Atlantic
Coast (N.C.) — History, Military — 19th century. 9. United States —
History — Civil War, 1861–1865 — Occupied territories. 10. United
States — History — Civil War, 1861–1865 — Social aspects. I. Title.
F264.B37B76 2011
975.6′192 — dc22
2010034639

15 14 13 12 11   5 4 3 2 1

To my mother and father:
JOANN BROWNING
(1946–1992)
JASON BROWNING
(1945–1994)

CONTENTS

ILLUSTRATIONS

ACKNOWLEDGMENTS

So many people read all or parts of this manuscript at different times and offered valuable comments and criticisms that I fear I cannot thank them all enough. John Inscoe read every chapter minutely and always gave sound advice and extraordinary encouragement; he is both a mentor and a good friend. James C. Cobb, Kathleen Clark, Peter Charles Hoffer, Thomas G. Dyer, Ronald E. Butchart, David Perry, Solomon K. Smith, Bruce Stewart, and Tim Silver each provided direction, suggestions, and constructive criticisms that greatly improved the final product. Jane Turner Censer and Robert Kenzer commented on part of this manuscript when it was a paper delivered at the Southern Historical Association, while George Rable and Susannah Ural did the same for various paper presentations at Society for Military History conferences. I thank Steve Batterson, a gifted writer in another genre, who constantly challenged me to become a better writer. I also thank the two anonymous readers for the University of North Carolina Press for offering significant commentary that helped me revise, refine, and polish the manuscript.

This book could not have been written without much financial aid to fund many research trips. I would particularly like to thank the University of Georgia (UGA) for a Presidential Fellowship and a Dean's Award in Humanities; the North Caroliniana Society for an Archie K. Davis Scholarship; the Southern Historical Collection for a J. Carlyle Sitterson Research Grant; the Colonial Dames for an American History Scholarship; the U.S. Center for Military History for its generous fellowship; Appalachian State University for a University Research Council Grant; the UGA History Department for a Warner-Fite Scholarship, and especially Dr. Robert Pratt, who, as UGA's History Department chair, granted me several individual travel funds to aid me in my research.

The research for this project required me to go many places up and down the eastern seaboard, and I have been fortunate to be helped by numerous friendly and knowledgeable archivists along the way. I thank the staffs at the American Antiquarian Society, Massachusetts Historical Society, Beverly Historical Society, Worcester Historical Museum, Baker Library of the Harvard Business School, National Archives (both in Washington, D.C., and in College Park, Maryland), Library of Congress, U.S. Army Military History Institute in Carlisle, Pennsylvania, North Carolina State Archives, Southern Historical Collection and North Carolina Collection at the University of North Carolina at Chapel Hill (UNC), Duke University Special Collections, Emory University Special Collections, East Carolina University Special Collections, and Carteret County Historical Society. The Connecticut Historical Society and the Simsbury Historical Society in Simsbury, Connecticut, greatly assisted me by photocopying and mailing me documents.

Certain members of these repositories require special mention. John White, Richard Schrader, and Laura Clark Brown of the Southern Historical Collection have offered invaluable help during my numerous visits over the years. Jason Tomberlin provided me with companionship and, of course, expert assistance while at the North Carolina State Archives, then later in his new position at UNC's North Carolina Collection. I wager that no one knows the collections at the North Carolina State Archives better than the recently retired George Stevenson, who was an immense help to me there, as was A. Christopher Meekins, who always cheerfully led me in the right direction, especially when I thought I had encountered dead ends. Keith Longiotti guided me through the North Carolina Collection's photographs and provided reproductions for this book; Kim Cumber did great detective work to find some elusive images from the North Carolina State Archives, and David Montgomery provided assistance and a photograph from the Carteret County Historical Society in Morehead City.

I am indebted to many friends who allowed me to stay with them, some on multiple occasions and some for weeks at a time, while on these research junkets. Mike and Corliss Bradley graciously hosted my wife and me in Beaufort. Lindy Aldrich generously let me stay two weeks with her in Medford, Massachusetts, during a brutal heat wave in the summer of 2003. Jessica Anders provided lodging at her apartment in Washington, D.C., and much encouragement during my visits. Ms. Beverly Kelchner ("Aunt Bev") opened her home in Carlisle, Pennsylvania, to me for a week. Michael Thomas Smith deserves special mention for letting me stay with him at Penn State while traveling on research, for joining me on weekend excursions to Civil War battlefields, for not suing me when I accidentally lined a softball into his eye necessitating dozens of stitches, and for being an intellectual companion to sound ideas off of both grand and ridiculous. Michael and Rachel Noto have graciously allowed me to stay with them on many, many research trips to the Raleigh area and have pretended that they never get tired of seeing me. Chris Hoch probably has the distinction of letting me sleep under his roof in Washington, D.C., the greatest number of times over the last ten years. Chris has been a close friend and supporter since we first met in Mrs. Hicks's fifth-grade classroom in 1984. I enjoy every conversation, tennis match, softball game, and baseball road trip we undertake.

Finally, I thank my wife Greta for all her love, support, and patience. As this work goes to press, we are basking in the joy that is our beautiful infant daughter, Bethany. These certainly are the two most important women in my life. Regardless of how my academic career turns out, asking Greta to marry me was easily the best decision I have ever made.

INTRODUCTION

As soon as the Civil War ended in the spring of 1865, northern journalist Sidney Andrews embarked on a tour of the recently defeated southern states. As he made his way through the coastal towns of Beaufort and New Bern, North Carolina, that summer Andrews was struck by the Janus-faced loyalty of local whites, many of whom had lived quietly under Union occupation for the previous three years. He described a puzzling irony in the region: "The North Carolinian calls himself a Unionist, but he makes no special pretence of love for the Union." Andrews already detected a streak of southern nationalism in the Beaufort–New Bern region only weeks after the southern nation had been laid to rest. He sensed that white professions of Unionism were fragile at best. The journalist employed an apt metaphor to describe the waning strength of national allegiance in the region and state, proclaiming that the North Carolinian "wears his mask of nationality so lightly there is no difficulty in removing it."[1]

Indeed, many North Carolinians, but especially whites in the Beaufort–New Bern region, had been wearing masks and changing one for another for the previous five years. Local whites had professed themselves Unionists before the war. Though New Bern residents began calling for secession soon after Abraham Lincoln's election, their Beaufort neighbors maintained a steady conditional Unionism until Lincoln summoned troops on April 15, 1861. Then residents of both towns removed their Union masks and eagerly put on Confederate ones. Only a year later, when the Union army arrived to occupy the region, many of those same residents, on being promised enhanced economic benefits coupled with the social status quo antebellum, quietly put their Confederate masks into storage and donned the old, familiar Union masks once again. However, by the time Andrews visited in 1865, he sensed that many of those same residents had already taken their Confederate masks down from the attic and dusted them off. If the new postwar Union included emancipation, enfranchisement, and education for blacks, as well as the threat of social equality, then whites would strip off their Union masks and show their true allegiance — identifying with the ideals, especially white supremacy, of the defunct Confederacy.

Union forces marched into New Bern on March 14, 1862, and Beaufort on the twenty-fifth, marking the beginning of a military occupation that would last the rest of the war. With Union occupation came thousands of Federal soldiers, government officials, and northern missionaries and teachers. For the next three years, residents of Beaufort and New Bern would question their own loyalties and negotiate with their occupiers and each other in an effort to carve out social, cultural, and political identities. African Americans utilized the northern agents to change the circumstances of their lives despite passionate white resistance. A study like this invites many questions: How did the lives of these whites and blacks change? How did they adapt to new stresses? How did they negotiate with their occupiers to create their own space? How did the occupiers react to the local population, whose values were so foreign to their own?

This book focuses the lens on one place to better understand the long-term impact of the Civil War on local civilians, while analyzing the effects of war on society and the nature of civil-military relations, as well as offering a social analysis of both military and civilian participants. Thus, this work employs a bottom-up approach to top-down books on military occupation policy, and it supplements the broad strokes painted by more comprehensive works on Union occupation throughout the South by offering a concentrated point of perspective in order to see how occupation played out on the local level.[2] It also holds Federal soldiers, northern benevolent society members, and the residents themselves — white and black, men and women — accountable for their actions; it does not view them simply as pawns in a larger power struggle or as passive victims of impersonal historical forces. This work not only explores why white residents, slaves, missionaries, and soldiers took the actions they did; it also analyzes how their actions affected the economic, social, political, and cultural dynamics of the region.

Especially important to this story is the experience of the black population. Much has been written about African American life during wartime and military occupation; however, most scholarly works have been concerned with how Union agents proscribed black freedom and autonomy. Instead of examining how events affected blacks, this work treats blacks as savvy pragmatists who used the Union army and agents of northern benevolent societies to attain the four pillars of their empowerment: escape, employment, enlistment, and education. Blacks gained much success in those years of the war when they were able to assert their independence, confident in the support of the Federal government. These very actions, however, led to the white backlash against occupation. Race became central to the hostile white reaction to occupation.

AT THE OUTBREAK of war, the white residents of North Carolina's Craven and Carteret counties were largely representative of those from the eastern, coastal region. They historically voted Whig, were not major cotton producers, and felt they had much to lose from secession due to their mercantile ties to the Atlantic world. Initial resistance to secession evaporated in the aftermath of Fort Sumter in April 1861. When President Lincoln called for 75,000 volunteers to help put down the southern rebellion, Carteret and Craven residents joined their North Carolina brethren in rejecting Lincoln and embracing the cause of the Confederacy. By June, hundreds of local whites had enlisted in companies to fight for the South.

Yet for all this initial enthusiasm, Union occupation in March 1862 forced the creation of another new identity as white residents tried to portray themselves as loyal to the United States. The president and his cabinet anticipated that the majority of white citizens would be loyal and expected to draw on this sentiment to foster a harmonious restoration. In May 1862 Lincoln appointed a native son, Edward Stanly, as military governor of North Carolina, with orders to enforce state laws as they existed prior to the war. Early results seemed positive, but the experience of Union occupation would ultimately lead to complicated relations between occupiers and occupied. Residents (even Unionists) altered their allegiances over perceived abuses of Federal power and serious disagreements over racial policies. Some studies of military occupation, even in certain counties of eastern North Carolina, have seen unrestrained class warfare between planters and nonslaveholders as a result of the arrival of Union forces.[3] In the region comprising Carteret and Craven counties, however, local whites did not turn on each other but rather unified in their opposition to Federal policies. Ultimately, these citizens demonstrated that race was far more important than their economic interests.

The complicated nature of loyalties pervaded the coast of eastern North Carolina. A few white residents maintained a strong streak of southern nationalism throughout the war. As historian Anne Sarah Rubin has argued, this nationalism was not so much a regard for the Confederate political state as it was an emotional and sentimental attachment to the sense of a unique and special culture, history, and social perspective that came with being a southerner. Occasionally these whites negotiated with Union forces, but that did not abnegate their sentiments; as Rubin suggests, "Placing themselves first did not necessarily indicate a rejection of the Confederate nation." For the most part, these few individuals took pride in resisting Federal occupation either physically or verbally. Similarly, some people maintained a steadfast loyalty to the Union, resisting or speaking out against the Confederacy—often at their peril—before the Union forces arrived. Yet, despite their loyalty, many of these Unionists resented some Federal policies. As Margaret Storey has written in her study of Unionists, "Though Southerners' loyalty to the Union represented a rejection of the Confederate state, it did not necessarily represent a rejection of Southern culture or values." Hence, these Unionists still placed a premium on honor, duty, and the maintenance of strict social divisions, which often confused Union authorities. Scholars have often separated white citizens of the South into one of these two camps—southern nationalists, who occasionally placed self-interest above their southern state, and staunch Unionists, who nevertheless adhered to southern values.[4]

Loyalty, however, was often quite fluid and driven by practicalities. An individual could have multiple loyalties with varying degrees of attachment to each, depending on his or her circumstances and agenda.[5] By far the majority of white citizens in eastern North Carolina had flexible loyalties— that is, they simultaneously adhered to a sense of southern nationalism while proclaiming an honest attachment to the Union. They had a form of dual citizenship, if you will. After all, they were southerners but also Americans. For these confused people, the strength of their convictions rested on a sliding scale—liable to be more pro-Union or pro-Confederate at any given time, depending on their individual circumstances.[6] This explains why some residents joined the Confederate army in 1861 but then deserted and signed up with the Union army in 1862; how Union soldiers could be so confused by contradictory actions of residents; and how people could profess Unionism, only to later take violent action against Union authorities. They believed in each of their competing allegiances at the different times they were pledging them. When the occupation began, these citizens did not even know themselves which allegiance would win out. Their loyalties were forged in the crucible of military occupation. At the end of that occupation, a great many of those with flexible loyalties shifted to the Confederate side in response to what they perceived as harsh enforcement of Federal principles and rejection of long-standing social values of southern society.[7]

African Americans were a fourth group of protagonists who complicated the occupation. Unlike in the case of whites, there was no ambiguity about black loyalties. African Americans clearly repudiated the ideals of the Confederacy (as well as the sense of white southern uniqueness associated with it) and wholeheartedly embraced the spirit of freedom, liberty, and autonomy that came with attachment to the United States. The difficulty was that many Union soldiers had a profound distaste for this group of staunch Unionist allies and did not welcome their assistance as readily as they could have. Military occupations are messy and complicated undertakings, made all the more so by multiple groups of competing nationalists with decidely different ethnic backgrounds.[8]

ONCE THE OCCUPATION BEGAN, whites and blacks forged new identities for themselves in the tense atmosphere of change. Freedpeople sought to attain autonomy over their own lives and assert their independence, especially from their former masters. Whites took oaths of allegiance and proclaimed themselves Unionists, though such claims did not necessarily show ideological motivation. Both whites and blacks sought to create circumstances that would give them the best means to support themselves and their families. Both knew what they wanted and were cognizant of the risks inherent in their choices. Though each group sought to protect their own interests, their actions revealed multiple, often divergent motives. Many wealthy white merchants found themselves initially embracing their occupiers, largely for financial reasons. Other locals gave lip service to the Union in order to protect their personal property, while their true allegiance remained ambiguous. Those without property to protect—local poor whites—took advantage of the Union army's arrival and invitations to improve their economic and physical situations. In time, many of these whites would change their attitudes in response to Federal actions.

Unlike the economic and survivalist pragmatism that motivated whites, African Americans who migrated to or inhabited the Beaufort–New Bern region demonstrated a multifaceted array of motivations for their actions. Repudiating their slave heritage, blacks sought control over their own bodies, minds, and material conditions. They asserted their independence, validated their manhood/womanhood and self-sufficiency, and improved the educational and material conditions for themselves and their children. Their actions, both symbolic and physical, often led to violent conflict with local whites, confrontations that strained the Union occupiers' ability to govern the region and preserve the peace, especially as white residents became increasingly hostile toward black assertions of self-determination. African Americans also had to negotiate with the Union soldiers and northern missionaries who entered the region with their own preconceptions of African Americans' innate abilities. While utilizing northern agents to help gain their freedom and autonomy, freedpeople had to endure soldiers' virulent racism and missionaries' sense of northern, middle-class, social, and spiritual superiority to achieve their objectives.

Union soldiers also found themselves changed by their time in eastern North Carolina. Practically nothing has been written about how occupation revised the views of Union soldiers who served in the region. The few studies of the military side of occupation analyze policy decisions from within the Union command structure.[9] This study offers a firsthand, ground-level account of how those decisions affected the Union soldiers who carried out Federal policies. For these Union troops, the experience of occupation altered their understandings of national and racial identities. Many of them—even some of the hardiest abolitionists—could not immediately overcome their long-standing racial prejudices. Many found their convictions tested and their patriotism weakened in the face of the local hostility, petty tyrannies of army life, and unrelenting monotony of occupation. Regardless of the strength of their commitment to ultimate victory, Union soldiers found that their attitudes and perspectives had changed significantly, especially their initial idealistic views of the war, their understanding of the enemy, their perceptions of African Americans, and their government's national policies.

TO TELL THIS COMPLICATED story in a comprehensible fashion, I have structured the book in a loosely chronological format with specific thematic emphases along the way. The opening three chapters are more traditionally linear in time line, while the last four explore specific themes within the overall chronological format. The first chapter examines the antebellum background of the two communities that experienced long-term military occupation during the war. It lays out the social, economic, political, and cultural milieu in Carteret and Craven counties (and specifically their county seats of Beaufort and New Bern). Chapter 2 focuses on the first year of the war and how each county mobilized its citizenry to fight for the Confederacy. So much about the region was shaped by that first year, before occupation, that it provides the context for and even foreshadows what was to come when the Union forces actually arrived. The third chapter examines the developments upon their arrival and the initial, largely positive responses of the region's communities to the occupying troops.

Chapter 4 begins the first thematic examination: how African Americans reacted to and used the northern forces to improve their physical, economic, and social situations. The fifth chapter explores the role played by northern benevolent societies in helping to uplift the supposedly degraded blacks they expected to find in occupied coastal North Carolina. Chapter 6 shifts the focus onto the northern soldiers who occupied the region, examining how that experience affected and changed them. The seventh and final chapter studies the local white reaction to prolonged Union occupation; it reveals how the initially benign response of white citizens shifted to a more belligerent tone by the end of the war due to social, cultural, and political conflicts during the occupation.

In short, this is a story of whites and blacks, men and women, soldiers and civilians, rebels and Unionists, all trying to carve out a social and cultural space for themselves during a tense time. It is the story of northern soldiers and benevolent societies imposing their distinct principles of civilization on a society with conflicting ideals. It is the story of local whites alternately accepting and rejecting Union occupation depending on the policies instituted. It is the story of how blacks sought to take advantage of these two conflicting cultures to improve their own situation, with a varied mix of successes and failures. Ultimately, this is a story of Americans trying to define their roles in a reconfigured country.

CHAPTER 1

Antebellum Antecedents

In 1524 Giovanni da Verrazano, an Italian explorer in the service of the French king, became the first European to view the southern tip of the Outer Banks. He painted a romantic picture of the tall sweeping grasses and majestic evergreens of Bogue Banks, the twenty-five-mile-long sandy island that teemed with dozens of species of exotic birds and sheltered tranquil Beaufort harbor from the tempestuous Atlantic Ocean. In 1585 Sir Richard Grenville, a captain in Sir Walter Raleigh's first English-sponsored colonization effort, became the first European to sail into Pamlico Sound and the mouth of the Neuse River, a few miles from present-day New Bern. Though Raleigh's colonization attempt ultimately failed, just over a century later Europeans began settling and developing the coastal areas that would become Craven and Carteret counties.[1]

Over the course of the colonial and antebellum periods, New Bern and Beaufort and their respective counties, Craven and Carteret, developed in different ways, yet maintained certain core similarities. Beaufort became primarily a fishing society, integrally attached to the surrounding waters, while New Bern grew into an agricultural and mercantile society connected to both the state's interior and the greater Atlantic world. In the 1850s both counties championed different political parties — Whigs for Carteret and Democrats for Craven. Despite a long history of Unionist sentiment in that tumultuous decade, Craven residents began calling for secession soon after Abraham Lincoln's election. Carteret residents maintained their Unionist leanings much longer. Though both ultimately supported secession, it took an extreme external threat to unite these two counties. Yet their residents had many fundamental similarities. They shared a powerful attachment to racial slavery and a fervent desire for commercial prosperity. Both had strong economic reasons for avoiding war, but equally strong social reasons

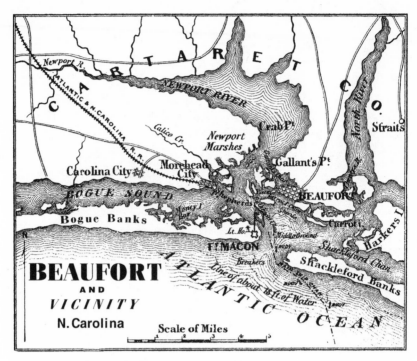

Map of Beaufort and surrounding area based on an inset from J. H. Colton, *Topographical Map of North and South Carolina, a Large Portion of Georgia, and Part of Adjoining States* (New York, 1861)

for acceding to secession. Though they had their differences, their social, cultural, and economic congruities ultimately shaped their experience of military occupation during the Civil War in very similar ways.

FROM THE EARLIEST DAYS of European settlement, New Bern was a more active, thriving port than Beaufort, though the latter possessed the best harbor in the state. With the widest mouth of any river in the continental United States, the Neuse made New Bern a gateway into the colony. Ships passed through Ocracoke Inlet and sailed through Pamlico Sound into the Neuse River to New Bern, where goods could be moved either up the river or overland on a system of roads that emanated from the port town. The town of Portsmouth was established at the northern tip of Core Banks at Ocracoke Inlet to aid New Bern's commercial trade. In a procedure known as "lightering," Portsmouth residents used their lower draft vessels to take half the cargo off a deep-draft vessel, which could not pass through relatively shallow Ocracoke Inlet while fully loaded, thus allowing the vessel to cross the bar and sail to New Bern.[2]

Oceangoing vessels could also opt to pass through the less dangerous Topsail Inlet farther south and sail into Beaufort's deep harbor with less difficulty. Twelve feet deep at low tide, and deemed "very safe and Navigable for Vessels of Great Burthen" by a 1766 act, Topsail Inlet offered greater access than its northern sister, Ocracoke, which only had a depth of nine feet. However, once merchants landed their goods at Beaufort, they found further distribution much more difficult. The North and Newport rivers flanking Beaufort were merely glorified creeks—five feet deep and extending less than fifteen miles into the interior. Moreover, no simple overland route existed between Beaufort and New Bern or other points in the interior. To get to New Bern, travelers from Beaufort either had to sail through the shoal-infested, shallow Core Sound (ranging from a few inches to seven feet in depth) to Pamlico Sound and the Neuse River, or travel over muddy roads that were intersected by creeks, bays, and bogs, and suffered from poor drainage. Road upkeep was nearly impossible. For all practical commercial purposes, Beaufort was cut off from North Carolina's interior from the time the first European settlers ventured into the region in 1696 until the eve of the Civil War.[3]

The tiny village that grew in the Core Sound region around 1709 was dubbed "Fishtown," before being officially named after England's duke of Beaufort in 1713. Whatever its official name, Beaufort was truly a "fish town." The opportunity for residents to make a living from the sea was great. Thousands of acres of estuaries created one of the most productive fishing regions on the Atlantic coast. On the eve of the Civil War, 95 percent of the inhabitants of Harkers Island, located in Core Sound near Beaufort, were fishermen. In 1860, 637 of the 1,029 (62 percent) white working men in the county earned their living on the waters.[4] In contrast, rapidly developing New Bern, named by a group of Swiss and German settlers in 1710, benefited from several agricultural, commercial, and political advantages in the eighteenth century. It was conveniently situated between the northern and southern coastal settlements of Edenton and Wilmington, and the surrounding rich lands also attracted settlers. The county developed improved transportation networks, constructing roads and ferries that provided many more commercial trade conduits than Beaufort. By 1766, nearly 90 percent of the region's exports left through New Bern.[5]

During the American Revolution, previously unimportant Beaufort briefly gained significance as a safe haven for merchant ships seeking to avoid British cruisers.[6] After the war, however, Beaufort resumed its somnolent ways while New Bern grew quickly. Francis Asbury, an itinerant Methodist minister, noted in 1796 that New Bern was "a growing place" and predicted a bright future: "Should piety, health and trade attend this Newbern, it will be a very capital place in half a century from this." Indeed, New Bern (and Craven County as a whole) grew substantially, along with its coastal neighbor, throughout the nineteenth century. By 1860, Craven County had a population of 16,268, including 6,189 slaves; Carteret County had 8,186 residents, of whom 1,969 were slaves.[7]

While one-third of Craven's population lived in the New Bern census district, the majority of Carteret's residents lived outside of Beaufort, along the waterways and in the lowland countryside and pine forests. Whereas fishing dominated Carteret's commerce, Craven residents tapped into their agricultural and forest industries. Craven County possessed far more slaves than Carteret, reflecting its citizens' greater involvement in both agriculture and naval stores production. Thanks to a nearly nine-month growing season — due to the proximity of the Gulf Stream and its moderating effect on the climate — and the larger proportion of arable land (compared to the poorly drained pocosins that dominated Carteret), a vast proportion of Craven residents identified themselves as farmers. Yet Craven's land was not well suited to large-scale cotton farming. Instead, much of the county's wealth came from its woodlands — especially in the form of naval stores. In fact, by 1860 Craven County was the second largest producer of naval stores in North Carolina. As a result, Craven's farms were generally small. In 1860, nearly 80 percent of the 690 farms in that county consisted of fewer than one hundred acres. Only eleven farms were larger than one thousand acres. While merchants and planters may have dominated the local economies and held positions of community and political power in both counties, the majority of people lived a yeoman existence, relying on neighbors and kinship networks to survive and prosper.[8]

BY THE TIME OF the Civil War, Carteret and Craven had a fairly similar proportion of slaves to their white population. Though Craven far exceeded Carteret in ownership of slaves, slaves as a proportion of the white population had been on a steady decline in Craven since 1830. By 1860 slaves accounted for 38 percent of Craven's population and 24 percent of Carteret's, far below the percentage of the heavy slaveholding counties in the state. Although the total slave population increased in both counties, individual slave ownership decreased. A similar pattern developed throughout the South in the antebellum period, as fewer landowners held slaves between 1830 and 1860 when price had outstripped the ability to buy. By the late 1850s, with rare exceptions, the price of slaves effectively excluded yeomen from joining the slaveholder ranks.[9]

Like most white southerners, residents of Carteret and Craven recognized that racial slavery was essential to their commerce and communal identities. In both counties slavery buttressed a multitude of agricultural and forest industries. Unskilled slaves tended rice, a little cotton, corn, and potatoes in the fields, or blazed pine trees and collected sap — which they distilled into tar — from the forests. Skilled slaves, as well as the growing free black population in Craven, served as mechanics and carpenters on merchant vessels and farm buildings; as coopers making barrels to transport the tar, pitch, and turpentine; or as mill operators, sawing thousands of feet of lumber or grinding corn into meal. In addition, slaves served as seamstresses, housekeepers, and fishermen. Because the majority of slaves in this region were not field hands, they enjoyed more freedom of movement and interaction with both races than bondsmen and bondswomen in other slave-majority counties.[10]

Yet greater responsibilities and freedom of movement did not place these slaves beyond the scrutiny and concern of the white population. For all their differences, whites in Carteret and Craven counties were in absolute agreement that slaves should be confined to the lowest social strata. They were acutely aware that coastal slaves were exposed to outside ideas and influences — influences that could potentially lead to a flight to freedom. Many slaves became infused with the ideas of freedom in the larger world introduced by black seamen who frequented the ports. Coastal communities like Beaufort and New Bern were not insulated from outside influences, but instead brought black sailors from all over the Atlantic world who shared stories of recent developments outside of North Carolina. Ideas of freedom would often inspire slaves to seek some form of control over their lives under the peculiar institution, including, of course, escape from their enforced servitude.[11]

To the dismay of local whites, slaves constantly sought some measure of autonomy over their lives within the confines of slavery. Some attempted to strengthen familial bonds, some drew on their specialized skills to hire themselves out, and others surreptitiously pursued education. But while each of these actions represented relatively passive inconveniences and symbolic forms of independence in white minds, what angered owners the most, and certainly caused the greatest economic burden, were the slaves' frequent attempts to flee from bondage. Advertisements for runaways dominated antebellum North Carolina newspapers, especially in the coastal region, where slaves could gain access to boats to leave the area. Some runaway slaves did not travel far from their masters, but instead set up hidden camps in nearby swamps and communicated with one another. Occasionally poor whites helped runaways escape. In 1857 William Kinnegay ran away and hid in the swamps south of New Bern. There he killed and dressed hogs for poor whites and traded with them for supplies. But poor whites were not the only ones willing to help runaway slaves. In the 1830s the son of a local slaveholder often hid slaves in ships carrying timber to Philadelphia. Indeed, the best means of escape for coastal slaves was a northern-bound vessel, and many slaves took advantage of this route.[12]

While Craven and Carteret residents worried about runaways, a much more controlling fear was that their slaves might rise up in rebellion against them. The dread of armed revolt by servile blacks had long dominated southern society and helped hold together disparate economic and social classes of society. Yeomen and poor whites who served on slave patrols saw their own social station in life enhanced by their elevation above blacks in the southern caste system. Several rumors of slave insurrections in eastern North Carolina heightened the general anxiety. In 1821 there was a brief scare in Carteret County caused by "a number of slaves and free persons of colour who had collected arms" and were "committing thefts and alarming the inhabitants" in isolated areas. The county militia mustered to put down this renegade band. Craven residents had discovered a planned insurrection in 1775; when word arrived of the successful slave revolt against the French at Santo Domingo in the West Indies in 1792, New Bern whites became even more frightened. One wrote that local slaves had decided "to rise against their masters and to procure themselves their liberty.... The inhabitants have been alarmed and keep a strict watch to prevent their procuring arms."[13]

More fears emerged in 1829, when copies of David Walker's influential *Appeal to the Coloured Citizens of the World* appeared in Craven County. Written by a former slave, the document denounced slavery and prompted the state to pass the "Free Black Code," a body of legislation that restricted their already limited freedoms and proscribed many actions of free blacks.

New Bern residents became concerned when, on the heels of Walker's *Appeal*, a Quaker preacher arrived from New York to deliver incendiary sermons regarding slavery. According to one planter, white witnesses agreed "that his observations respecting our Slaves were highly improper and most of them say he used the following strong language 'that the Slaves of the South were a degraded & oppressed People that the just judgment or vengeance of God was now hanging over the heads of their masters on account of it and that the time would soon come when they would all be free.'"[14]

The Nat Turner uprising in southern Virginia in 1831 further heightened anxieties. At New Bern residents' request for arms, the state's adjutant general sent two hundred muskets from Raleigh's arsenal. The Craven County Superior Court ordered all firearms of local slaves to be confiscated, and agents kept a vigilant watch on free blacks. Ten years later New Bern experienced another episode of paranoia regarding their slaves. William H. Bryan, a local politician, wrote a friend: "There has been considerable alarm in Craven on account of a supposed conspiracy of the Negroes, and from what I learn they had been talking about it. It is a terrible state of things especially for the female portion of the community to be subjected to such horrible apprehensions."[15]

While white men feared the results of male slaves unleashed on the female portion of society, the women themselves played a key role in maintaining the dominance of racial slavery in southern society. When a male friend expressed bitterness at the rush toward secession provoked by slaveholders, Catherine Ann Devereux Edmondston, who owned slaves in coastal Halifax County, North Carolina, proclaimed that she believed all whites would support the South and the slave system. "I call it patriotism," Edmondston averred, "for I should like to know what is to become of the country when our slaves are free." While lamenting that owning slaves was "a heavy responsibility on our shoulders which we do not discharge aright," she and many other southern women justified their ownership of slaves by the belief that their slaves wanted nothing more than to be properly governed. Referring to her female slave and nurse, Gatty, Edmondston remarked: "In her eyes their manifest destiny is to wait upon white folks. . . . She drew a harrowing picture as to what they would [be] if they didn't have no Master & Missus to give [food and supplies] to them."[16]

Though white women reinforced white superiority, elites across the South were generally concerned with interactions between lower-class whites and slaves. In coastal North Carolina, as in most every other region where slaves and lower-class whites lived in proximity, informal social encounters took place as whites and blacks worked, drank, traded goods, and slept together. Yet, no matter how often or freely lower-class whites interacted with blacks, even on intimate levels, such liaisons did not overcome white unity. This was demonstrated by the fact that in 1861 thousands of nonslaveholders from coastal North Carolina—including hundreds from Carteret and Craven counties—filled the Confederate muster rolls. Although those enlistees were prompted by a variety of factors, white superiority was certainly one implicit motivation.[17]

Racial slavery intricately intertwined the experiences of elites, yeomen, and even poor whites, as well as the economic, political, cultural, and social milieus, creating a southern society that exalted white superiority. While simultaneously granting slaves certain latitude, whites relied on slave patrols, militias, intimidation, and the court system to maintain racial boundaries and control slave behavior. Whites could not deny that slaves contributed greatly to their prosperity and kept the agricultural and commercial engines of society running smoothly.

IN THE 1840S CRAVEN COUNTY commerce went into sharp decline, due largely to the rise of Wilmington, which benefited from the new Wilmington-Weldon Railroad. New Bern residents decided that the only way to reverse the slump was to get a railroad line connecting New Bern with the state's interior. Carteret County joined New Bern's call for a railroad that would take advantage of Beaufort's capacious harbor. Beaufort had always been a struggling town. In 1840 its streets and sidewalks were "continuous banks or drifts of sand"; it had only "a few stores . . . no market house, a courthouse, and but one church." Visitors noted that the town lacked any social graces as well. Colonel John Rogers Vinson, commandant of the Fort Macon garrison in 1844, commented: "There is not one family in the place where our officers visit on terms of social interest." Reverend John Edwards, who preached there in 1839, remarked: "Beaufort in those days, was as nearly out of the world as a town could well be. [Yet] communication with New York, Boston, Philadelphia and Baltimore was more direct and frequent than with Newbern."[18]

Throughout the antebellum era, leading Carteret citizens tried to bring the railroad and other technological improvements to Beaufort in order to take advantage of its harbor and improve their commercial prospects. Many local and state politicians advocated completing the Atlantic and

North Carolina Railroad to Beaufort so western North Carolina's produce and agricultural goods could be transported to market via Beaufort instead of through Charleston, South Carolina, as was the current method. Local physician James Manney asserted that the completion of the railroad was a manifestation of "the loftiest spirit of patriotism, [and] of state pride." The profit from North Carolina goods should be reserved for North Carolina people. And, of course, the establishment of Beaufort as a major trading port would not hurt the town either, as Manney acknowledged: "Our merchant princes would have their splendid palaces, at this great seaport, one of the healthiest in the Union." When the General Assembly passed acts in 1850, and again in 1852, to run a railroad line from Goldsboro to Beaufort by way of Kinston and New Bern, residents in both Carteret and Craven rejoiced, pledging hundreds of thousands of dollars to the enterprise.[19]

However, construction of the railroad became an issue that bitterly divided the two counties. Some problems quickly arose, not the least of which was Beaufort's diminutive physical capacity to serve as a major entrepôt for commerce, unlike the much more developed New Bern. In 1854 Walter Gwynn, an engineer who surveyed the best possible routes for a line into Beaufort, warned Governor David S. Reid: "The harbor of Beaufort undoubtedly possesses many advantages . . . but to make it the center of a trade, now dispersed to other places, a city must be built up in a day, everything, Minerva like, must spring into existence in full perfection of matured vigor." Instead, he recommended placing the terminus at the small, newly established village of Morehead City on the western side of the river. Until Morehead could be properly developed, New Bern would serve as the primary commercial hub of the railroad. Angry Beaufort residents felt betrayed by the members of the railroad board — many of whom, including the chairman, were New Bern residents — and cut their monetary contributions in half. As one citizen complained, "Are we to consider that the eastern division of the [railroad] has a 'sliding' terminus, and if so, is it not to be feared that it will eventually 'slide' so far up the line, as to be *finally* fixed within the corporate limits of Newbern?" The conflict over the railroad led to bitter recriminations and verbal feuding in the competing county newspapers; it stopped just short of prominent residents of both towns settling the dispute by the *code duello*. Despite the tension, the railroad was finally completed, reaching New Bern in 1858 and Morehead City in 1860.[20]

In addition to the railroad, citizens attempted to improve the economic situation of Carteret in other ways. Some tried, unsuccessfully, to add industry, while others sought a more adventurous route to riches. "There is great excitement here about California. Some of our young men have started from Beaufort for the Gold Region," James Manney Sr. wrote in early 1849. His son James joined nine others in the California expedition with the hope of getting "into some kind of profitable business there," as the "young men have poor encouragement in the 'Old North State.'" However, as one later observer noted, "Nearly all of the ambitious ten found the wave washed shores of old Carteret far more attractive, if not more profitable, than the golden shores of California."[21]

In fact, those "wave washed shores" of Beaufort proved to be its biggest attraction and one of its more profitable assets — not for commercial traffic, but for personal recreation. Wealthy socialites in North Carolina chose Beaufort and its developing resort hotels as a vacation destination to recoup their health and enjoy the cool sea breezes in the height of summer. After returning from a seventeen-day stay in the seaside town in 1858, a congressman wrote Governor Reid: "Beaufort has become quite a favorite summer resort with North Carolinians. From all parts of the State, there is a constant inpouring of the people, who wish to see the finest harbor south of the capes of Virginia, and to enjoy the health-giving breezes of the Atlantic." Elites throughout state, including politicians, planters, and even William Woods Holden, editor of the *North Carolina Standard*, came to enjoy the scenery, the pleasant walks along Front Street, and the cool ocean breeze, which, during the summer months, according to one citizen, "sets in about ten o'clock in the morning & blows with refreshing coolness throughout the day."[22]

Visitors from Greensboro in the late 1850s found a thriving town taking advantage of the tourist trade: "Beaufort ... has a population of some twelve or fifteen hundred — contains three very neat Churches — three Hotels, all said to be good houses, and at either of which, comfortable lodgings, and plenty to eat can be had." The travelers encountered "an active, good looking, thriving and intelligent population, men of character and stability, who were putting forth all their energies to avail themselves of the many advantages and the great market facilities with which nature had so bountifully blessed them." Even New Bernians touted the vacation spot. A reporter for the *New Bern Daily Progress* who joined a New Bern militia company in an excursion to Beaufort in August 1860 issued glowing reports of the town when he returned. "Indeed," he wrote, with a bit of hyperbole, "Beaufort ... was as pleasant a place as could be found anywhere in the habitable world." He heartily encouraged others to visit and lauded the town's future prospects, stating unequivocally, "The truth is, Beaufort is destined to be *the* place for Summer recreations." Perhaps such glowing praise helped to assuage Beaufort's bitter feelings over the railroad debacle. The economic boosts from the tourist trade led some merchants to open small shops, while others invested even greater amounts of money to entice vacationers to visit their fair city. By 1860, Beaufort sported three luxurious hotels, and many made a living renting out rooms to boarders.[23]

PARTISAN POLITICS HAD prevailed in the Carteret-Craven region since the development of the first parties in the 1790s, but by 1840, both counties had thrown their support to the Whigs, as had much of the state. Whigs supported an activist Federal government that used its resources to improve transportation and commercial facilities. From 1836 through 1850, the Whig Party maintained supremacy in hotly contested elections. Craven and Carteret illustrated the state's vibrant, partisan two-party system as well. From 1836 until the outbreak of war in 1861, Carteret was staunchly Whig, only voting Democratic once—in 1858. Nevertheless, the Democratic Party maintained a strong presence in the county, and margins of victory were often narrow. Craven reflected similar political divisions. Whereas the county voted Whig in the gubernatorial elections through 1850, the Democrats took over from 1852 to 1858. One reason Craven returned the Democratic Party to power was that by 1852, state Democrats had overcome dissenting voices within their own party and, according to political historian Marc W. Kruman, "evolved toward an endorsement of the positive state." As another historian of the Pamlico region has pointed out, "Advocacy of a railroad became a bipartisan matter from which there was little discernible dissent."[24]

Though Craven voted Democratic in the 1850s and Carteret stood by the Whig Party, both counties harbored strong Unionist feelings during the crises of that decade. One of the first serious moments of distress for the Union occurred in 1849, when the controversy over the admission of California as a free state heated the secessionist rhetoric in Congress and in parts of the South nearly to a boiling point. When southern Democrats called for a Southern Convention in Nashville, Tennessee, in June 1850, many of North Carolina's coastal plain counties began holding "Southern Rights" meetings in support of the convention. Neither Craven nor Carteret convened such a gathering, suggesting that their interest in the preservation of the Union outweighed any concern for the southern rights issue over the expansion of slavery.[25]

Many local citizens believed the secessionist calls for disunion were absurd. "We are devoted to the Union, in the 'Old North State,'" wrote James Manney in February 1849. "We would rather all the abolitionists and negroes should be drowned in the Atlantic Ocean, than our glorious Union-cemented by the blood and toils of our forefathers, should be dissolved." The Beaufort physician denounced both "the crazy abolitionists at the North and the crazy pro-slavery men of the South" who had brought on the crisis. Manney undoubtedly spoke for many Carteret residents who condemned the heightened passions over slavery and those who threatened to tear the Union apart: "I am willing to lay down my life at any hour, rather than see our stripes torn or one star blotted from our glorious banner."[26]

The strong appeal of the Union continued in the state and the Pamlico region through most of the decade. In 1851, when Southern Rights Democrat Thomas Ruffin challenged incumbent Whig congressman Edward Stanly for the Eighth District seat in Congress, Stanly wrote a letter to the citizens of New Bern advocating a Unionist stance: "I sincerely believe that any candidate, an avowed advocate of secession or disunion, who would without equivocation proclaim his wish to dissolve our Union, would be driven into retirement amidst the execration of our people." Craven voters supported Stanly, casting their ballot for the Union as much as for the candidate, as even Stanly recognized. "It is a victory of the friends of the Union," he observed of his triumph. "It has proved that the people of this district condemn those who advocate even the 'abstract right of secession.'"[27]

Similarly, in the presidential election of 1856, the fate of the Union and southern interests dominated political discourse in the South. A troubled friend wrote to New Bern's John D. Whitford, "The question is as to the *perpetuity of the Union*, and no sophistry or artifice can hide it from a thoughtful, calm man who loves his country more than party." Concern had grown rapidly over which party was strong enough to thwart the newly formed northern Republican Party and its platform explicitly opposing the expansion of slavery. Several former Whigs had gravitated to the American Party, but ultimately Craven and Carteret (and the state as a whole) backed Democratic candidate James Buchanan — a Pennsylvanian who embraced southern values — as more likely to protect southern interests and prevent radical southerners from advocating disunion.[28]

Some attitudes began to change in the fall of 1859, when word of John

Brown's October raid on Harpers Ferry, Virginia, spread into eastern North Carolina. In New Bern, newspaper editors advocated keeping a vigilant eye on potential outside agitators, particularly northern booksellers: "No doubt but all such are abolition agents in disguise and we can conceive no remedy likely to prove of so much efficacy as *tar and feathers*." In addition, northern merchants came under intense scrutiny. "No southern merchant should buy a dollar's worth of merchandise from a nigger freedom shrieking abolitionist under any circumstance," proclaimed the *New Bern Daily Progress*. When local citizens learned that two of the men in John Brown's band had been free blacks from North Carolina, some legislators proposed evicting all free blacks from the state. The New Bern paper supported this measure entirely, reprinting an article that declared free blacks to be the "meanest people" and implored the state to "get rid of such nuisances."[29]

Craven County residents, primarily in New Bern, prepared for drastic measures, taking military precautions against abolitionist insurrections winked at by northerners. Denouncing the treasonous northerners who were "openly applauding" Brown and his crusade, Duncan K. McRae, a gubernatorial candidate in 1858, organized a local militia company, the "Newbern Light Infantry" on November 30, 1859. A month after John Brown's execution, citizens of Craven County met at the courthouse in New Bern and appointed a delegation to inform the governor of "the condition of the 'Depot of Public Arms' at this place, and also to request your aid in obtaining for the State, her full quota of all arms of the latest and best improvements." Joining the New Bern Light Infantry and the Elm City Cadets (a militia company that had formed in 1858), New Bern men created a volunteer cavalry company in March 1860 to be even better prepared for the next crisis.[30]

Well before Lincoln's election, Craven citizens believed that the next crisis was looming. "Even the most careless observer of the signs of the times, must be aware that danger not only threatens us, but it is imminent," three New Bern leaders warned Governor John W. Ellis in January 1860. In the event of secession, they advised, "Our geographical position will not permit us in this or any contest involving the South, to be neutral or indifferent, even if we were craven enough to desire it. Whenever Virginia and South Carolina act, North Carolina must take her part."[31]

Not everyone in Craven shared this sentiment. John L. Pennington, editor of the *New Bern Daily Progress*, a politically independent newspaper, supported Stephen A. Douglas, the pro-Union Democratic candidate for president. In July 1860, after the Democratic Party had split and nominated two competing candidates for president — John C. Breckinridge by splinter group southern Democrats and Stephen Douglas by the rest of the party — Pennington condemned President James Buchanan and his radical southern manipulators for effectively destroying the national party. "The election in November will show to the world how complete has been its destruction," the editor presciently predicted. Pennington's press opposed Breckinridge, who it believed "has no chance of election by the people," and supported Douglas for pragmatic reasons. "The fact is, while Douglas is not likely to be elected," the editor admitted, "his being run will most certainly prevent the election of Lincoln by the people and throw it into the House," where moderates hoped a more suitable compromise candidate could be named. In this way, Pennington hoped to preserve the Union.[32]

In Beaufort, Stephen Decatur Pool, a schoolteacher and former editor of the *Beaufort Journal*, and one of the most outspoken antagonists in the Atlantic and North Carolina Railroad disagreement, joined his New Bern counterpart in seeking to preserve the Union. On August 25, 1860, Pool established the weekly *Union Banner* to promote the Constitutional Union Party ticket of John Bell and Edward Everett. This pro-Union sentiment prevailed at the polls in November, as both Carteret and Craven residents voted strongly in favor of Bell. The results of that year's gubernatorial election further demonstrated Union sentiment in the region. The Carteret and Craven electorates gave majorities to opposition party candidate John Pool over Democratic incumbent John W. Ellis, even though both counties had voted for Ellis in 1858 (and despite the fact that Ellis had married a New Bern belle that summer). Word that Ellis would support secession in the event of a Republican victory in the presidential election turned many voters in the region against him.[33]

When that Republican victory came to pass in November, the *New Bern Daily Progress* made no secret of its stance: "We believe in holding on to the Union as long as it is possible to do so with honor." Though Lincoln's election might not have immediately changed the position of some Craven residents, it did transform the attitude of many others. From New Bern on December 2, 1860, State Supreme Court justice Matthias E. Manly wrote fellow justice Thomas Ruffin: "Our political surroundings make me sad and apprehensive." Though he held out a slim hope that Lincoln's election might "present an occasion of having a better understanding with our northern neighbors," he uncompromisingly declared: "If they insist upon regarding slaves at the south as a *moral taint* which it is *their* duty to eradicate, we must quit them."[34]

Other New Bern citizens were more proactive in the course they believed the state should pursue. On December 12, 1860, more than a week before South Carolina declared its secession from the Union, a group of residents met in the city theater to vent their feelings on the "present alarming state of National affairs." These individuals resolved to send a proclamation to Governor Ellis asserting that "the state of North Carolina has suffered from the aggression of the North upon the institution of slavery until the burden has become intolerable" and that the Union no longer afforded North Carolina the "welfare, equality and tranquility which it was intended to secure." They recommended that the state should simultaneously not only prepare itself militarily to resist any attempt by the national government to coerce the southern states that chose to secede back into the Union, but also quickly institute the process by which the state legislature could call for a secession convention. In the wake of such declarations, and of developments around the country, even Pennington altered his Unionist attitude. By December 17 he announced, "If the Union cannot be preserved upon principles of equality, for which all good men should devoutly pray, let it be smashed and let it be smashed now."[35]

The fervor of secessionism swept up men and women in the coastal portion of the state. Catherine Edmondston had defiantly proclaimed to her Unionist mother in October 1860, a week before the presidential election, that "if S[outh] C[arolina] did secede & there was any attempt made to coerce her, I would go to South Carolina & load guns for her men to shoot!" Such sentiments infected residents of Craven County as well. By early 1861, New Bern had restocked its armory with over 1,600 rifles, and several local companies of men prepared to take them up in the cause of the South if North Carolina were to secede. As New Bern men gathered in February 1861 to nominate delegates to the secession convention, a resident wrote: "The time has come when we should no longer submit to the tyranny of the detestable abolitionists, but should defend our rights, even if it costs us the last drop of our blood." Come what may, Craven County was prepared, and some even welcomed a conflict.[36]

Carteret County took none of these steps of its sister county, reflecting the depth of its Unionist sentiment. While leading New Bern citizens issued prosecession proclamations, several prominent Beaufort residents held their own pro-Union meeting on December 15. "Taking strong grounds in favor of the Union," the participants decided that the state should assemble a convention that would embody "that spirit of moderation, conciliation and compromise, which becomes the character of North Carolina." Though not condemning the action that any other southern state might take regarding secession, the Beaufort residents proclaimed: "We believe that the people of North Carolina should never adopt such a course" without cooperation with all other southern states, including the border states. Like conditional Unionists throughout the South, they did not deny the right of secession, but rather viewed it as the absolute "final remedy — after all other remedies . . . have been tried and failed." When a citizen offered a resolution that called for North Carolina to secede if South Carolina seceded, "it was rejected by an almost unanimous vote."[37]

Carteret's Unionist sentiment continued to prove deeper and stronger than Craven's in the following months. Whereas Craven approved a secession convention in February 1861 by over 500 votes, Carteret cast only 21 votes in its favor. Though a small majority of eligible Carteret voters had approved a secession convention, this did not translate into a call for action. Craven had elected two secessionist delegates to attend the convention, but Carteret had sent a Unionist. Carteret, like many counties throughout the state, called for prudence. In contrast to Craven County, no local companies of eager young men were formed in Beaufort during these anxious months; no wealthy resident financed an organization or tried to captain a vigilance committee; no letters were penned by Beaufort leaders welcoming the secession movement.[38]

Instead, Carteret residents were content to see what course the new president might take before they condemned the venerable Union to destruction. As Governor Ellis had written to the South Carolina governor before the election of 1860, "Some favor Submission, some resistance and others still would *await the course of events that might follow*." Few favored the former; by early 1861, most residents of Craven supported the middle course, but Carteret residents preferred the latter. All hinged on what course the Lincoln administration would pursue. The climax of the waiting was coming soon, as Confederates in Charleston, South Carolina, prepared to fire on Fort Sumter and force its Union garrison to surrender. Though Carteret residents were reluctant secessionists, Lincoln's actions after Fort Sumter surrendered would unite them with their more ardent Craven County neighbors and mobilize North Carolina for war. The threat of the use of force by the national government against their state, their region, and potentially their communities — thereby disrupting economic progress and threatening to overturn the racially stratified foundation of their society — would unite these two counties in a common bond. Like two companions joining hands as they jumped off the precipice together, they would leap into the war to resist the tyranny of the Federal government, not knowing what awaited them in the abyss below.[39]

CHAPTER 2

The First Year of War

Sitting in his home in Raleigh on the evening of February 13, 1861, Governor John W. Ellis closed his day by writing in his diary about the pervasive fear that had preoccupied his thoughts since South Carolina seceded from the Union nearly two months earlier. "Coercion is all the talk. Whether that will be the policy of the incoming administration &c &c," Ellis wrote. The despised word even came out of the mouth of Ellis's babe. "Sitting at dinner to day our little daughter Mary about 20 months old overheard this word 'coercion' and pronounced it quite distinctly, and of course, we thought, very sweetly," Ellis recounted. "But alas! How ignorant of its terrible meaning." The North Carolina governor, along with many other inhabitants of the Upper South states, adopted a watch-and-wait attitude in the days before the firing at Fort Sumter. These conditional Unionists believed that Lincoln's election alone did not justify secession. But they did agree with the right of secession, and their pacifism would endure only as long as the Federal government did not attempt to forcibly compel the seven seceded states to rejoin the Union. As Ellis penned in his diary, the term everyone used to represent that potential use of force was "coercion."[1]

The word's terrible meaning became clear on April 15, 1861, three days after Confederates fired on Fort Sumter, when President Lincoln issued a proclamation calling for 75,000 troops to put down the rebellion. When Secretary of War Simon Cameron sent a telegram to Ellis formally requesting North Carolina's contribution to the national levy, the governor indignantly asserted that the call to arms against the seceded southern states was "in violation of the constitution and a gross usurpation of power." He confirmed the state's resistance to Lincoln's action with his unequivocal statement, "You can get no troops from North Carolina."[2]

Lincoln's proclamation also alienated other Upper South states, prompting Virginia, Tennessee, and Arkansas to secede along with North Carolina, and induced many conditional Unionists to throw their lot in with the secessionists. Carteret and Craven residents represented just a fraction of those southerners provoked into joining the war by this call to arms. But inhabitants of the two counties supported the Confederacy with varying degrees of enthusiasm. Craven residents rejoiced at the event and embraced the opportunity to join their brethren in arms. Carteret's citizens showed the proper support at a surface level, though their conviction proved to be not only shallow in depth but also limited by numerous conditions. They demonstrated that they would fight, but only if they could dictate the terms of their service in a localized way. Together, these adjoining communities would face many trials over the next year that tempered their enthusiasm and tested their loyalty to the Confederate nation.[3]

THE NEWS THAT Fort Sumter had surrendered arrived in New Bern at around 9:30 P.M., Sunday, April 14, on a special train from Goldsboro. Over one hundred residents greeted the train at the depot and shouted their excitement as a messenger read the reports aloud. Many of the white residents in town poured into the wide, tree-lined city streets to celebrate. At 10:00 P.M., seven guns were fired in honor of the seven seceded states, and the townspeople lit up the night sky with several bonfires. A group of young men hung Abraham Lincoln in effigy from the ruins of the recently burned courthouse; a sign around its neck read, "May all Abolitionists meet the same fate." Boys pelted the effigy with rocks. John L. Pennington, as editor of the *New Bern Daily Progress*, announced in fiery rhetoric that the firing on Fort Sumter should cement local support for the South: "The South is now our country and our country demands our allegiance; our section, our honor, our Interests and all that we hold dear upon earth calls [us] to arms! Are there any whose craven hearts will shrink from a duty so palpable?" Pennington asked. "We will not believe it."[4]

If any did still shrink from war after April 14, news the next day stiffened their backbones. At noon on April 15, another express train brought word of Lincoln's proclamation calling for troops. In response to this report, the *Daily Progress* declared that "a war of *coercion* has been openly proclaimed." "There is no division of sentiment in our community now. All are for defending our rights as Southern citizens to the death," Pennington further expounded. "If divisions existed before upon the true policy of the county, the proclamation of Lincoln has served to disperse them and make

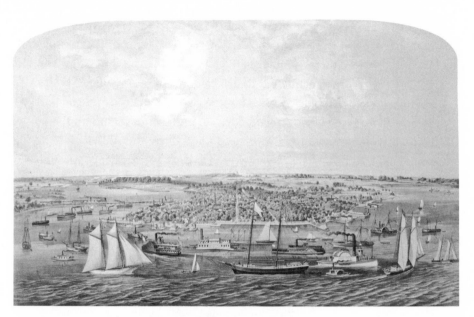

New Bern, 1864 (Courtesy of North Carolina Collection,
University of North Carolina at Chapel Hill)

our people unite." A large, enthusiastic crowd met at a local hall where the
people voted, without state authorization, to send a committee of men to
capture Fort Macon. That night, a New Bern militia company, the "Elm
City Rifles," paraded through the town carrying a hastily made flag of the
Confederacy, while ladies crowded the windows and doors of downtown
establishments, waved their handkerchiefs, and cheered the soldiers deliri-
ously. The next day, the company marched down the road toward Beaufort
and Fort Macon while the "whole population" saw them off with "deafen-
ing shouts."[5]

In New Bern, months of nervous anticipation had given way to a climactic release. One local planter expressed relief that the tension had finally
been broken: "I was glad to learn . . . that the Confederate States had taken
Fort Sumpter [*sic*], and hope since war has actually began [*sic*] between the
two sections, that the border States will no longer hesitate about uniting
her destiny with that of the Confederate States." The call to arms seemed
to mobilize and unify the county's entire population. As the *Daily Progress*
proclaimed, "Great excitement prevails in our midst seasoned with genuine
patriotism and an unyielding love of our own institutions." Even those who
had opposed war now appeared to surrender, momentarily at least, to their

regional pride. Such enthusiasm convinced the local editors: "We think we can safely say that there is but one party here now and that is for the Independence of a Southern Confederacy."[6]

Carteret residents manifested similar elation. On the evening of Friday, April 12, upon hearing that South Carolina had commenced firing on Fort Sumter, more than 120 citizens attended a meeting of the Southern Rights Party of Carteret County in Morehead City, where they declared: "The honor and best interests of North Carolina demand that her connection with the present Union be dissolved, and that she should unite her destiny with her sister States of the Southern Confederacy." News of Fort Sumter's surrender on Sunday further fueled their excitement. In addition to public cheering along Front Street, many men gathered at the Atlantic Hotel, where its proprietor, Josiah Solomon Pender, rallied them to follow him, in imitation of their southern brethren in Charleston, and capture the Federal fort in their harbor, which they did on April 14. Their task was not difficult, as only one individual—a maintenance man—inhabited the fort.[7]

Pender's precipitate action stunned even the war hawks in New Bern. City leaders could scarcely believe that the Unionists of Beaufort could have struck a blow for the Confederacy before New Bern's martial-spirited men. Indeed, residents of Carteret displayed the instant transformation in attitude that swept the state and prompted former governor Charles Manly to avow on April 22: "All are unanimous. Even those who were loudest in denouncing secession are now hottest & loudest the other way." On April 16, a surprised John Pennington praised "the gallant people of Beaufort" for their actions and demanded, "When will Newbern send down her quota?"[8]

Pennington did not have long to wait. Numerous Craven County leaders got into the martial enlistment spirit immediately after the outbreak of hostilities. On April 18, two prominent New Bern men informed Governor Ellis: "Alive to the emergency of the times, forty-six gentlemen have already pledged themselves to take up arms in defence of the State and Southern Rights." Calling themselves the "Beauregard Rifles" after the commander of the Fort Sumter bombardment, the men asked Ellis for arms to outfit the new company, in which one of the "gentlemen"—twenty-four-year-old former customs collector Edward K. Bryan—would serve as second lieutenant. Lest Ellis have any doubts, they assured him: "The citizens of New Bern are thoroughly aroused and patriotic in the Southern Cause." The number of men who flocked to the Confederate banners in the late spring of 1861 overwhelmingly supported their contention.[9]

New Bern businesses closed early every day to allow men to enlist and train on the city's fairgrounds. Bryan's Beauregard Rifles were the first to form, electing thirty-five-year-old tailor Daniel W. Hurtt as captain. Quickly joining the Beauregard Rifles in the service were the "Gaston Rifles"—organized by twenty-three-year-old Hugh L. Cole, son of one of the largest landowning farmers in the county—and the Elm City Rifles militia company, which boasted twenty-two-year-old George C. Lewis as captain and twenty-one-year-old Alexander Miller as first lieutenant. Lewis and Miller lived together and worked for Miller's father in his successful rosin oil distillery. These three companies formed the nucleus of the 2nd North Carolina Regiment and would serve in Virginia throughout the war.[10]

Forty-year-old attorney and 1858 gubernatorial candidate Duncan K. McRae formed a unit that eventually became Company D of the 5th North Carolina Regiment on June 3, 1861. McRae's neighbor, engineer Henry T. Guion, served as captain of Company B, of the 10th North Carolina Regiment, which mustered into service on June 13, 1861, and comprised part of the garrison at Fort Macon. During the summer, several more companies were organized and detailed to man the defensive lines below New Bern. Pennington served as lieutenant of Company I, 10th North Carolina, which elected John N. Whitford, a twenty-four-year-old New Bern merchant, as captain. Some companies even formed and disbanded during the summer. Henry R. Bryan, a twenty-five-year-old attorney, enlisted a company for twelve months' service, but when Confederate authorities declined to accept any but companies that enlisted "for the war," Bryan reluctantly disbanded his unit, stating, "I would be physically unable and my business would be entirely ruined." Nonetheless, six Craven companies entered service in the initial *rage militaire*, and several more materialized in response to Union expeditions that threatened the North Carolina coast in the fall and winter.[11]

Thirty-nine-year-old Peter G. Evans, the wealthiest landowner in the county, canvassed Craven and neighboring Lenoir County for volunteers to join his cavalry company, the "Macon Mounted Guards." Evans's unit consisted of scions of the economic elite in the region, with an average wealth valuation of $26,481 per man, four times larger than any previous company. Simultaneously, James S. Lane organized over one hundred men into what became Company D, 40th North Carolina Regiment, in October 1861. Though he recruited at the same time as Evans, Lane lured men from a different economic class, as his company possessed one of the lowest average wealth valuations. Thirty-one-year-old merchant Joseph Whitty organized the last group of Craven men to enlist in 1861, forming Company K of the 31st North Carolina Regiment on November 21, 1861. Confederate authorities ordered the 31st to Roanoke Island, where on February 8, 1862, the regiment, including Whitty's company, would be captured by Union general Ambrose Burnside's expeditionary force.[12]

With Burnside's expedition sailing down from Virginia in January 1862, the *Daily Progress* declared that this was no time for sunshine patriots. "He who refuses to act now," the editor wrote, "is a traitor to his country, a traitor to his home, and a traitor to his God!" Two more companies enlisted soon afterward. Nearly 950 Craven men joined Confederate units during the first ten months of the war, prompting the *Daily Progress* to boast: "No county in the State . . . has done as much as Craven has toward the object of self-protection and Southern independence." Over the course of the four-year conflict, approximately 1,100 men, or nearly 70 percent of men of military age, would join fourteen companies from the Craven area.[13]

Carteret did not match Craven's enlistment output either in total numbers or in proportion to its population, nor could it duplicate Craven's enthusiasm. Yet enough county residents enlisted to suggest that they did not lack patriotism — at least initially. In the weeks after Lincoln's call for troops, three Beaufort men formed companies. A close examination of their efforts at enlistment, however, reveals suspect sentiments and various motivations for joining up. Naturally enough, Josiah Solomon Pender, the captor of Fort Macon, was the first to begin recruiting a company for military service. Pender, whose more famous cousin was Confederate general William Dorsey Pender, combined a charismatic personality with a natural commanding presence — standing a slender six foot two, with dark hair, heavy eyebrows, and blue-grey eyes. Born in 1819 in Tarboro, North Carolina, Pender had attended schools in Rome and Paris, had dabbled in the arts as painter and poet, had briefly attended West Point, and had seen duty for a few weeks in the Mexican War. Though not a Beaufort native, the well-traveled Pender had immediately established himself as a leader in the community when he arrived with his family in 1856. With business partner Stephen Page, Pender constructed the enormous Atlantic Hotel and appeared to be prospering handsomely. In the 1860 census Pender claimed $50,000 in real estate and $20,000 in personal property, including seven slaves.[14]

Though many admired his hotel and his wealth, Pender had amassed substantial debts along with his impressive assets. In July 1860, only a few days after the census taker visited Pender's home, the local credit agent expressed his concerns to the national bureau. "They have expended a large amount in the erection of this hotel," the agent wrote, "they must be in debt to no small amount. My advice is caution." Court records revealed that Pender had been sued for debts by a number of businessmen. In January 1861 Pender bought out Page (who then left the county) and continued the hotel on his own, but he was still dilatory with his creditors. By February 1861 the credit agent characterized him as a "very slow pay." Only two months later, Pender would be the aggressive captain of the Fort Macon raiders.[15]

While Pender's martial activity may have stemmed from a strong sense of regional solidarity with South Carolina and patriotism for the nascent Confederate nation, it is also quite plausible that he rattled his saber the loudest to deflect public attention away from his financial difficulties. Capitalizing on his standing as a community leader, Pender actively championed secession. He served as secretary of the meeting of the Carteret County Southern Rights Party on April 12 that called for North Carolina's secession, before orchestrating the capture of Fort Macon on April 14 and recruiting a company of local boys. Eventually 101 young men would join his company, which officially mustered into service at Fort Macon as the aptly named "Beaufort Harbor Guards" on June 1, 1861. Pender's conspicuous military activities simply cemented his image in the community as a natural leader imbued with enthusiasm for the southern cause.[16]

Another company leader had more practical incentives to display his martial ardor than just patriotic zeal. Forty-two-year-old Stephen Decatur Pool, a Pasquotank County native who had moved his family to Beaufort in the mid-1850s, sought to enhance his flagging prestige within the community. Prior to April 1861, Pool was the least likely candidate to raise a company for Confederate service. In fact, he appeared to be as firm a Unionist as lived in the county. He had edited the antisecessionist *Union Banner* in Beaufort, served on the committee of the pro-Union meeting that met in December 1860, and refused to participate in the Southern Rights Party meeting on April 12. But after Lincoln called for troops, he quickly championed the southern cause. Unlike the wealthy Pender, Pool experienced a more economically tenuous existence. According to the 1860 census, Pool owned no property and claimed just $1,000 in personal value. As the local credit bureau agent reported, Pool's income as newspaper editor and schoolteacher at the town's female seminary had progressively declined before the war. While acknowledging that Pool was "married and of very fine character," the agent deemed him a "slow pay" on his debts and, more to the point, "a bad manager [who] has but little means." In 1860 the agent wrote that Pool was "a hard case[;] consider him insolvent (or he won't pay his debts which is worse)." Finally on February 19, 1861, the agent concluded that Pool was "not worth anything."[17]

Though he had tried to maintain his role as a community leader, Pool had been unable to secure a post even within the county court system since February 1859. The county commissioners did not trust him in a position of fiscal responsibility. The sense of shame and loss of honor, in a society that respected men for their ability to materially provide for their families, must have been severe to this father of ten. One way southern society allowed one to save face was through the display of manly, martial acts. Enlisting a company for the war served as a public commitment to combat on the field of honor. For Pool, the war could not come fast enough for him to regain respect and perhaps rehabilitate his professional reputation in Beaufort society.[18]

Carteret citizens must have had enough regard for Pool's education and leadership skills — despite his financial woes — to welcome him as company commander of their sons. One hundred and one young men, whom Pool deemed "the flower of Carteret County," including the sons of some of the wealthiest and most prominent citizens in the county, served in his outfit. Pool recruited his company, dubbed the "Topsail Rifles" after the name of the inlet that led into Beaufort harbor, concurrently with Pender in the days after Fort Sumter and tendered it to the state on May 21, 1861. Pool and his men garrisoned Fort Macon, where on June 1 his troops watched Pender's company muster into service. Three days later, however, the Confederate War Department ordered Pool's company to Camp Advance, near Garysburg, North Carolina, on the Weldon Railroad, less than ten miles from the Virginia border. Once there, the company was assigned to the 2nd North Carolina Infantry Regiment, where three Craven companies already served. August found the men north of Richmond. As they passed through New Bern on their way to camp in June, Pool assured community leaders that his men "would only return to their homes and friends when victory and independence shall have been achieved for the South."[19]

But time would prove the men's devotion to be not nearly as strong as Pool proclaimed. Within one year half of Pool's company abandoned the unit. Likely enlisting under the tacit assumption that they would join their comrades in Pender's company serving at home, within the brick walls of Fort Macon, some of the men undoubtedly were dismayed that they were being sent to fight so far from home. Though Pool's company would be reassigned to Fort Macon before autumn, their departure during the summer probably affected the recruiting efforts of the next officer to follow Pender and Pool.[20]

In June 1861 Benjamin Leecraft, a successful Beaufort dry goods merchant with prominent, long-standing family ties to the community, set about raising a company to join Pender and Pool in the Confederate war effort. In a foreshadowing of the county's lukewarm commitment to the cause, he found much of the initial enthusiasm for enlistment to be tapped out. Most Carteret men abandoned the Union only after Lincoln's call for troops. Job L. Kinsey, a native farmer who would serve as a Confederate spy in the region during the latter part of the war, acknowledged that "I was a Union man at first, but afterwards went into the Confederate army." Similarly, farmer William Rowe told postwar Federal investigators, "At first I was a union man," but "afterwards my sympathies were with the confederacy." Clifford Simpson testified that he was "strictly loyal until the state seceded and went out of the union and I then followed my State."[21]

These statements not only illustrate the shift from Unionist sentiment as a result of Lincoln's action, but also reveal the flexible loyalties in the region. Many residents had been Unionists, but what they perceived as an intolerable abuse of power by Lincoln had increased their loyalty to the South. Yet even that allegiance, with some exceptions, initially proved more conditional than absolute. As William A. Blair asserted in his study of Virginia's Confederate identity, "People may not fight for the nation but for the community or neighborhood." However, "when local goals fall into line with national purpose, the combination creates a powerful motivating force." Carteret enlistment patterns imply that most men in the area considered their foremost loyalty to be to their own community. But by fighting for their own small corner of the Confederacy, they were, by extension, defending the nation.[22]

When Leecraft began recruiting, he encountered resistance, as potential recruits dictated enlistment terms in a localized way. In other words, these conditional Confederates would serve only if they could remain in their home region. Most had never been away from their corner of the world and were less concerned with the potential dangers of Union armies marching through the fertile fields of the Shenandoah Valley, or sailing down the waters of the Mississippi River, than they were with the real dangers of the Union army marching through the marshy fields outside of Beaufort or sailing through the waters of Pamlico Sound and Topsail Inlet. Leecraft's difficulty, even though a large proportion of able-bodied men were still available for service, suggests the superficial commitment to the Confederate cause in Carteret.

On June 25, 1861, three weeks after Pool's company departed, Leecraft admitted defeat, telling Governor Ellis that his "endeavors to raise a company . . . have been unsuccessful." Leecraft lamented that he "could not succeed in raising a company to go any where on Southern Soil to repel the invader," but "I find that a large number would enlist for the War provided they could have the assurance that they would be retained in the County." Duty only went so far. For these men, if duty to country and family could not be made compatible, then their obligations to family were much stronger than their obligations to a country that had held their nominal citizenship for only a month. Stressing the importance of defending the state's coastline, Leecraft urged the governor to allow him to enlist a company to guard the shores of Carteret. Ellis consented to the captain's suggestion, and Leecraft enlisted sixty-nine men by October 12, 1861, when his company was officially mustered into service as a battery of heavy artillery. It would serve in Carteret until ordered to New Bern on the eve of the Union attack in March 1862. In addition to Leecraft's unit, about sixty more Carteret men joined other assorted companies that arrived in Beaufort in the autumn of 1861. Specifically, seventeen Carteret men enlisted in "Andrew's Battery" of heavy artillery, originally organized in nearby Wayne County, which arrived in Beaufort in July 1861 to help garrison Fort Macon. In October 1861, amid heightened anxiety over a possible impending Union invasion, forty more Carteret men went with "Herring's Artillery," another company sent to defend the canals around Beaufort.[23]

In all, Carteret County sent over 350 men into service, approximately 31 percent of the population of eligible military age. The editor of the *New Bern Daily Progress* was sufficiently impressed by Carteret's enlistments in June 1861 to declare: "It is madness and folly longer to say that those who were for the Union a short time ago, were not truly solicitous for the honor and happiness of our country, for Carterett [*sic*], though a small county and one of the strongest for the Union, has, now, two companies in the field and another almost completed." Despite the editor's praise, the numbers suggest that the martial spirit in Carteret was not nearly as incandescent as it was in Craven. While Craven men willingly volunteered to serve the Confederate nation wherever it needed them, Leecraft's lament to Ellis reveals that Carteret's men lacked this level of commitment. Carteret could put up an impressive facade, but behind it there was no real depth of Confederate sentiment.[24]

An economic and demographic analysis of the enlistees from each county further illuminates the disparity in commitment. At the time they enlisted in the Confederate army, the vast majority of Carteret recruits had not established independent households and possessed no real or personal property of their own. Of the 295 men who can be found in the census, only 69 soldiers (or 24 percent) were heads of households. Few had any association with slavery either, as only 3 percent owned slaves and 24 percent lived in slaveowning households. Only 50 men (or 17 percent) claimed any real or personal property of their own. Though most of the enlistees were neither independent nor possessed any wealth of their own, nearly 68 percent did come from landowning households, and 83 percent were from households that could claim either land or personal property of some kind. In contrast to Carteret, over 41 percent of Craven enlistees were heads of households, and over 37 percent claimed personal ownership of land or property. While only 7 percent of Craven enlistees owned slaves themselves, 31 percent lived in slaveowning households. In addition, 75 percent of these recruits came from landowning households and 91 percent from households that possessed either land or personal property.[25]

These data suggest the level of commitment to the southern cause for each county. In Carteret, primarily unattached youth flocked to the banners, probably because they found the excitement of service more enticing than the continued drudgery of farm or sea work, especially given that they would not have to leave the county. Their fathers generally stayed out of the war; in fact, only 12 percent of Carteret enlistees were older than thirty (compared to 25 percent of Craven enlistees). In Craven, established citizens matched the zeal of the youth, and they did not demand to stay in the region; they were willing to serve anywhere the Confederate authorities needed them. The war was not a lark to these men, but an earnest defense of their way of life. Their commitment was deeper; they fought to preserve their homes and households. Lincoln's call to arms could either damage their livelihood through coastal blockade or threaten their homes, property, and loved ones through invasion. For many, their honor demanded that they take up arms to defend their families, homes, and livelihoods.

Carteret and Craven did share some characteristics of enlistment, however. In both counties, those who enlisted during the initial excitement following Fort Sumter tended to come from more financially secure households. Just as in Carteret, Craven companies experienced a generally steady decline in the average household wealth and slave ownership over time, with two exceptions. George Lewis's Elm City Rifles was a prewar militia company that had attracted many prominent citizens as much for social reasons as martial ones in the years before the war. Peter Evans's Macon Mounted Guards was a highly selective cavalry outfit that had recruited mainly among elites (certainly those who could furnish their own horses) in Craven and Lenoir counties.

The officers who organized these companies, with a few exceptions like Stephen Decatur Pool, were wealthy, landowning slaveholders and thus inhabited a different economic stratum from the enlisted men. The economic, political, and social leaders of local communities often became the military leaders. The enlisted men elected as their officers citizens from the community whom they had worked for, traded with, and trusted with positions of civil authority. Indeed, nearly every officer in both Carteret and Craven had held some position of civic responsibility (either at the state, county, or municipal level) in the two years prior to the war. These civic leaders-cum-military leaders reflected a higher degree of slave ownership as well as a higher average wealth valuation than the common enlisted man.[26]

The officers and enlisted men knew each other well, hailing from the same communities or localities. Sarah Trenwith, a New Bern teenager, remembered that of the Confederate troops constantly passing her house and stopping to call in 1861 and 1862, several of them "were young men we knew who lived in the neighborhood." They were neighbors, schoolmates, and business colleagues, as well as fathers, sons, brothers, cousins, uncles, and nephews. They worked together, played together, drank together, and worshipped together. The war also served as an avenue for many of the young boys to come of age and to earn the privileges of adulthood and community citizenship. There was no mistaking the fact that they were preparing for something momentous and exhilarating. After the war, a sober, reflective Trenwith recalled the intoxicating excitement that infused all the young men of the Carteret and Craven region in 1861: "They were young fellows who thought it fine fun to go to war, were full of fun and frolic and didn't know what war meant."[27]

WHILE CARTERET AND CRAVEN residents rallied to enlist in the war effort, Governor Ellis turned his attention to organizing the state's defenses against Federal forces. He directed that the forts guarding the North Carolina coastline be confiscated and Fort Macon be captured. When he learned that Pender had already taken the fort, the governor praised him. This was just the beginning of a long, cumbersome process of mobilization for a war for which the state was hopelessly unprepared. Over the course of the next several months, thousands of men — short on equipment, military skill, or patience, but long on braggadocio, exuberance, and moxie — hurriedly organized into companies and flooded into hastily arranged training camps around the state capital and its surrounding communities. Ellis was soon overwhelmed by his responsibilities, and the strain was fatal. He died on July 7, 1861, while traveling to a mountain retreat to recoup his failing health. His death would leave the state with even more organizational and administrative difficulties. But in the last weeks of his life, Ellis tried to prepare the state for war as well as he could.[28]

Of prime importance to residents of Beaufort and New Bern, the governor attempted to bolster the woefully inadequate coastal fortifications. Immediately after the capture of Fort Macon, Ellis had instructed his agent to do all he could to improve the fort's defenses. "You will take the most active measures for the defence of the post under your command, and hold it against all comers," Ellis instructed Marshall D. Craton, captain of the "Goldsboro Rifles" and the fort's temporary commander, on April 17. Knowing that the weaponry at the fort was either outdated, dilapidated, or nonexistent, Ellis assured Craton that heavy batteries had been ordered to the fort and that an agent was in Richmond purchasing cannon to fill the casemates and parapets. Over the next few weeks, a concerted effort was made to improve the condition of Fort Macon.[29]

The sense of martial excitement reached a fever pitch in the first week of May, when a contingent of Morehead City ladies presented the fort with a new Confederate flag. Nine guns saluted its ascent to the top of the flagpole while the men of Pender's and Pool's companies cheered. And when the state's ordinance of secession was read aloud on the evening of May 21, the soldiers exhibited "the wildest and most enthusiastic demonstrations of joy," boisterously singing "Old North State Forever" and "Dixieland" well into the night. Yet, despite all the soldiers' giddy martial activity and the slaves' backbreaking labor, repairs to the fort progressed slowly.[30]

In late May, engineer Walter Gwynn was forced to admit to Governor Ellis that "I find Fort Macon much more exposed than I had supposed." Not only were there very few serviceable guns mounted, but also "there are no land defenses, and the guns on every face of the Fort, both by land and sea, are exposed to an enfilade, or flank fires. No traverses have been erected to protect them. The guns are all in barbette without merlons to protect either them or the men." This meant that the gun positions had neither blocking walls on either side to protect the men from shrapnel from indirect shell bursts nor solid walls in front of the gunports. Outside the walls, the topography compromised the fort's integrity and military value. Gwynn stated that he was spending as much time "leveling the sand banks adjacent to the Fort" as he was trying to improve its interior. But lacking equipment, the work was "most expensively conducted — the earth being removed by hand barrows." Though local authorities continued to call for more aid, state and national officials moved lethargically with little sense of urgency throughout the warm summer months, almost as if their torpor were in direct proportion to the sultry summer heat.[31]

An event at the end of August jolted the state leaders out of their daze. On August 29 U.S. Navy steamers appeared at Hatteras Inlet, and within twenty-four hours combined Union naval and land forces had captured Fort Hatteras and its 550-man garrison, thereby controlling access to Albemarle and Pamlico sounds and the rivers that led into the state's interior. Many coastal residents probably shared the sentiment of eighteen-year-old Elizabeth Collier, living in the coastal plain off the Neuse River, who bemoaned in her diary in the finest tradition of the Psalms, "Quick oh God! Save us from the enemy. Surely thou hast not forsaken us."[32]

Hoping to protect residents like Miss Collier, and most importantly the port cities and valuable hinterlands connected by railroads, Governor Henry Toole Clark (Ellis's successor) dashed off an urgent message to the Confederate secretary of war acquainting him with the serious implications of the attack. Clark then informed the adjutant general of the inadequate defenses at the other important coastal points, which included only "five companies at Fort Macon . . . one regiment and two battalions at New Berne," and "a light battery at New Berne, but no ammunition." Even if they could send warm bodies to the coastal areas, the state of North Carolina did not have enough resources to equip and arm them adequately.

Clark had two regiments in Raleigh ready to move and "any number of volunteers offering, but very scarce of arms." If the Confederate government wanted to protect the coastline of one of their largest, most populous states, they had better send supplies, and fast. North Carolina faced too many internal difficulties to do it alone. If the coast were lost, all of its ports would be cut off and become havens for the Union blockade fleet; the rivers that drained into the coastal sounds could then serve as avenues of invasion for the entire coastal plain, almost one-third of the state.[33]

By September, Beaufort and New Bern were seriously alarmed, as rumors swirled that a Union invasion fleet would attack at any moment. From Beaufort, Henry King Burgwyn Sr., whom Governor Clark had sent as his military aide to inspect defenses and procure weapons from a British steamer lying off Beaufort, wrote to Confederate secretary of the navy Stephen Mallory that merely having men in the garrison at Fort Macon would accomplish nothing if they could not effectively man the guns. "Fort Macon has not one practical gunner," Burgwyn wrote on September 4, "and only raw troops without proper supplies." If it was not "supplied at once with a competent naval ordnance officer," Burgwyn warned, then without any doubt "it must fall." Clark added his concern that the fort's officers "are all taken from the ordinary occupations of civil life, with no military instruction or education except what they have acquired amidst the labors of camp life." Except for Captain Pender's very brief stints at West Point and in the Mexican War, no officer had adequate military training, much less possessed the technical expertise needed to service the guns in the event of an attack. Even the colonel of the 10th North Carolina and current commander of the fort, an Edgecombe County native named John L. Bridgers, acknowledged his ignorance in such matters. A Confederate naval officer recounted a conversation in which Bridgers admitted that "he knew nothing about heavy artillery or the defense of fortified places. 'I only know,' said he, 'that the flag must not come down.'"[34]

Though no attack came in the autumn of 1861, such urgent appeals did at least succeed in prompting Confederate authorities to redouble their efforts to strengthen these coastal defenses. In late August the War Department recalled Captain Stephen D. Pool's company of Carteret men from Virginia and sent them to Fort Macon. By September several new guns had been added to the fort, and new troops were slowly arriving. The first unit to arrive in Beaufort at this time was the 26th North Carolina Regiment, led by future governor Zebulon B. Vance and lieutenant colonel Henry King

Burgwyn Jr., a precocious nineteen-year-old former Virginia Military Institute cadet. Many rumors were spreading about the increase in forces; residents eighty miles away in Hatteras warned Union colonel Rush Hawkins that the area had been fortified so strongly that Beaufort and Fort Macon now held 4,500 rebel soldiers, and sections of the fort had been reinforced with railroad iron. The numbers were grossly inflated; in reality, not nearly enough had been done to protect the coast.[35]

Such problems were not unique to North Carolina or Beaufort but, in fact, were endemic throughout the Confederacy. Every state and every fort called for guns, ammunition, troops, uniforms, and experts. But in the opening months of the war, state governments and the Confederacy generally were in short supply of many of the necessary munitions of war. North Carolina was as unprepared materially as the Confederate government to wage war. The state, which had relied on the North and Great Britain for almost all of its manufactured goods, had next to no manufacturing capabilities. Out of nearly one million people, barely fourteen thousand were engaged in any sort of manufacturing trade. North Carolina could not supply its own people with clothes, shoes, or saddles, much less such military necessities as iron, lead, guns, or swords.[36]

In addition to material shortcomings, confusing and conflicting administrative domains made the task of defending North Carolina's extensive coast even harder. The division of responsibility between the states and the Confederate government had not yet been clearly defined, and communities not knowing whether to plead for aid from their state capitals or from Richmond usually appealed to both, causing confusion over which supplies had been sent and by whom. North Carolina's situation was made even more problematic when Governor Ellis unexpectedly died in July. Henry T. Clark had to assume a job for which he was ill prepared at a time when the state government was even less equipped for the logistics and supply demands of wartime mobilization. Not only was the manufacture of arms, clothing, and munitions difficult to contract, their suppliers had to be paid. Moreover, some North Carolina banks had ceased loaning money to the state government, causing supply shortages, bankruptcies, and unrest among the unpaid troops, including those stationed at Beaufort. Two weeks after his 26th North Carolina Regiment arrived in Beaufort, Colonel Vance wrote to Governor Clark: "I am sorry to say that a portion of my regiment are [sic] almost in a state of mutiny on account of the non-reception of their pay."[37]

Through all the assorted complications, the state and Confederate authorities continued to send reinforcements to improve the Beaufort and New Bern defenses. The Confederate War Department assigned General Daniel Harvey Hill, a West Point graduate, and, later, Lawrence O'Bryan Branch, a political general, to coordinate the North Carolina coastal defenses. Hill threw himself into the task, traveling all over the region inspecting defenses and alternately demanding, cajoling, and pleading for more men, guns, powder, and ammunition. Nearly every request was met with plaintive replies of regret from both Raleigh and Richmond.[38]

Some local pressure was being put on young men who had not signed up in the spring. After the Hatteras attack, Elizabeth Collier wrote: "Men of NC Arise! Arise! Let the cry be 'Victory or Death.'" No doubt New Bern and Beaufort ladies echoed her sentiments, especially with the enemy potentially at their door. During this time of heightened anxiety, Captain Benjamin Leecraft's company officially mustered into service, and forty Carteret men enlisted in Herring's Artillery near Beaufort. In New Bern, under a recent Confederate Congress act for local defense and special service on the coast, Peter G. Evans organized the Macon Mounted Guards; James Lane and Joseph Whitty had already formed their companies. Twenty-three more Craven County men enlisted in Captain Whitford's company, and a handful of Carteret County men came forward to join established companies at this time of imminent peril.[39]

On October 23, 1861, the Confederate War Department sent ominous warnings of a 15,000-man Federal expedition possibly sailing for New Bern. Soldiers in the region exhausted themselves in physical and mental activities. Rumors spread that the enemy had landed or appeared in the distance. Drums would beat calling the troops to arms, and the soldiers on the banks and the garrison in Fort Macon would form in line, on edge, their nerves becoming increasingly frayed, only to find once again that it was a false alarm. Seeing Federal blockade squadron ships sailing on the horizon only added to the stress. "Every thing begins to look Seriously like an attack soon," Vance wrote in October. "The ocean is smooth & a great many ships are seen every day cruising around." A few days later he added: "We are in constant doubt here. . . . We may be here till Spring without being molested, and then a day's carelessness might see us surprised and ruined." Another soldier agreed, writing home: "We cant tel what a day will bring forth[.] The next time you hear from us we may have had a hard battle or may be prisners bound for New York or some other port." The strain of constant vigilance took a toll on the men's psychological health and dulled their edge.[40]

The climate and the ubiquitous mosquitoes did not help the soldiers' physical health. Some men brought communicable diseases like measles and mumps, while mosquitoes brought malaria; terribly unhygienic camp conditions, fostered by the ignorance of amateur officers, caused near epidemics of typhoid. Lieutenant Colonel Henry K. Burgwyn Jr. of the 26th North Carolina spent most of the fall in a hospital, stricken with typhoid fever. Local merchants did not give the soldiers many breaks either, as a review of the price of foodstuffs shows that patriotism did not come with a financial discount. A soldier of the 37th North Carolina Regiment stationed in New Bern commented, "We Get plenty To Eat but have To pay for it." He went on to say: "Butter is selling at 60 cts a Pound in Newburn, but we Don't Eat any butter At that price." As far as the overpriced chickens and eggs were concerned, "We can Doo very well without." Farmers demanded twenty cents a pound for pork. When Confederate officials offered only sixteen, the farmers left town without selling their wares. Many troops could not have purchased goods anyway, as the payroll was often months behind. One Carteret soldier from Pool's company complained in November 1861 that he had been enlisted for about four months without receiving a penny, which was causing great hardship for his family who depended on his pay. Those who did have money to spend found that it was becoming increasingly worthless. In February 1862, the New Bern branch of the Bank of North Carolina refused to take state Treasury notes—the currency in which the soldiers were paid—on deposit. The bank feared for the soundness of the currency with the prospect of invasion and potential defeat looming. So the soldiers, from both local companies and other regiments from around the state, fought the rumors, diseases, local price gougers, and financial institutions to the best of their abilities, all the while digging trenches until their hands were raw.[41]

The soldiers detested this last duty, and they blamed their generals, though local slaveholders were also culpable. Generals Hill and Branch worked tirelessly to establish defenses along the lower coastal region throughout the fall and winter of 1861–62. Branch implored the slaveowners to send their slaves to help dig the fortifications that would protect their towns. But those who had offered their slaves in April no longer wanted their valuable property in the hands of anxious, hard-driving officers. Hill denounced citizens in New Bern and Beaufort who did not seem to be taking an active enough part in their own defense. "There is much apathy among the people," Hill proclaimed. "They do not want to have their towns destroyed, neither are they disposed to do much for their protection." He could not understand how the local populace could appear so unconcerned with its own defenses. Imbued with a strong sense of patriotism himself, Hill had little tolerance for those who did not share his commitment. Therefore, he ordered the entire labor force at his disposal — the white soldiers — to dig trenches and fortifications throughout the region, much to the soldiers' indignation. "The spade has been set again everywhere I have been," he wrote. Sardonically, he commented of his most difficult task: "I have also got the promise of a little work from Beaufort. Should it be done, the miracle of the ages is not yet over."[42]

THE APATHY AND INDIFFERENCE that Hill and Branch encountered in the region were reflections of the lukewarm enthusiasm toward the Confederacy displayed by many local people, especially in Carteret County. Even as men enlisted in Confederate companies after Lincoln's call for troops, evidence of dissent lurked beneath the community's secessionist surface. Many youths flocked to Confederate companies, while their fathers, regardless of class, remained much more guarded. Some protested their sons' enlistment out of a personal concern, but others ideologically opposed the Confederacy. Reuben Fulcher, a humble Beaufort fisherman, testified that he "begged [his eighteen-year-old son, Wallace] not to go in the service, but he would not listen to me." Wallace joined Captain Leecraft's company on November 9, 1861. Early in 1862, Elijah Whitehurst and a couple of loyal friends had "frequently met and discussed the better way to get to the federal Blockade fleet off Beaufort Harbor in case they were drafted in the Rebel army." Naturally, he was despondent when his seventeen-year-old son, Samuel, "left against the wishes of his family" and joined the Confederate service in the spring of 1861. Five months later, however, Elijah was able to get Samuel discharged for being underage.[43]

Jesse Fulcher of Beaufort had no legal recourse when his twenty-five-year-old son, William, joined Pender's company in April 1861. When the elder Fulcher applied to Federal authorities after the war for compensation for his confiscated fish house, he reluctantly admitted: "I had a son in the Confederate army." The memory must have been painful to Fulcher, since William had died on December 17, 1862, fighting a Union force near Goldsboro. Overcoming his personal grief, Fulcher asserted that he "contributed nothing to supply him with military equipment or money," and that his son had joined "without my consent or approval." Nevertheless, his compensation was rejected.[44]

Some parents managed to persuade their sons to avoid the siren song of war, at least temporarily. James T. Lewis, of Craven County, had served in the Elm City Rifles before the conflict began. When war broke out, Lewis and his mates reported to the training camp where his company was incorporated into the 2nd North Carolina Regiment. "I was only at the camp three days when I got a letter from home begging me to return, so I got on the train next day and came home," Lewis admitted. But his parents could not keep him out of the war for long. "I remained at home till about 12 or 13 months after the capture of Newberne, and then crossed the lines, in opposition to the wishes of both my parents, and joined the State troops." A neighbor confirmed that Lewis's father was, on both occasions, "bitterly opposed to his son for going into the confederate service." Gabriel Hardison, another Craven County farmer, likewise deplored the departure of his sixteen-year-old son, Council, to Confederate lines. According to a relative, "When [Gabriel] came home and found [Council] gone he said he would rather have found him dead." As the parental laments of Fulcher, Whitehurst, Lewis, and Hardison reveal, many sons joined the Confederate army over the objections of their Unionist fathers. Historian Amy Murrell Taylor has argued that these father-son divisions throughout the South resulted from "rational political calculation" on the part of the sons, though the fathers preferred to view them as "a familiar, yet lamentable, generational conflict." Though these divisions challenged the cherished American notion of strong family unity in times of crisis, it was just one manifestation of dissent in eastern North Carolina.[45]

Dissent could run the gamut from vigorous Unionism to simple disaffection, but the result was the same — a determination to resist Confederate authorities, either actively or passively. In addition to protesting enlistments, some locals, as we have seen, demonstrated such resistance by refusing to give soldiers price breaks and to let their slaves serve as manual laborers for the army. Eastern North Carolina, of course, was not alone in having dissenters within its midst. Scholars have demonstrated that the state was home to significant numbers of Unionists in the western mountains, central piedmont, and eastern coastal plain.[46]

It is difficult to define what constituted a Unionist in the South, much less in eastern North Carolina. As many studies have argued, Unionism could stem from an abstract, ideological conviction or from more concrete, practical concerns. A contemporary, William "Parson" Brownlow of Tennessee, offered a rigid definition: a Unionist was one who showed "unmitigated hostility" to Confederates, "uncompromising devotion" to, and a willingness to risk life and property in defense of, the Union. Though scholars have discovered such sentiments in Appalachia, Alabama, and other regions, few eastern North Carolinians fit Brownlow's description. Such diehard Unionists were few and far between in Carteret or Craven counties during the first year of the war. This was an onerous time for those who vocally stood up for the old Union and condemned the Confederate experiment. Quiet resistance or passive noninvolvement was a more prudent tactic, while many southerners were simply unsure of their convictions and chose neutrality. But a few found their disagreements with the Confederate representatives in the region too strong to suppress. These few vocal Unionists elicited swift reaction from Confederate officials, who were dismayed that, in addition to preparing to fight off the approaching armies of Federal soldiers in the anxious autumn and winter of 1861–62, they had to quell the ominous stirrings from enemies within their lines.[47]

These stirrings came not only from Carteret County, where a prewar Unionism existed in strength, but also from strongly secessionist Craven County. Alexander Taylor, a poor Craven farmer whose brother joined the Confederate army, had been a vocal opponent of secession from the beginning. In early 1861 he declared to "a party of gentlemen that if they did not put a stop to the war they would be as poor as I was." And on July 19, the interim editor of the New Bern Daily Progress (John Pennington had enlisted) denounced those who were trying to disrupt Confederate enlistment, calling them "traitors" to the cause. The editor warned: "Having determined to hazard our life in the struggle for independence we are as willing to encounter traitors at home as to meet the common enemy of the North, and we should take more deadly aim at a Yankee sympathizer here than we would at old [Union General Winfield] Scott or even Lincoln himself." That the paper would dedicate its lead column to such episodes of local "treason" on the eve of the war's first major battle suggests that there was more than just an isolated incident of dissent in the region. The warnings became more numerous through the winter of 1861–62, as rumors of Union invasion circulated.[48]

Local Confederate officials tried to intimidate those who publicly maintained their fidelity to the Union, using traditional southern methods for community discipline — social ostracism, humiliation, and violence. In late May 1861, the New Bern paper reported an incident from neighboring Jones County, where illiterate sixty-year-old laborer James Griffin was "tarred and feathered and rode on a rail" for his "unsound sentiments and incendiary words and conduct." Similar examples of intimidation were taking place in Carteret and Craven counties, even if the local papers, wishing to present a united front, declined to publish them.[49]

In Carteret, Beaufort fisherman Jesse Fulcher, whose son had joined Captain Pender's company against his father's wishes, ran afoul of the captain, who "threatened to put a gag in my mouth and place me in close confinement." Unlike this isolated threat to Fulcher, railroad supervisor Isaac Hill and his family experienced continued harassment at the hands of Confederate soldiers because he "vehemently opposed the actions of the secessionists." In 1861, a soldier of the 7th North Carolina Regiment "cocked his gun at him and told him he was a damned Yankee," while another "drew his bayonet and attempted to strike him with it." Hill was "injured by threats to burn my house, and the burning of the bridge in the immediate vicinity of my house." He claimed such abuse did not hurt him personally, but they "frightened my wife so much that she died here days afterward."[50]

Hill's close friend, David W. Morton, a Morehead City grocer, got into trouble as well for his words and actions against the Confederate cause. One spring day in 1861, Morton angered a pro-Confederate crowd in Beaufort. As a companion later related: "One time we were out at the brickyard where they were drilling the Confederate malitia [sic] [.] Something was said concerning the Northern people and about how many Northern soldiers it would take to whip the crowd and [Morton] said three would whip the crowd, and they wanted to ride him on a rail for what he said. They called him a 'dam abolitionist.'" Morton further undermined the Confederacy by convincing his nephew to leave the army. News of his actions reached Confederate authorities. Morton testified after the war that in February 1862, his friend Isaac Hill had warned him that "I was reported at Havelock & that I must be cautious & say as little as possible or else I would be arrested & put in prison." Morton was not the only one threatened. Henry Covert, a "decidedly loyal and outspoken" ship carpenter from New Bern, angered residents with his Unionist talk. A friend begged Covert "not to speak so freely as he might get into difficulty. I have heard him say he considered the southern leaders in getting up this war were the biggest fools in the world."

In the fall of 1861, a New Bern mob arrested Covert and "threatened [him] with tar and feathers for talking on the Union side."[51]

Thomas Hall, who had purchased a Morehead City hotel on the eve of North Carolina's secession, claimed that in the summer of 1861 he "was threatened with imprisonment by Mrs. Vance, wife of Col. Z. B. Vance." In response to his unpatriotic sentiments, the soldiers of Vance's regiment "burnt my boat & part of my fence and robbed my kitchen, and one of them threatened to take my life." Hall refused to back down, and was menaced by the wife of another Confederate officer and even Governor Clark's military aide, Henry King Burgwyn Sr., father of the 26th North Carolina's lieutenant colonel. Hall remembered: "Generally, I was very much annoyed on account of my Union sentiments, especially by being called a 'whitewashed yankee.'"[52]

Even African Americans were singled out for their Union sentiments. The potential fifth column they represented caused fear among the locals, who used every opportunity to keep them in check through intimidation. Black boatmen developed a reputation as bolder, more assertive, and more independent-minded than other slaves, due to their jobs, which allowed long periods without white supervision and constant interaction with outside sailors.[53] This assertiveness, which whites had considered a nuisance during peacetime, became a threat during wartime. John Chapman Manson's slave, Caesar, was one boatman who was singled out for being too vocal. "Always a bold, outspoken man," Caesar made many trips to Fort Macon, where his master served as a lieutenant in Captain Pool's company. There, his words or actions angered the garrison, and "they threatened to tar and feather him for his Union sentiments." Manson did actually suffer humiliation at the hands of Captain Pender. Though Pender had allowed his own slaves certain latitude in peacetime — he permitted his skilled slaves to hire themselves out and keep much of their wages — during wartime he took a dim view of the nature of slave loyalty to masters. Pender publicly shaved Manson's head in order to "disgrace him and cow him down." Confederates could not afford to allow whites or blacks to continue to speak treasonous statements, lest it lead to open insurrection against the Confederacy.[54]

FOR ALL THEIR DIFFICULTIES in dealing with supply shortages and recalcitrant residents, Generals Hill and Branch did manage to modestly improve the Confederate defense in the region. Under their command, before the year 1861 was out, properly trained naval officers arrived at Fort Macon to train the garrison and its officers on how to properly lead their men. But Josiah Pender would no longer be one of those officers. On December 19, 1861, Pender was dismissed from the service by a sentence of general court-martial for being absent without leave and then lying about it. The story of his dismissal reveals the amateur nature of the fighting forces and under-scores the men's belief that because they served in their home county, they could tend to business at home during an emergency. Pender was a bit of a contradiction. Outspoken on behalf of the Confederacy, Pender had held everyone accountable for their actions and tried to intimidate those who dissented from the southern party line. Yet he broke the rules himself when he left his post at Fort Macon without permission to visit his wife, who was slowly dying at the Atlantic Hotel in Beaufort, within easy view of the fort. When his superiors asked him who gave him permission to abandon his post, Pender lied, stating that he was absent on General D. H. Hill's au-thority. When Hill denied the claim, Pender was charged with being absent without leave and brought before a court-martial. It must have been a dif-ficult week before Christmas for Pender. On the evening of December 18, he stood by the bed of his wife, Marie Louise, as she died of an undisclosed disease at the age of thirty-five. The next day, Pender stood in front of the court-martial that found him guilty and dismissed him from the service. James Manney — a prewar opponent to secession who had been a commit-tee member of Beaufort's December 1860 Unionist meeting, but had en-listed in the Confederate army after Lincoln called for troops — assumed command of the company and the rank of captain on Pender's discharge. Though Pender was gone, Manney continued the work of training his men and preparing them for the battle that would inevitably come.[55]

Throughout the Pamlico region, the new year of 1862 opened with more of the same anxiety that closed the old year. Word spread that a Federal ex-peditionary force was headed for New Bern, and General Branch ordered the 26th North Carolina, along with several other companies, to Craven's county seat in late January. Once General Ambrose Burnside's expedi-tionary force had captured Roanoke Island on February 8, Branch expected the next attack to be on New Bern and therefore called all the remaining troops from Beaufort, except for five companies (including the Carteret contingents of Pool's, Manney's, and Andrew's battery), which he left to garrison Fort Macon under the command of twenty-seven-year-old, West

Point–trained Lieutenant Colonel Moses J. White. Branch dispatched the rest of his troops along a defensive line south of New Bern.[56]

New Bern had two sets of defensive fortifications south of the city along the Neuse River. The farthest line, about ten miles below New Bern, was known as the "Croatan line." It ran west from Fort Dixie on the bank of the Neuse to a nearly impenetrable swamp. General Branch considered this line to be his strongest defensive position, but it was too exposed. If the main enemy force landed upriver, it could attack the defenders from behind and cut them off from New Bern. Because he did not have enough men to protect this advance position, Branch concentrated on a closer defensive line — that of Fort Thompson — about six miles south of the city. These primary defensive fortifications anchored the army's left flank on Fort Thompson, an underprepared earthen fort on the west bank of the Neuse. Branch detailed most of his troops to defend a line of fortifications extending from Fort Thompson west to Bryce Creek. Between these two streams ran the likely avenues of attack, the main Beaufort road and the Atlantic and North Carolina Railroad. However, the position was weaker than it appeared on paper, because ten of Fort Thompson's thirteen guns faced the river. Engineers had laid out seven forts to guard the river approaches to New Bern, but no forts effectively protected the more likely land approaches. One Confederate officer complained about the "miserable manner in which our works were constructed. . . . They are a disgrace to any engineer." Nevertheless, the soldiers directed all their efforts to improving these works. Troops constantly marched back and forth from camps near New Bern to work on the fortifications, all the time keeping alert to any sign of Federal forces on the rivers and creeks. The strain of constant vigilance took its toll. To a New Bern friend Colonel Vance wrote, "I am exceedingly tired of watching and waiting behind ditches."[57]

Eastern North Carolinians feared a Union attack every day. From nearby Edgecombe County, a young woman wrote in her diary: "Uncle and Aunt have the 'Blues' now the Yankees are gaining on us so rapidly. . . . Tis fearful to think of[,] but pining does no good." In January 1862 one Confederate soldier stationed in New Bern wrote a friend, "Exciting rumors have been afloat all day and we are on the lookout for an attack almost constantly." The soldier downplayed these rumors, stating: "I still am of [the] opinion that Newbern is too small a place for so grand an expedition to seek." In late January another soldier informed his father, "There is a good deal of excitement down here among the citizens [as] they expect Newbern to be attacked dayly." But the soldier, suffering from a disease that would soon take his life, was confident that the southern defense was stout. "I guess it will be hard for the yankees to get possession of this country," he wrote. The waiting became stressful, and men feared that the Union battalions might pass them by. On February 4 one Confederate noted: "Day after day we have been looking for the enemy, but as often have been disappointed. Since our fortifications have been rendered somewhat efficient, and there is a probability that we can make the enemy land below them[,] we are rather anxious than otherwise that Newbern should be assailed, & if the Yankees pass us by, we will certainly be very much disappointed."[58]

Keener minds, and not just military ones, held a different view. One New Bern lady perceptively surmised that an attack by water would likely be devastating: "We have no naval force to meet them on water[;] they have every advantage of us in that respect and unless God fight for us we must be defeated." Even some military minds agreed that only the intercession of a divine power could prevent a rout. The garrison's works were poorly designed, the men were poorly trained, and several of the officers were poor leaders. In January 1862 Henry Burgwyn Jr. believed that "none of our Regiments are as efficient as they should be." For his own regiment's faults, Burgwyn blamed Vance: "His abilities appear to me to be more overated [sic] than those of any other person I know of." Despite his best efforts, Burgwyn still found his regiment's discipline "wretched." Not only was Burgwyn "heartily tired of being under [Vance's] command," he also saw even greater dangers in the region's defensive scheme.[59]

Unable to divine precisely where the next Federal attack would come, and overwhelmed by urgent appeals from citizens all along the coast to send troops to their locality, state and Confederate authorities spread their forces too thin, dispatching isolated detachments to many different points along the coast. As a result, whenever Burnside concentrated his attack at any one location, few rebel reinforcements would be available to help the defenders ward off the intruders. Burgwyn railed against this setup, dictated by local interests, telling his mother that it was a "very great mistake . . . to divide our troops so as to expose the detachments to a certain defeat just whensoever they may be attacked." As for his own location, Burgwyn took a dim view, telling his father in late February: "It appears to me therefore to be plain that whenever New Bern is attacked by the force Burnside will have it will fall." On March 12, when news arrived that the Federal in-

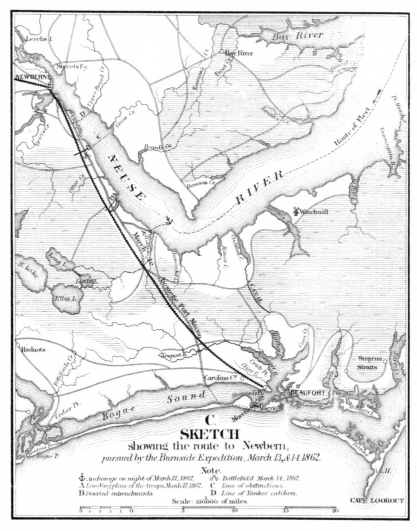

Map of General Burnside's expedition route to capture New Bern, March 13–14, 1862, in William T. Sherman, George Henry Thomas, John Pope, John G. Foster, A. J. Pleasanton, Ethan Allen Hitchcock, Philip Henry Sheridan, James B. Ricketts, and Norman Wiard, *Supplemental Report of the Joint Committee on the Conduct of the War: Supplemental to Senate Report No. 142*, 38th Cong., 2nd sess., vol. 2 (Washington, D.C.: Government Printing Office, 1866)

vasion force was sailing up the river toward New Bern, Burgwyn reaffirmed his misgivings: "My opinion is and has been from the start that New Berne ought to be abandoned." Within forty-eight hours he would have confirmation of his fears, when the Union soldiers appeared and attacked the defensive line.[60]

The first year of the war had seen Carteret and especially Craven boldly pronounce themselves against Lincoln's coercive tactics and in favor of the newly established Confederacy. Yet as the weeks and months wore on, residents had to deal with the enlistment of their young men, ill-prepared defensive fortifications, and dissent and opposition to the Confederacy within their own neighborhoods. In addition to quelling the internal threats posed by these dissenters, they were constantly troubled by the rumors of an impending invasion by Burnside's expedition. That sobering prospect forced residents to declare where their true allegiances lay, for once the Union army occupied the region, local whites had to choose whether to abandon their property, livelihood, and perhaps families, or renounce their southern allegiance. Both choices came with potentially dangerous consequences.

CHAPTER 3

The Beginning of Military Occupation

When advance scouts brought the word on March 13, 1862, that Union soldiers had disembarked from ships on the Neuse River about ten miles south of New Bern, excitement and dread gripped the town. The residents had been anticipating this moment for several months. In January, newspaper editors complained that rumors of a Yankee landing fueled a "cruel and unnecessary panic now raging in our town, crushing up furniture and driving crowds of people from their homes." In February, the Bank of New Bern stopped accepting North Carolina Treasury notes, fearing that Union capture would render them worthless. Even the weather seemed to portend something ominous; on March 6 it snowed all day in New Bern — a rare occurrence. As if divining disaster from the heavenly signs, citizens hustled to load up on supplies. The next day, the *New Bern Daily Progress* editors witnessed "the greatest rush we have ever seen on a store in Newbern."[1]

Though some panicked, other residents demonstrated their resolve. Editors of the *Daily Progress* had vowed to continue publishing the paper throughout the war: "Though the war be brought to its very door *it shall not suspend*." In January, a "worthy gentleman" publicly bet five hundred dollars that the Yankees would not invade New Bern. There was no word on how many took him up on that losing wager. Few people left the city on March 13, though many did prepare a train for a quick departure on the morrow if necessary. These residents exuded confidence in their defenders. On the morning of the fourteenth, Confederate soldiers reinforced this belief with their jocosity. Many suggested that local ladies prepare meals to feed them on their triumphant return from the morning's battle.[2]

Mary Norcott Bryan had risen early to prepare extra dinners, "expecting to feed the Confederate soldiers." But late morning brought sounds of heavy fighting and messengers relaying the grim news of Confederate defeat. Instead of sitting down to a midday meal with gray-clad officers, Bryan got caught up in a "perfect panic and stampede, women, children, nurses and baggage getting to the depot any way they could." Years later, Bryan reflected: "Our homes and hundreds of others were left with dinners cooking, doors open, everything to give our northern friends a royal feast." A Union soldier laughed over similar situations throughout the city: "The troops which left the city in the morning told their folks to get a good dinner ready for them as they should whip the Yankees in two hours." However, as Mary Bryan had witnessed firsthand and the soldier drily remarked: "They returned whipt & had not time to eat even a hasty plate of soup."[3]

The retreating soldiers had indeed been "whipt" in what was their first taste of battle. New Bern fell on March 14, Beaufort capitulated without a fight eleven days later, and Fort Macon surrendered on April 26, setting the stage for a Union occupation that would last the rest of the war. The experience of defeat altered the allegiance of numerous Carteret and Craven combatants. When the Union army asserted command over the region, many residents chose to forsake their allegiance to the Confederacy. Seeking to take advantage of new economic opportunities while simultaneously maintaining the social status quo, they wedded themselves to the Union. But just as the Confederates learned that not everyone in the area was a secessionist in 1861, Federal authorities would discover that not everyone was a Unionist in 1862. Many of those who did profess Union sentiments believed in a conditional form of Unionism; that is, they would be Unionists provided that they were returning to the Union of 1860. Even during the initial honeymoon phase of military occupation, dissent emerged as local whites disapproved of certain Union policies, especially regarding race.

ON THAT FATEFUL fourteenth of March, the outnumbered Confederate forces manning the defensive works south of New Bern, stretching from Fort Thompson on the Neuse River west to Bryce's Creek, held the Union army in check briefly during the early morning. But General Branch had unwisely placed his least reliable troops — the militia — in the least fortified point in the line — the center, where the Atlantic and North Carolina Railroad ran to New Bern from Morehead City. When the fighting reached its hottest, the militia line broke, exposing the rebel defenders on the left and right to flanking and rear attacks. Confusion ensued; orders did not get passed properly, and some units beat a hasty retreat while others doggedly held out, unaware of the turn of events. Colonel Zebulon B. Vance's 26th

North Carolina Regiment, defending the Confederate right, remained oblivious to the fact that the rest of the line had broken, and only began to retreat after it was cut off from the roads to New Bern. The future governor of North Carolina was forced to flee to Bryce's Creek, scrounge for boats, and ferry his men across the swollen stream, nearly drowning himself in the process. They barely escaped capture. The Federal soldiers exulted in their victory and the pell-mell retreat of the Confederates. The rebels "could not stand the Yankees," wrote one Connecticut soldier. "They ran into the city and got into the [train] cars—all that could, the rest running through the country as if the devil was after them." One of the fleeing soldiers admitted, "We all had to run like the very mischief to keep from being taken by the enemy."[4]

Indeed, as the Confederate soldiers retreated back to the town, panic set in among the remaining residents. Hundreds frantically packed and hastily fled in wagons, on horseback, on foot, or piled into the train cars that had been specially stationed in town for just such an emergency. It was often a pitiable scene. "It was an affecting sight," wrote one resident, "to see ladies, both young and old . . . trudging along the road in mud and water, on foot, carrying immense loads of their household articles, perhaps those most highly prized, and with tears, beseeching for some mode of conveyance to enable them to escape from the ruthless invader." The locals left in such haste that they abandoned much valuable property inside their homes or out in the open. A Union officer recalled that "I saw on one of the streets a handsome piano, which, evidently, the owner had attempted to carry away, but in his haste had thrown from his load." Many residents fled without their slaves. The Union soldiers witnessed and heard much of the flight as they approached from below the city. By Federal estimates, seven trains, with at least 120 cars, left the city on the day of the battle, carrying away most of the town's white (and some of its black) population.[5]

Unprotected homes fell prey to local African Americans and incoming soldiers with an inclination to gather the spoils of war. One soldier lamented, "I visited some of the private residences in the city and it was sad to see the waste and confusion that no doubt our soldiers had made[;] furniture broken and damaged Bureaus with the drawers smashed in with the but [sic] of the Musket or pried open with the Bayonet and rifled of their valuables." The troops celebrated their conquest by taking advantage of the finer things left behind by residents. Daniel Read Larned, General Burnside's personal secretary, entered the vacant and well-furnished home of a former secessionist and joined in the exultations. He recounted, "I found a piano there & sat down & played 'America' and such a chorus as I had the soldiers on the street took it up and the woods rang with it." As soon as possible Burnside imposed martial law on the city to put an end to all plundering, whether by soldiers or civilians. He posted sentries and forbade the men from entering private dwellings, though one officer noted that they still "do it on the sly and pick up many relics."[6]

For much of March 14, Burnside's army sought to extinguish the fires that threatened to destroy the city. As their last act before abandoning it, Confederates had put the torch to all structures of value to the enemy, including the long wooden railroad bridge over the Trent River. From the other side of the river, the entire city appeared to be engulfed in flames. A Rhode Island officer marveled at the sight as he steamed up the Neuse on a gunboat: "The great arches of the bridge, with every post, rail and brace, all ablaze, and ever and anon, great timbers falling with a hissing crash into the water below, sending up showers of golden sparks scintillating in the great black cloud above them." Intending to use New Bern as their major base of operations in North Carolina, Federal forces quickly gave up the chase of the retreating Confederates and expended all their energy in dousing the fires. After many hours of toil, the soldiers and sailors succeeded in saving the city; only a turpentine factory and New Bern's largest hotel were destroyed. At least one soldier appreciated the irony of the situation: "It was a splendid sight—a beautiful moral example. The men that fought the enemy's [*sic*] of their country a few minutes before were now fighting for their Enemy's Homes and property." Indeed, their efforts to save the city not only served a practical end—as they could better utilize it as their base—but also demonstrated to the few remaining white residents that the northern army was not bent on the destruction of southern property.[7]

Though it is impossible to determine the exact number of residents who fled, Union soldiers were impressed by the extent to which whites utterly abandoned the city. A Federal officer estimated that "only about two hundred out of a total population of seven or eight thousand white people, remained at their homes." Larned concurred that "all but the poorest residents have left," suggesting that only those who lacked the means to move remained. In the ensuing weeks, many other soldiers offered their observations of the town, and its lack of white residents, coupled with the preponderance of blacks and soldiers. "It was not the kind of place I had expected to see," a New Jersey soldier wrote. "A New England town on a fast day, I imagined, would be a cheerful place in comparison. . . . To me it seemed as though every one had gone to a funeral, or was arranging for one. The windows of the houses were darkened, and it appeared as if the destroying angel was hovering over the place." Another soldier voiced the complaint shared by nearly everyone who wrote from occupied New Bern during the war: "One meets nobody but soldiers and niggers." The overwhelming presence of military men and destitute black refugees, the fire-damaged structures, and the strict imposition of martial law prompted one Massachusetts soldier to comment that the city more closely resembled a "despotic power of monarchal Europe than that of a free democratic government."[8]

Most soldiers were able to appreciate the beauties of the city despite its forlorn appearance and the ubiquitous presence of the military. Many agreed with Connecticut soldier Oliver Case, who wrote his sister that New Bern "is one of the pleasantest cities I ever saw for its streets are shaded by large trees which meet overhead which makes the streets pleasant that otherwise would be uninhabitable." Many Union troops did not stay long after the fall of the city. Burnside turned his attention southeast to Beaufort and, more importantly, the capture of Fort Macon, which guarded its harbor. Less than a week after taking New Bern, he ordered Brigadier General John G. Parke to lead a force to subdue any resisting Carteret towns and set up the approaches to the fort.[9]

Beaufort residents, as well as the Confederate garrison at Fort Macon, had known the Union army was on its way ever since March 14. Throughout that morning the townspeople could hear the boom of the cannons as the Union army assaulted the Fort Thompson line, about thirty miles away. Citizens also knew the Union navy plied the waters somewhere over the horizon as well. The crew of the Confederate blockade-runner *Nashville*, which had recently arrived from Bermuda, had hurriedly shoveled coal into its boilers on the evening of Monday, March 17, and steamed out of the deep harbor and past the fort. Its departure ended Beaufort's contact with the outside Confederate world. Lieutenant Colonel Moses White and his 441-man garrison at Fort Macon, which included three companies of Carteret and one of Craven men (Guion's company), knew they would inevitably face a Union attack. White, who felt it was his duty to hold out as long as possible, warned the townspeople that he would turn the guns of the fort on Beaufort if Union troops attempted to enter it. This caused a great stir among the populace and the citizen-soldiers from Beaufort in the fort's garrison.[10]

On Monday, March 24, two Federal officers under a flag of truce from General Parke arrived in Beaufort to invite local representatives to speak with Parke. James Rumley, the clerk of the Carteret County Superior Court, and D. W. Whitehurst, a farmer, met with the Union commander over the next two days at his headquarters near Morehead City. Rumley tried to dissuade the general from sending troops to Beaufort, saying that it had no supplies for the soldiers and barely enough for the civilians; moreover, White had threatened to fire on the town if the troops came. Undisturbed, the general informed the two representatives that the town would hear from him shortly. Probably heeding Rumley's warning about White's threat to fire, Parke ordered a small force to take the port by stealth. During the wet, foggy night of March 25, two companies from the 4th Rhode Island Regiment shoved off from Morehead City, quietly rowed past Fort Macon, landed at Beaufort's wharf, and marched into the town, encountering no resistance.[11]

Union forces began preparing to besiege Fort Macon. When Lieutenant Colonel White declined General Parke's preliminary call for surrender, Parke directed troops to approach Fort Macon from its land side, on Bogue Banks, while constructing batteries on other islands in the harbor. On Parke's signal, the army batteries would join the Union naval squadron in bombarding Fort Macon into submission. Parke spent nearly a month laying the groundwork for the assault. During that time things grew increasingly tense for the 22 officers and 419 men inside the beleaguered fort. White, an intelligent and able twenty-seven-year-old West Pointer, suffered from poor health and even poorer discipline in his garrison. Stricken with epileptic seizures and rumored to be fond of the bottle as well, White was strict and inflexible with his men, brooking no dissent from his hold-at-all-costs stance. A Union officer heard that White had supposedly claimed that "he would not surrender until he had eaten his last biscuit and killed his last horse." White's threats to bombard Beaufort if residents allowed the Union army to enter the town earned him the enmity of many of his men. In an effort to maintain discipline, White ordered several soldiers placed in confinement for "expressing their dissatisfaction" with his decisions. Daniel Larned, repeating gossip, asserted that the Beaufort members of the garrison "will mutiny if an attempt is made to destroy the city."[12]

The murmurings of disquiet grew louder as the April days passed. White admitted that "some discontent arose among the garrison" during the siege, including complaints about their fare and other quibbles. But

White touched on the more incisive point when he observed that the garrison "seemed to be dissatisfied with being shut up in such a small place, so near their relations and friends, but unable to communicate with them." Even Union soldiers recognized the fort's impossible situation. "It seems a pity that they should attempt to hold it," wrote a Connecticut soldier, "when they themselves know they cannot and it will probably cost them a great many lives."[13] Some local soldiers agreed and decided to abandon their hopeless prospects. On the night of April 9 three Carteret farmers, Owen and William Foreman and John D. Phillips, stole away from the fort. The next night two poor mariners and Beaufort neighbors from Manney's company, Joseph Bloodgood and George W. Scott, followed their comrades. Charles P. Willis, a private in Pool's company, was mourning the loss of his brother Martin, who had died of pneumonia in the fort on February 27, when he too decided to desert. Willis joined three other members of the company, and together this disgruntled contingent made good their escape to Union lines in the days before the assault began.[14]

When the actual bombardment commenced, it was a more powerful demonstration of force than anyone in Beaufort or Fort Macon had ever witnessed. At 5:40 A.M. on the morning of April 25, the guns opened up. The shelling lasted nearly eleven hours, with the concussions from the mighty 10-inch siege mortars jarring the earth and reverberating through the wooden buildings of Beaufort. Residents watched the action from their windows or perched on rooftops. What they saw were the Confederates desperately, yet hopelessly, returning fire. The garrison could only fire out to sea, as no cannons challenged land approaches to the fort. In a small, yet meaningless accomplishment, its gun crews managed to drive off the Union ships that had come in close enough to fire on the fort. But the land batteries wreaked terrible havoc. Throughout the long bombardment, the fort kept returning fire, under the particularly diligent efforts of Captains Pool and Manney. When the Union shells threatened to blow up the fort's magazine, White finally hoisted a flag of truce, ending the attack. White formally surrendered the fort and its garrison on the morning of April 26, 1862, after having negotiated terms with General Burnside.[15]

The terms were highly favorable to the men in the garrison, who were immediately paroled on their surrender. Those from the area were allowed to return to their homes in Craven and Carteret counties, while those from outside the region were transported to the Confederate port of Wilmington under a flag of truce, so they could also return home. Each captive was

Beaufort citizens watch the bombardment of Fort Macon, April 25, 1862. From *Frank Leslie's Illustrated Newspaper*, June 7, 1862. (Courtesy of State Archives, Division of Archives and History, Raleigh)

charged with not taking up arms against the Federal government until they had been formally exchanged. The result was more lenient than any local men could have hoped. Instead of spending months inside northern prisons, they were allowed to return to their homes and loved ones. "Sightseers say that they had a great time over in Beaufort Saturday when the garrison was set free," wrote a Connecticut soldier. "Children looking for their parents, wives for their husbands, fathers for their children and when they were recognized in the crowd such a hugging and kissing as was not often seen was carried on."[16]

The generous surrender terms in Beaufort were similar to the mighty efforts to douse the fires in New Bern. In both cases, Union officials hoped residents would see that the men who took such pains and risks to accommodate them and restore order were not the evil minions of a despotic regime, as southern newspapers had portrayed invading Union soldiers. Such leniency was part of the Federal government's larger goal to convince local whites that the Union army would be benevolent during its occupation. Though the Federals would ultimately abandon their policy of conciliation in late 1862 for a variety of reasons — from Union military reversals to inveterate southern hostility — it was their overarching approach to southern civilians during the first year and a half of war, including the initial occupation of the Carteret and Craven region.[17]

Major General George McClellan, for a brief time commander of all

Union armies, had encapsulated the goal of the conciliation policy in November 1861, when he wrote: "It should be our constant aim to make it apparent to all that their property, their comfort, and their personal safety will be best preserved by adhering to the cause of the Union." McClellan had a friend and an advocate of conciliation in General Burnside. In February 1862 Burnside had issued a proclamation to the citizens of North Carolina stating that he wished to protect native interests and property and did not seek to confiscate anything, including slaves. Burnside announced: "The Government asks only that its authority may be recognized, and, we repeat, in no manner or way does it desire to interfere with your laws constitutionally established, your institutions of any kind whatever, your property of any sort, or your usages in any respect." He earnestly hoped that his efforts to protect property, restore order, and make the occupation as nonintrusive as possible would encourage residents to return to their former allegiances.[18]

Daniel Larned was confident that the locals would appreciate Union efforts: "I have no doubt when these people become better acquainted with us, and our intentions, they will come out in support of our Government." Larned saw evidence of Unionist sentiment coming to the surface after the fighting was over. When the victorious forces raised the stars and stripes over Fort Macon, he noted, "from Beaufort came the hearty cheers of the Union people." As a gesture of appreciation, "a 'union lady' from Beaufort sent the General a magnificent bouquet." Despite their misgivings about releasing hundreds of paroled Confederate soldiers into their midst, Union troops took some comfort in such demonstrations of affection for the Union. Most of them believed that the region's populace would appreciate their efforts. Such expectations were not unique to local Union observers, however, as the same general sentiments emanated from the highest offices in the nation as well.[19]

PRESIDENT ABRAHAM LINCOLN and many other Federal authorities anticipated that the majority of local white citizens in eastern North Carolina would be loyal, and expected to use this sentiment to return the state to the Union fold. Initial appearances along the North Carolina coast seemed promising.[20] When northern soldiers arrived in New Bern and Beaufort in the spring of 1862, they were convinced that they witnessed loyalty to the United States. New Bern was largely deserted of native whites, and much of Craven County was in no-man's-land—hinterland regions just outside either Union or Confederate military control, and subsequently visited and inhabited by both Confederates and Union men. Much of Carteret County, however, was under Union military control, and most of its native white population remained. The populace that the soldiers encountered in Beaufort seemed, in Daniel Larned's opinion, to be "loyal to a great extent." On March 31, 1862, a reporter for the *Philadelphia Inquirer* observed: "There appears to be more real Union sentiment at Beaufort than in any other place in North Carolina yet occupied by our troops." A Rhode Island soldier noted that the white residents "welcomed our troops, in many instances with seeming cordiality." U.S. Treasury agent John A. Hedrick arrived in Beaufort on June 12, 1862; after a week of interacting with the residents, he noted: "Some are Secessionists but the greater number are Union men now and I think always have been." If they were not all Union men yet, Massachusetts soldier Joseph Barlow was convinced that "this State will be in the Union by fall."[21]

Union troops noticed that even more citizens had started warming to their occupiers when northern merchant vessels laden with goods began arriving at Beaufort and New Bern docks by June 1862. On the eighth, one soldier in New Bern acknowledged: "Business is getting to be very lively in the city. Nearly all the Stores have been opened and it makes the city look very much like the northern cities, only most all the business is connected with Military matters in some way or other." The resurgence of commerce and the promise of future profits produced a telling effect on white attitudes. A Rhode Island soldier in Beaufort saw local businesses reopen "with cheerfulness and profit"; according to him, "Many of the most rabid among them soon dropped their patriotic allusion to the Confederacy, and began to consider themselves as part and parcel of the U.S. government once more."[22]

Union soldiers witnessed the latest shift in the flexible loyalties of the local citizens. When Federal forces drove the Confederate army out of the area, many Carteret and Craven residents changed their allegiances, falling back into the more comfortable role of supporter of the old and venerable Union. For most in Carteret and many in Craven, acceptance of secession had come very late—only after Fort Sumter and Lincoln's call for troops. Many had spent the years leading up to secession vehemently opposing it, only displaying a grudging acceptance in the spring of 1861. They had a sense of southern nationalism, but also a long and strong attachment to the Union. Most of these residents, and many Unionists throughout the South, simply wanted the status quo antebellum complete with Federal protections for southern slavery. In fact, many of those Unionists had argued against secession, claiming that the Union offered the greatest protection for southern rights and their "peculiar institution." South Carolina's James Chesnut Sr. remembered: "Without the aid and countenance of the whole United States, we could not have kept slavery. . . . That was one reason why I was a Union man. I wanted all the power the United States gave me—to hold my own." At the Virginia secession convention, a Unionist delegate pointed out that much of the world condemned slavery, "and it is nothing but the prestige and power of the General Government now that guarantees to the slaveholder his right."[23]

As North Carolina Unionists warned in 1861, abandoning the United States "jeopard[iz]ed the institution of slavery a thousand-fold more by secession, than by carrying on the contest under the old government." Alexander Taylor, a nonslaveholding farmer from Craven County, had admonished some of his slaveowning neighbors for their outspoken support of secession in February 1861. After the war, Taylor said: "I told a party of gentlemen that if they did not put a stop to the war they would be as poor as I was." Indeed, to maintain white supremacy and avoid the potential disasters of a social upheaval among their slaves, many masters had opposed leaving the Union; now many more advocated throwing their support behind the Union quickly, before the war could take any radical turns.[24]

In occupied Carteret and Craven counties such Unionist support was apparent, though it often had more practical than ideological foundations. Turpentine distiller Elijah W. Ellis claimed he had opposed secession but admitted that when secession came he "went with the State." However, he was much more concerned about maintaining his business interests in the naval stores industry than involving himself in the military conflict. When the Confederate army fled from New Bern and burned a large amount of supplies in their wake, Ellis abandoned his tenuous allegiance to the Confederacy. In the confusion and panic of hasty retreat, Ellis claimed, "I was cut at by a Confederate officer while I was endeavoring to put out a fire" that threatened to engulf his warehouses. When the Union army arrived, Ellis applied for and was granted protection from General Burnside, acknowledging his allegiance to the Union. Yet a friend later aptly characterized Ellis's stance during the war: "I cannot say that I ever heard him express himself pro or con about the war, he did not talk politics much[;] he talked more about turpentine than politics."[25]

Ellis's friend Solomon Witherington also exhibited the passive tendency toward Unionism. Once the U.S. Army arrived in March 1862, Witherington chose to take an oath of allegiance to the Union. However, this did not indicate any strength of conviction. Characterizing Witherington as a "quiet, peaceable, and inofficious man," Ellis testified that during the war "[Witherington] told me that he did not think he had an enemy in the world—that he liked our side as well as he did the other—that when the Southern troops came to his house he treated them as gentlemen and when the Northern troops came he treated them the same—that he knew no difference." After the war, the Federal government deemed the Unionism of Ellis and Witherington too passive and denied their claims for reimbursement. But Ellis and Witherington simply demonstrated that many residents negotiated just as freely with Union soldiers as they had with Confederates.[26]

Residents of all classes negotiated with the local wielders of power to preserve their property and livelihood. Many businessmen allied with the Union army to protect their economic interests, especially after witnessing how secessionist property was treated. Immediately on arriving in Beaufort, northern troops quickly took possession of Josiah Pender's Atlantic Hotel. After liberating it of its most valuable furniture, the Union army converted the hotel into a major hospital for much of the war. The army's retribution against Pender prompted other merchants in town to quickly assess their own allegiances. Seeing the treatment of the Atlantic Hotel, George W. Taylor, proprietor of the rival Ocean House, let few daylight hours pass before he had secured an arrangement with the Federal troops.[27]

Though Taylor left behind no writings to suggest his ideological convictions, he certainly had practical business reasons for declaring his allegiance to the occupying army. Taylor had moved from New Bern to Beaufort in 1853, just as the latter was beginning to develop its reputation as a resort area. Taylor sought relief from his financial woes by running a hotel, which offered the greatest opportunity for profit in the resort town of Beaufort. In 1857 he bought the Ocean House from D. W. Whitehurst and tried to appeal to the vacationing wealthy elites during Beaufort's summer season. Though the unrelenting stress of his financial condition probably led Taylor to the bottle—a contemporary noted that he "*drinks* hard" and "rather freely"—by January 1861 his hotel gamble seemed to be paying off. A credit bureau agent reported that Taylor had "been exceedingly cramped, but is getting out of his difficulties." Then the Civil War began, drying up the tourist trade at a time when Taylor desperately needed the continued profitability of his hotel.[28]

Taylor recognized the economic benefits to be derived from cooperating with and catering to a northern clientele. He immediately agreed to operate his establishment as a boardinghouse for Union officials. Military officers, government agents, and benevolent society members all took advantage of the Ocean House's hospitality. When John Hedrick, the newly appointed U.S. Treasury Department agent for Beaufort, arrived in June 1862 from Washington, D.C., he took a room in Taylor's lodging, noting that it was the only hotel in town that remained open. One Massachusetts soldier remarked that Union troops frequented the Ocean House, "where we used to get those famous dinners for fifty cents." Though the soldier claimed, "I hardly think the landlord made much on us as we had unbounded appetites," Taylor would have respectfully disagreed. His decision to ally with the Union secured his financial stability through the war years. By December 1865, his net worth had tripled to nearly $15,000, and he was "doing good business." Taylor owed his wartime prosperity to the choice he made in April 1862.[29]

The other major hotel owner remaining in town, Benjamin A. Ensley, proprietor of the Front Street House, did not make such a clear choice as Taylor. Ensley did not immediately take the oath of allegiance, and as a result Union forces shut down his hotel and forbade him from traveling outside of Union lines. This was particularly difficult for Ensley, who in addition to owning the hotel and a house in Beaufort had a farm in Craven County (where he claimed residence in 1860).[30] In March 1863 he petitioned for a pass to leave Beaufort and visit his Craven farm. The Union provost marshal denied his request because Ensley had not made his allegiance plain. "Mr. Ensley has not taken the oath," wrote the provost marshal, "on account, as he says, of particular reasons." Ensley was reluctant to renounce the Confederacy, fearing severe retribution from his secessionist-sympathizing neighbors and southern forces if they recaptured Craven. John Hedrick admitted as much, observing that many residents who openly supported the Union "were afraid they would be punished under State law" if the Confederates returned. In addition, their property "would be confiscated by the rebels immediately."[31]

Ensley felt compelled to enter the Union fold in October 1863 after a kitchen fire destroyed his primary residence in Beaufort. Without a home or the means to make a living since his hotel had been confiscated, he made peace with the Union forces. On January 28, 1864, he wrote to the provost marshal: "Being desirous of obtaining the possession of my 'hotel' I am willing to allow the US Government to put a building on the ground where I was burnt out on Front Street for use of a commissary." After maintaining his neutrality, with considerable difficulty, for nearly two years, Ensley ultimately joined the occupying forces in order to stabilize his tenuous economic situation.[32]

Military occupation forced the other merchants in town to quickly decide where their true allegiances lay. Retribution was immediately taken against those who were known secessionists. Thus, Benjamin Leecraft's store received the same treatment as Josiah Pender's hotel. In June 1862 the Union provost marshal granted a Boston merchant permission to occupy Leecraft's store because "the owner [had] joined the CSA Army." Union officials also commandeered Leecraft's home. James Rumley helplessly looked on as slaves expropriated bed and table furniture and "even the dresses of Mr. Leecraft's deceased wife and child." Rumley was incensed, yet, trying to preserve his own interests, he did not report such outrages to the Union authorities.[33]

The impressive number of soldiers in the occupying army — which usually had several companies stationed in and around Beaufort, with anywhere between 5,000 and 30,000 troops in New Bern at any given time — helped convince the local population that the Union army intended to remain in the vicinity for the duration of the war. This prompted many people to openly proclaim their Union allegiance and induced secessionists to keep their dissent private. A perfect example of the latter was James Rumley, whose diary reveals him to be an unreformed Confederate. Yet Rumley befriended John Hedrick, the U.S. Treasury Department collector, and projected a neutral facade in public interactions with Union officials, while secretly spouting his rage in his diary. As a result, Rumley gave no outward indication of his anger at the Union treatment of Pender's and Leecraft's property. Both men suffered because they were away when the Union army arrived. Yet Federal forces demonstrated the ability to forgive those who had initially supported secession if their contrition seemed genuine. Joel Henry Davis was a prominent merchant who showed such repentance.[34]

Davis provides an illuminating example of how local whites negotiated with those who were in power — either Confederates or Federals. A prosperous, slaveowning Beaufort merchant at the outbreak of the war, the fifty-seven-year-old Davis initially accepted secession. His had been the quint-

Leecraft House at 307 Ann Street, Beaufort, March 1862 (Courtesy of North
Carolina Collection, University of North Carolina at Chapel Hill)

essential success story as he turned small means into large gains through
thrift and hard work. Claiming no slaves and only $2,000 of personal value
in 1850, the "industrious" and "hardworking" merchant possessed $4,000
in real estate and $10,000 in personal property, including fifteen slaves, in
1860. Davis had earned the respect of his peers and had mentored young
men along the way, most notably Henry Rieger, a mechanic from Germany,
who married Davis's oldest daughter, named his first-born son Joel Henry,
and eventually became a business partner of Davis. When North Carolina
seceded in May 1861, Davis supported the Confederacy. Two of his sons,
twenty-two-year-old James and eighteen-year-old Joel Jr., had made an even
more public demonstration of their allegiance by enlisting as privates in
Pool's company on May 25, 1861. Thus, many economic, social, and familial
reasons encouraged Davis to support the Confederacy in the first year of
the war.[35]

Nevertheless, the elder Davis was quick to back Union officials when
they occupied Beaufort. Like George W. Taylor, Davis immediately took

the oath of allegiance and opened his store to Union currency, even allowing Treasury agent Hedrick to use a room in the store as an office. Ever the pragmatic merchant, Davis swiftly recognized the benefits that accompanied allegiance to the Union. While his store maintained a steady trade with Union soldiers, he still managed to export goods through the northern blockade. Of course, in April 1862 no one was certain who would win the war, but Davis felt that his best chance of protecting his property and business interests lay with the Union. John Hedrick applauded Davis's public stance at the same time he bemoaned the fact that other prominent citizens were not very demonstrative in their support. "Mr. Joel H. Davis, Mr. [Rieger], and a few others of some wealth and standing have contended for the Union all the time," Hedrick wrote in September 1862, "but I can tell that men of their stamp are few and far between." Davis even accepted some of the duties that came with being a prominent Unionist in town. At a meeting that September, he introduced Charles Henry Foster, a staunch Union promoter and orator, to the gathered assembly. In fact, Davis had developed a reputation as perhaps the foremost Unionist in Beaufort, even though he and his sons had previously supported the Confederacy without much hesitation. Davis successfully negotiated with those in power — whether they were Confederate or Union authorities — to protect his personal and business interests.[36]

Davis's sons followed their father's example. After surrendering with the Fort Macon garrison on April 26, 1862, James and Joel Henry Davis Jr. forsook the Confederate army and swore allegiance to the United States. James opened a billiard parlor and bowling alley behind the provost marshal's office in Beaufort where he entertained Union soldiers. The two Davis sons were not the only ones who retired their Confederate uniforms after they surrendered. Levi Woodbury Pigott, a former teacher and a private in Pool's company, took the oath of allegiance and successfully applied to John Hedrick for a position with the U.S. Treasury Department. After his parole, John W. Day, a former mariner, operated an inn about seven miles outside of Beaufort, hosting several venues of entertainment, including a well-attended fandango in 1865, for northern soldiers. Of the 177 Carteret men who were captured and paroled at Fort Macon, 56 (32 percent) did not return to their units after their exchange, and 30 more (17 percent) who did return soon deserted.[37]

Benjamin Leecraft's company had not been at Fort Macon, but experienced similar abandonment at the battle of New Bern. In the retreat from

New Bern, his battery fled in such disorganized haste that it virtually ceased to exist. In his after-battle report, Leecraft observed that he had "no intelligence" about several men who had subsequently "strayed off in New Bern" during the retreat. When his company reassembled at Kinston on the evening of March 14, 1862, he only fielded twenty-one of the original sixty-nine men in his command. Confederate authorities reassigned his remaining men to another company. Leecraft resigned in protest on April 12 but did not venture back to his home in Beaufort, though undoubtedly many of his soldiers had. Ultimately, of the 356 Carteret men who had enlisted for the Confederate cause, 131 (37 percent) permanently abandoned their units during the war.[38]

These actions suggest that the ideological convictions of many Carteret men were never that strong for the South. They had joined the Confederate army hoping to stay close to home and had been granted that wish, but when the army abandoned their home county, many soldiers in turn abandoned the Confederacy. Several Craven County residents experienced a similar lack of commitment. Of the approximately 1,100 Craven men who enlisted during the war, at least 219 (20 percent) abandoned their regiments. For these troops, an ideological attachment to the Confederate nation either did not exist or was too weak to sustain in the face of hardship. These men, many of them of lower-class status, undoubtedly left their units and returned home to protect their property and economic investments, or they sought to improve their economic opportunities under Union authority.[39] Whether for economic or other reasons, those who left their Confederate units to return home demonstrated that their primary allegiance was to their families and community rather than to the nation. This further reveals the tenuous nature of southern nationalism among many inhabitants of eastern North Carolina. Each of these men who joined the Confederacy in 1861 had felt an attachment to the shared culture, history, and social system of the South, but it was not a spirit that controlled their lives. Instead, their southern nationalist spirit resided simultaneously with an abiding attachment to the Union, and it was not difficult for that Union sentiment to win their hearts once their circumstances had changed.

While some Carteret and Craven men demonstrated their loyalty to the Federal government by leaving their units, taking the oath of allegiance, or just resuming business as usual, others actively aided the Union army. James B. Roberts, a Carteret farmer who had refused to join his two brothers in the Confederate army, acted as both a cavalry guide and a pilot for Union ships plying the Neuse River toward New Bern. Other citizens served as pilots for Union naval vessels in the coastal rivers and sounds. Isaac Hill, who had been threatened by Confederate soldiers in 1861, worked as a Federal naval stores inspector in Carteret County.[40]

Some men took a more overt step by enlisting in the Union army. In June 1862 the Federal government authorized the raising of an infantry regiment of native North Carolinians, the 1st North Carolina. In November 1863, the government authorized the creation of a second regiment of native white volunteers. In each regiment, individual companies formed in the occupied towns along the North Carolina coast. One company of the 1st and three of the 2nd organized in Beaufort, while another company of the 1st was established in New Bern. Nearly 1,500 men all along the North Carolina coast joined these two regiments, earning the derisive but obscure nickname "buffaloes" from unsympathetic residents. Unionists from throughout the state's coastal plain made their way to these port cities and enlisted. However, many local people also joined up. Thirty-three Carteret men and sixty-nine Craven men enlisted; many others applied but were rejected due to physical disabilities or advanced age. Six of the thirty-three Carteret Union enlistees and twenty-five of the sixty-nine Craven enlistees had previously served in the Confederate army. Most of those "turncoats" who left records revealed that their Confederate sympathies had been suspect to begin with, and most had been coerced into the southern army.[41]

Easton Arnold, a turpentine maker, claimed: "My service in the Confederate army was a force of circumstances." He was "engaged peacefully" in making turpentine until Union forces captured Hatteras in the fall of 1861. Then he could no longer find willing distributors for his products and was unable to move the goods himself. "I shunned Confederates until I was reduced to a state of starvation," Arnold later testified. Ultimately he had to deal with the devil in order to gain his salvation. "As a last resort I joined Confederate forces with a view of escaping and joining US forces, which I did at first opportunity."[42] Similarly, William Fillingum of Craven County said he was compelled to join Captain Joseph Whitty's Company K of the 31st North Carolina Regiment in November 1861 against his wishes. He asserted, "I never fired a gun with them and left at the first chance." He joined the 1st North Carolina (Union) Regiment on September 27, 1862. John Lincoln, also of Craven County, asserted that he was nearly forced into Confederate service. He "was never a regularly enlisted man in the Confederate service," but said Confederate officials confined him and eighty-five others at Stonewall, a tiny village on the northern Craven line, for six months "with a view to putting us in the Confederate Army." Soon after the Federals invaded Craven County, "the matter was abandoned and we all went home." Three months later he joined the Union army.[43]

Craven County farmer Henry Sawyer experienced Confederate intimidation as well. Sawyer had desperately sought to avoid rebels agents, claiming that "I lade in the woods over a month to keep way from them but then they took me." In January 1862 Confederate soldiers forcibly took Sawyer from his home and, "after many protests," compelled him to serve at Fort Thompson near New Bern, preparing the breastworks for the impending Union attack. Sawyer unwillingly participated in the battle on March 14, 1862, and when his company was forced to retreat, he "runaway and lade in the woods until I could get to the United States army." He enlisted in the Union army in June 1862. When Confederates learned of his actions, they took their vengeance. Sawyer later related that Confederate pickets destroyed "all most everything I had and even cut my beds open and burned my fence down."[44]

Local poor whites, like Arnold, Fillingum, Lincoln, and Sawyer, took advantage of the Union army's arrival and of the invitation to improve their economic and physical situations. The northern army arrived with preconceived notions of poor whites as degraded and deluded by slaveholding elite and more than willing to welcome Union forces. Their first impressions of the region did not alter their view. A soldier in the 9th New Jersey wrote: "Nearly every family, especially the poorer classes ('white trash,' as the planters called them) possessed a love for the 'old flag,' and they joyfully hailed their deliverance from the bondage from which we had released them."[45] Most poor men recognized the many practical advantages of joining the Union army. They could provide food, clothing, shelter, and protection for their families. Secessionist James Rumley grudgingly admitted that recruiting efforts "[have] been materially aided by the establishment of a public subsistence store in Beaufort, where the families of volunteers are gratuitously supplied." A Union soldier also recognized this transparent motivation of many poor white enlistees. After troops from his unit gave provisions to a destitute man and his family, the exuberantly thankful recipient announced that he would join the local native Union regiment to "help defend his family." The Union soldier remarked somewhat cynically, "That is the spiret [*sic*] that is gaining ground here fast [especially] amongst the poor class if it is not through love for freedom it is because Uncle Sam will furnish them provision and that is a greight thing to them."[46]

As important to potential enlistees as the material provisions was the very attractive economic opportunity to be paid in Union currency, whose inflation rate was much lower than that of Confederate scrip. While the average household wealth of men who joined the Confederate army from Carteret was $3,076, the average wealth valuation of men who joined the Union army from Carteret was merely $489. The figures for enlistees in Craven County were even more astonishing. The average household wealth of Craven men who joined the Confederate army was $7,102, whereas the average valuation of those who joined the Union army was $413. In both counties, only one Union enlistee lived in a slaveholding household.[47] Lieutenant Colonel James McChesney, commanding officer of the 1st North Carolina Regiment, argued: "The majority of these men have large families who are entirely dependent on the thirteen dollars per month for the supply of all their wants." Records indicate that many men were the breadwinners for their increasingly destitute families. Farmer Joseph Fulcher recognized that the war had severely disrupted his family's agricultural livelihood. He joined the army to support his family and freely admitted to friends that he devotedly "gave all his wages to his father because he had a family to maintain and was not able to work." Federal money also enticed local fishermen, especially as they headed into their first winter under occupation. On October 21, 1862, one recruiting officer in Beaufort wrote: "The Fishing season is now nearly over and I expect to be able to fill up the Company very soon from the large number of men whose business will then be suspended." Indeed, several Carteret men and nearly two hundred more white men from neighboring counties who had fled to Union lines on occupation, joined the Federal army during the winter months of 1862–63.[48]

THOUGH MANY WHITES appeared to accept Federal occupation, readily taking the oath of allegiance and even joining the Union army, northern soldiers discovered that not everyone was a Unionist. Local women were particularly outspoken in offering insults. When a Union officer tried to talk with a white lady in New Bern shortly after the battle, she became agitated and defiant and "remarked that she Could blow Abe Linkon's Brains out with a pistol." Massachusetts soldiers were digging a grave to bury a fallen comrade in May 1862 "when one of those secesh ladies was passing along—she stopped and told them to dig it deeper. They asked why? She said that the journey to hell might be shorter." Such comments shocked northern soldiers unconditioned to hearing such aggressive and disrespectful talk from women. When a woman profanely railed at Union soldiers for allowing her slaves to run away, one officer commented: "I told her it sounded very strange to a northerner to hear such language from a lady." It would have sounded strange to most southern men as well, for such improper language broke most social conventions.[49]

Such aggressiveness by secessionist women against Union soldiers was not unique to North Carolina.[50] In many areas of the South, like Beaufort and New Bern, the local men had either fled or surrendered, but few Union soldiers would admit in 1862 that much of the female population had given up the fight. "The secesh ladies seem the most bitter enemies we have—I think if we had them to fight, we should find it warmer work," wrote a Massachusetts soldier in May. Two months later he reaffirmed, "I heard one fine looking and intelligent lady say that, never, never, would the southern people live under the 'stars and stripes.'" Recording his encounter with a local woman in June 1862, another soldier stated: "I'd bet you would have laughed if you had heard the lecturing I got from a woman in this city, she was talking about the mean contemptible Yankees and about Genl. McClellan. I told her she had better shut up and then she gave me what Paddy gave the drum"; that is, she slapped him.[51]

Many Union soldiers believed that overtly assertive southern women were more zealous in their support of the Confederacy, and hence more dangerous, than southern men. Nevertheless, such women were able to speak and act so boldly without serious repercussions primarily because they were women, even if they were enemies. Union social values—rooted in the Victorian ideals of women as innately pious, submissive, fragile, and inferior to men—found southern women to be nonthreatening and ultimately not a potentially violent force, regardless of what came out of their mouths. Similar words from the mouths of men, of course, would not be so benignly tolerated.[52]

Union authorities also demonstrated that they would not stand for attacks that were anything other than verbal. On June 24, 1862, when a New Bern woman standing on her front porch took out a revolver and fired into a crowded street, killing one person, "the guard immediately arrested every person in the house and carried them to jail." Again, Union men arrested not just the triggerwoman, but the men in the house as well, holding them equally accountable for the actions of anyone in the household. A month later a soldier wrote home of a new pastime in New Bern: "The citizens have commenced the game of firing on the sentries from houses in the night."[53] This "game" took a dangerous turn on July 25, when a soldier from the 23rd Massachusetts Regiment was seriously wounded while on night patrol in one of New Bern's districts "infested with suspicious persons." In swift response, General John G. Foster, then commanding the Union forces in North Carolina, ordered the regiment to destroy the house from which the shot was fired, as well as four houses nearby and all surrounding outbuildings. Foster arrested the six occupants of the suspected house, despite their plaintive protestations of innocence; among them was former Confederate lieutenant W. P. Moore Jr., who had surrendered at New Bern and taken the oath of allegiance. That afternoon the regiment leveled the house until "it was prostate [sic] finally amidst the loud cheers of soldiers, darkies, and some of the citizens" while the unit's band spiritedly played "Bully for You," "Yankee Doodle," and the "Star Spangled Banner." Foster, who sat comfortably in a chair in the shade of a tree enjoying his soldiers' handiwork, warned the crowd of citizens gathered around that he would "make a camp ground of the whole City if they don't stop shooting his men."[54]

Despite such reprisals, some locals continued to take potshots at sentries in August and September. One New Bern woman decried, "Some of our people are acting very impudently, in the suburbs of the town they have been shooting at the guards placed at the corners for the protection of the place." After witnessing Foster's retaliation in July, she wrote on August 21: "Would you believe it two nights ago, a guard was shot at again." When Union doctors in Portsmouth, Carteret County, suspected the few inhabitants there of plotting to capture the hospital, they directed soldiers to confiscate all guns from people who were not known Union men. Such actions indicate that although they hoped to cultivate amicable feelings among the people, Union authorities would impose order in the occupied zone by military force if necessary.[55]

FEDERAL AUTHORITIES TRIED mightily to bring North Carolina back into the Union by more palatable ways than the use of military force. To assist them, President Lincoln appointed Craven County native Edward Stanly as military governor of the state in May 1862. The former Whig congressman, who had represented the region in the late 1840s and early 1850s, had moved to California but returned when summoned by Lincoln. Stanly's appointment heartened some residents. New Bern's Caroline Howard told a relative in August 1862 that Stanly "is a real blessing to the citizens here, he has it in his power to protect, and defend them." She proclaimed, "God has sent him for the sake of these poor suffering people." Charged with helping reconstitute local self-government and reassuring the local population of the national government's limited and benevolent war aims, Stanly, with the supposed cooperation of General Burnside and the army, attempted to carry out Lincoln's conciliatory commands to enforce antebellum state laws. Being a native of the region, Stanly took these orders seriously, especially the ones that pertained to maintaining racial control. Stanly was aware that radical racial policies could damage the Unionism that was growing in the region in 1862.[56]

Stanly arrived in New Bern on May 26, 1862, "amid the most drenching rainstorm." The tempest was a fitting portent of his turbulent administration in the region. To his surprise, Stanly discovered that Burnside had been employing escaped slaves—paying them wages of eight dollars per month, plus rations and clothing—and allowing blacks to attend school under the supervision of a northern missionary, Vincent Colyer. Appointed superintendent of the poor by Burnside, Colyer had come to New Bern in early April from Washington, D.C., where he had worked in hospitals under the auspices of the Young Men's Christian Association. In New Bern, Colyer immediately set up a day school for white children and, more radically, two evening schools for blacks, which were soon "full to overflowing." One approving Union soldier remarked, "How joyful that a brighter day is dawning upon this down trodden race."[57]

Stanly found little joy in these practices. North Carolina law expressly forbade teaching blacks to read. Stanly, who sympathized with local slaveowners but opposed secession, admitted to James Rumley that "he deeply lament[ed] the bad effects of the war upon our slave population." Though Burnside initially informed Secretary of War Edwin Stanton that his views and Stanly's were "remarkably coincident," Stanly found some of Burnside's arrangements for the fugitives too radical for his tastes. The governor insisted that Vincent Colyer shut down the schools for freedpeople. While some of the eight hundred blacks who had been attending the schools "cried as if their hearts would break," Colyer stormed off and reported this injustice to Washington. The action angered many Union soldiers and prompted Burnside to diplomatically retract his early statement of being in complete agreement with Stanly's views; instead, he assured Stanton that he would

Edward Stanly (Courtesy of Library of Congress)

enforce the governor's dictums regardless of how unpopular they may be with his own troops.[58]

Meanwhile, when slaves escaped into Union lines, Stanly deemed them fugitives and subject to be returned to their owners as soon as the latter took the oath of allegiance. Residents had reason to believe slave property would not be bothered. On February 16, 1862, Burnside had issued a proclamation vowing not to interfere with North Carolina laws, institutions, or property. The *New Bern Daily Progress*, now run by Union soldiers, declared explicitly on March 26: "We are not fighting for the perpetuation or annihilation of the peculiar institution of the South. We propose to let the people of the South manage their Negro question as seems best to them." The paper further assured residents that the Federal government "shall not make war upon the peculiar institutions or reserved rights of a class, but shall adhere to all constitutional requirements under which our nation had thrived so long and happily." The practice, however, proved much more complicated than the theory.[59]

In the first test of the governor's authority, a local farmer named Nicholas Bray visited Stanly's headquarters in New Bern on May 30, 1862, less than a week after he took office, to report that a "rude" northern soldier had taken his four slaves against their will. Before responding to the complaint, Stanly insisted that Bray take the oath of allegiance. Then, suggesting the owner "use mildness and persuasion," Stanly granted Bray permission to search for and retrieve his slaves. One female slave, according to Stanly, "voluntarily returned" to her "kind master." But some Yankees, disobeying Stanly's orders, confronted the Brays that night. A Union soldier readily acknowledged: "A party of our men had made them a visit . . . held a pistol at the head of Bray and his wife — put the girl into a carriage and left — One of his houses was burned down and the fence of his own [set] on fire." Daniel Larned corroborated the story and related his assurances and advice to the distraught Mrs. Bray: "We have promised to place a guard at her house, but advised her to let her slave remain where she is. I think they will soon find out that the best way is to let their slaves be where they are." Powerless to command the army, Stanly also counseled the Brays to give up their quest. Stanly's impotence in the matter only further emboldened some Massachusetts soldiers. As one asserted, "So this kidnapping game has been played out in a brief and summary manner — It will soon be attempted again — the feeling is deep and bitter among the soldiers and many of the officers."[60]

To native residents, such actions by northern soldiers, though contrary to formal Federal policy at that time, foreshadowed more ominous initiatives in regard to African Americans and threatened the strength of Unionism in the region. Stanly argued that he was trying to prove to loyal citizens that the Union army did not intend to interfere with their property. When Stanton chastised Stanly for his handling of the Bray situation, the governor testily replied: "What are the 'constitutional rights and privileges' of the loyal inhabitants of this State? If their property is destroyed or removed before peace is restored, what 'rights and privileges' are they to expect!" Stanly embodied the beliefs of many Unionists in the region and throughout the South. He had opposed secession, not the institution of slavery; he had supported the Union, not abolition; he wanted a united nation again, but not with anything resembling social equality between the races. On May 31, 1862, Stanly presciently warned the Lincoln administration that unless he could give North Carolinians "some assurance that this is a war of restoration and not of abolition and destruction, no peace can be restored here for many years to come."[61]

Events in the summer and fall of 1862 would alter Union war goals, as the conflict slowly progressed from one of simple restoration to one of emancipation. When Lincoln announced the Emancipation Proclamation on September 22, five days after the bitter struggle at Antietam, the war had ostensibly become a war for freedom for all men. But many whites in occupied Carteret and Craven counties feared that Lincoln's proclamation was a sign that social equality and black empowerment — and the resulting potential for race-mixing — had become official Federal policies. While African Americans immediately took advantage of both Union protection and the promise of emancipation to seek autonomy in their own lives, local whites resisted this radical transformation of their society and culture. Those, like James Rumley, who already disdained Union occupation, simply saw a fulfillment of their dire prophecies. Yet even those who had embraced the arrival of Union forces found reason to equivocate. The tensions and conflicts that ensued began to change local white attitudes toward both their present Union occupiers and the nation to which they were trying to return.

CHAPTER 4

The African American Experience under Occupation

Wednesday, January 14, 1863, found Beaufort still drying out from a recent storm and getting colder by the hour. The weather had not been the only turbulent event that week. Captain William B. Fowle Jr., Beaufort's provost marshal, sat down that morning to write a letter to his department commander relating an event that had occurred just a few days earlier when an African American woman enraged two prominent Unionists, Joel Henry Davis and Henry Rieger. According to Fowle:

> Mr. Davis and Mr. Rieger together tied the woman to a tree[,] her arms over her head[,] and then whipped her severely, the flesh on her arms where the ropes went was badly lacerated and her arms covered with blood when I saw her — She was only released upon the peremptory order of a private of the 9th N. Jersey, who says the treatment was very cruel — Her crime was that she demanded her daughter whom Mr. Davis retained in slavery; she is a smart intelligent woman and quite able to support herself and children.[1]

This story illustrates one of the ways in which African Americans asserted their independence — and the violent reactions such assertions could cause — in the wake of the Emancipation Proclamation. Many slaves felt emboldened by the Proclamation, which was a direct acknowledgment of their right to freedom and, as a consequence, of their right to assert themselves. Perhaps it was under such influences that on a brisk January day this African American woman sought out Davis, a man she knew well, to insist that her daughter be released from servitude, provoking the incident that Fowle described.

As the captain of a company of nine-month Massachusetts militia volunteers (the 43rd Massachusetts Regiment), Fowle had only been in the service for a little over three months. On his company's arrival in November 1862, it was thrust into a complicated matrix of allegiances. Uncertain how to deal with Davis and Rieger's action, Fowle informed Davis "that the matter was one which I did not understand and about which I should be obliged to ask advice at Headquarters." As the town's military chief of police, Fowle would have been in charge of arresting those who broke the law, and beating a free citizen was clearly a criminal offense. But he did not arrest Davis and Rieger immediately, probably because he knew they were among the foremost Unionists in the region.[2]

The woman's ability to "support herself" and her assertion of her independence may have rankled the former slaveholder Davis as much as any Federal policy. In southern society, whites believed a black person's proper role, especially a woman's, was as a dependent. Independence and autonomy granted blacks a new psychological footing and, if allowed to go unchecked, such assertions could lead to a genuine belief in social equality. The woman's demand challenged Davis's traditional social authority. For financial reasons, Davis had embraced Union occupation, but he would not tolerate black assumptions of equal rights. The violent attack was his own personal attempt to stem the tide of racial equality that the Federal government seemed to be ushering into the region. It served a symbolic as well as a political purpose. By physically scarring the woman's body, Davis sent a visual warning to other blacks not to challenge their former masters. To fellow whites whose allegiance might be suspect, Davis's message revealed that although he accepted Union occupation, he would not countenance racial equality. To be a Unionist did not mean one renounced white superiority.[3]

Many scholars have written about the tensions inherent in the creation of a new order that began when Union soldiers arrived in southern communities. Most of their works have been concerned with how Union agents proscribed black freedom and autonomy.[4] Yet blacks were savvy pragmatists who used the Union army and agents of northern benevolent societies to attain the four pillars of their empowerment: escape, employment, enlistment, and education. While whites figure prominently here — as they were integrally involved with the black experience, and much evidence of black actions comes from white sources — African Americans are the leading actors in this drama. Some whites recognized freedpeople's strong sense of self-reliance and intense desire to achieve autonomy. H. S. Beals, a northern agent visiting a black church in the contraband camps just outside of New Bern in the summer of 1863, reported this attitude to the secretary of the American Missionary Association (AMA). Beals noted that the black congregants before him "appeared to feel that their only hope rested in *their own efforts*, mainly, for Freedom & Justice." When the AMA secretary published Beals's letter in the organization's flagship periodical, *American Missionary*, he carefully excised this provocative statement. The AMA did not want to give the impression that the freedpeople did not *need* the help of the white New England missionaries and were instead determined to gain their own autonomy, with or without assistance.[5]

Freedpeople were remarkably successful in achieving their empowerment goals during the wartime occupation and hoped that success would lead to greater opportunities for independence and autonomy after the war. In this, they were frustrated. Once the conflict ended, the Federal government withdrew much of its support, bequeathing power to hostile local whites who sought to deny many rights to blacks. Nevertheless, this should not diminish the story of the black struggle for autonomy under Union occupation. Blacks achieved a great deal during those wartime years, confident in the support of the Federal government. Repudiating their slave heritage, African Americans sought personal autonomy — control over their own bodies, minds, and material conditions — and asserted their independence, especially among their former masters.

Embittered local whites placed all the blame for such radical black actions on the Union soldiers and Federal government. Local slaveholders declared, like most southern planters, that their slaves were content within the confines of the peculiar institution and did not desire independence. Carteret Superior Court clerk James Rumley was convinced that slaves "would be faithful and contented if let alone." But Rumley conveniently ignored reality and history. For as he and other slaveowners well knew, African Americans had been trying to ameliorate their hardships and establish control over their lives for decades before the Union soldiers arrived.[6]

WHEN UNION SOLDIERS LANDED south of New Bern on March 13, 1862, they immediately encountered welcoming slaves, most of whom, as one officer remarked, were "laughing and so glad to see us." Some were more serious, recognizing the consequences of the soldiers' arrival. One slave woman, "her eyes shining like black diamonds," encouraged the Federal soldiers to defeat the rebels, defiantly commanding, "You Bomb 'un out." A Union officer summed up the emotions in the county when he wrote, "The slaves alone seemed rejoiced at our coming, and looked upon our victorious banners as signs of their approaching millennium." As their masters fled, slaves felt immediate relief from the institution of slavery and thanked the Federal forces. As one slave told a Union soldier three weeks after the battle of New Bern, "It seemed like Christmas to him," for "it was the most rest that he had seen in all his life." A Massachusetts soldier recounted after the war that slavery had "died a natural death wherever the stars and stripes were unfolded, and the moment we entered New Berne, the overjoyed slaves considered themselves free, and they were wildly free!"[7]

After seizing control of something as intangible as their own personal liberty, slaves turned their attention to more tangible items that had been so long denied them — such as their masters' property. In New Bern, on March 21, 1862, General Burnside informed Secretary of War Edwin Stanton that "nine tenths of the depredations on the 14th, after the enemy and citizens had fled from the town, were committed by the Negroes, before our troops entered the city." The efficiency of looting by local blacks impressed Union soldiers, who displayed remarkable skill in such work themselves. A Massachusetts soldier noted: "The Negroes take the advantage [and] became Masters of their Masters['] Houses and things and went in for spoils and things had to fly." "I have no doubt that tens of thousands of dollars' worth of silks, laces, books, silver, etc., was sent home by soldiers," Union officer William Draper admitted, but "from the style in which the negroes dressed afterwards it was evident that they did not suffer in the distribution of clothing, at least."[8]

In Beaufort, when Federal officers commandeered the comfortable home of the temporarily absent merchant, Edmund H. Norcom, an angry James Rumley claimed, "the kitchen and backyard [had] become a perfect den of thieving runaway Negroes" who "had free access to every part of the building." Some blacks took practical items from the houses of Norcom and Benjamin Leecraft, the absent commander of a Beaufort artillery company, such as food, beds, furniture, and clothing. Other liberties were more symbolic than practical. A Massachusetts soldier reported that in New Bern blacks "stole everything they could get hold of — some of the colored ladies now wear some very fine silk dresses — and seem to feel above the rest of man or woman kind." In Beaufort, Rumley complained that former slaves had taken the clothing of Mrs. Norcom. Perhaps more galling to Rumley's sensibilities as a patriarch and protector of the purity of white women was that "even her bridal dress has been worn by negroes!" This last garb held particular symbolic importance to the plundering bondspeople. Slaves had been denied any legal right of marriage, and though they took spouses, they had no protection against separation or white male sexual exploitation. Donning the silk dresses of city elites, and the wedding dress of a wealthy slaveowner's wife, was more than just an appreciation of quality tailoring; it was a public gesture of defiance and revenge.[9]

THE ARRIVAL OF UNION forces offered more than just prospects for plunder; it afforded slaves opportunities to attain the four pillars of their empowerment. The first and foundational pillar was escape, without which none of the others could follow. Despite local white protests, numerous slaves in the countryside fled from their masters and sought freedom under the protection of the Union army. Some cleverly duped their owners before gaining their freedom. Young Dehlia Mabrey of Edgecombe County wrote that her brother and a friend were going to take their slaves to Rutherford County in western North Carolina less than two weeks after New Bern fell. The surprised Mabrey recorded, "The negroes pretended they were very anxious to go and lo! and behold, they've gone, to look for the Yankees it is generally believed." Undoubtedly those slaves made their way the roughly eighty miles to the Union forces at New Bern.[10]

Union soldiers documented the flood of black refugees. From New Bern on March 28, 1862, Daniel Larned wrote: "Stealing in from every direction by land & sea — in squads from 6 to 30 each — they come and dump themselves by the side of the fence and 'wait orders from Mr. Burnside.'" Superintendent of the Poor Vincent Colyer confirmed: "The freed people came into my yard from the neighboring plantations, sometimes as many as one hundred at a time, leaving with joy their plows in the fields, and their old homes, to follow our soldiers when returning from their frequent raids."[11] A soldier suggested the risks that slaves took to escape their masters. "They are continually coming in," he wrote in April 1862, "in squads of from one to a dozen threading their way through the swamps at night, avoiding pickets, they at last reach our lines." Sutton Davis, a black fisherman, led the slaves on Davis Island in Pamlico Sound to freedom in New Bern. He found a small boat and rowed it to the fishing village of Smyrna, from which they escaped to New Bern on foot. James Emmerton of the 23rd Massachusetts was amazed at the numbers of freedmen flocking to the coastal port in 1862. He proclaimed, "There is perhaps not a slave in North Carolina who does not know he can find freedom in New Bern, and thus New Bern may be Mecca of a thousand noble aspirations."[12]

Freedpeople escape to Union lines at New Bern, 1863. From *Harper's Weekly*, February 21, 1863. (Courtesy of North Carolina Collection, University of North Carolina at Chapel Hill)

Some soldiers were less charitable in their language but nonetheless were impressed with the persistence of slaves in escaping to Union lines. In August 1862 William Lind, of the 27th Massachusetts Regiment, wrote to his brother: "The niggers are coming in as thick as sheep[;] there was 62 came in yesterday." In November Joseph Barlow, of the 23rd Massachusetts, told his wife: "The nigers still come into our lines, about a hundred came yesterday. What in the name of god will Become of them I don't know for there is more here now than can be taken care of. I expect by the first of January we shall be over run with them." In December, after a Union expedition toward Kinston, hundreds of African Americans followed the army back to New Bern. One soldier confirmed that Union expeditions always attracted more slaves from the countryside, who were so dedicated to escaping that they had no concept of what to do after they had accomplished this feat. "Possessed with the single idea of personal freedom," wrote James Emmerton, "they took no thought of how they were to be supported. Some of them seemed to have no idea that the change meant anything but a new and, they hoped, kinder master. A young mother brought a cart-load of her black pickaninnies to the lines, and, when asked to whom the horse and vehicle belonged, had no answer but 'To you all, Massa.'"[13]

Slaves also testified to their immense desire for freedom. George W. Harris, from Jones County, recalled that his master had concealed George and his fellow slaves in the woods, "mindin' hosses an' takin' care o' things he had hid there." George, his father, and several other slaves decided to leave together in a gang and "ran away to New Bern," about twenty-file miles away. Mary Barbour and her family came from a much greater distance. They originally fled from near Raleigh to Union lines in Chowan County. Federal officers instructed them to make their way to New Bern, where they would face better prospects. Mary and her family did so, traveling over two hundred miles on their circuitous journey to freedom.[14]

The irresistible impulse for freedom compelled many slaves to perform amazing feats to rescue friends and family members. Vincent Colyer related the story of a black woman and her children who took a canoe one night and headed for New Bern. "They rowed, after twilight, down the [Neuse] river, until a breeze came up, which rocked the canoe badly, and they rowed for the shallow water, where, however, the waves were higher," Colyer wrote. "She jumped out, and walking, kept the boat steady all the way — twelve miles — to Newbern." The boldness of a slave who had just escaped to New Bern in April 1862 astounded Massachusetts soldier R. R. Clarke. The slave "had just heard that his wife was about 7 miles above our pickets and that [the rebels] were going to carry her off upcountry. He wanted to go & get her — of course we gave consent & I have no doubt but that he will evade their pickets and get her within 48 hours." While testifying before the American Freedmen's Inquiry Commission at Fort Monroe, Virginia, on May 9, 1863, a Union provost was asked, "In your opinion, is there any communication between the refugees and the black men still in slavery?" The provost answered, "Yes Sir, we have men here who have gone back 200 miles" to bring others to the sanctuary of Union lines.[15]

Some of the slaves who won their freedom came from distinguished North Carolina families. Robert Morrow had been a personal body servant to Confederate general James Johnston Pettigrew. In fact, he had grown up with Pettigrew and had accompanied the young man to West Point and the University of North Carolina. Despite these ties, he fled to the Union lines when Pettigrew's unit was involved in an aborted attack on New Bern in the spring of 1863. Morrow went on to distinguish himself as a teacher and a soldier before he died of yellow fever in 1864. Though he had enjoyed favored status in the wealthy Pettigrew family, he deserted his master at the first opportunity "for liberty and Union." Many slaves had discussed freedom for so long that they could not pass up the chance to seek it out. Alex Huggins, who escaped to New Bern, remembered what prompted him to run away from his family at age twelve. "Twan'nt anythin' wrong about home that made me run away," he recalled. "I'd heard so much talk 'bout freedom I reckon. I jus' wanted to try it, an' I thought I had to get away from home to have it."[16]

Thousands of slaves likewise "wanted to try it" and flocked to Beaufort and New Bern from nearby coastal areas and even from the hinterland to experience it. Reverend Horace James, former pastor of Worcester's Old South Church and chaplain of the 25th Massachusetts Regiment who later became superintendent for Negro affairs for the Department of North Carolina, conducted a census in January 1864. Based on the results, he asserted that 17,419 blacks lived under Union protection in eastern North Carolina. Beaufort, whose total white and black antebellum population numbered about 1,600 (including 600 blacks), became home to nearly 2,500 blacks by January 1864 and over 3,200 by 1865, while New Bern housed over 8,500 freedmen in January 1864 and nearly 11,000 a year later (as compared to about 3,000 blacks in 1860). Slaves readily migrated to coastal cities like Beaufort and New Bern along the same water routes that many runaways had used in antebellum times.[17]

Slaves discovered that they had useful allies in the Massachusetts soldiers who would often directly intervene to ensure their successful escape, as happened in May 1862 when Bay State soldiers forcibly freed the female slave of New Bern's Nicholas Bray.[18] To local whites, such actions by northern soldiers to grant slaves de facto freedom only portended much more ominous initiatives. Indeed, when President Lincoln issued the preliminary Emancipation Proclamation in September 1862, it reaffirmed white fears, particularly because North Carolina was not exempted from the Proclamation, unlike most other areas under Union occupation. Though they bitterly opposed it, white citizens were highly cognizant that the Proclamation would grant de jure freedom to their slaves in the New Year.[19]

African Americans were also keenly aware of the Proclamation's meaning. In February 1863 a Union soldier in New Bern commented: "Although they could neither read nor write," slaves "were quite well informed upon the President's proclamation, at least the portion relating to their own immediate change of condition, viz. freedom." Another soldier concurred:

"The Negroes are on the whole so far as I have seen more intelligent and clear headed than I fancied and are considerably interested in the President's proclamation, which many of them understand very well." The Proclamation had a powerful and lasting effect in African Americans' collective memory. A northern missionary recounted that on January 1, 1864, local freedpeople held a mass meeting in which "they called themselves one year old on that day; because a year ago Pres. Lincoln set them free." A Union soldier who understood the black affection for Lincoln declared, "Still coming generations that come up will call him blessed." Horace James also recognized the slaves' appreciation of their legal freedom: "They know as we do not what slavery means and are truly grateful that they have escaped it."[20]

Some former slaves used their newfound independence to rectify previous wrongs perpetrated on them. William Derby, a soldier in the 25th Massachusetts Regiment, recounted the story of James Whitby, a slave who had married Emeline thirty years earlier and had watched eight of their fifteen children be sold away. In 1863 James and Emeline asked the regiment's chaplain to remarry them, making the act legal in the eyes of God *and* the law. Indeed, a new day had dawned for slaves, and their hopefulness and joy at future prospects became infectious. One northern missionary wrote that blacks beheld "visions of freedom and civilization opening before them," which "inspired my heart with unwonted enthusiasm."[21]

Often blacks' desire to assert their independence led to confrontations with local whites over the nature of what it meant to be free and occupy a place in this new civilization. James Rumley complained when "negroes looked on with indifference" as "delicate women and aged men" had to perform "drudgeries, to which they have never been accustomed." Understandably, ex-slaves felt little pity when their former owners were compelled to perform daily menial tasks for survival. Indeed, when the Union provost marshal in Beaufort, fearing a Confederate attack in February 1864, compelled many grumbling local white men to work on fortifications around the town, a northern missionary reported that the freedpeople "were in ecstasies upon seeing them pressed into the service."[22] Slaves also engaged in verbal rows with whites. One New Bern resident complained: "It is nothing unusual for the Negroes to curse their masters & mistresses in passing along the streets. They are allowed to do so [by the Yankees]." One white lady angrily vowed, "If any of her slaves were impudent again she 'would knock them flat.'" In at least one instance, a slave woman did the "knocking." When a runaway returned to her former mistress to get her child, the mistress refused the slave woman's request. At that, a disgruntled white woman wrote, "the impudent wretch drew off and gave her a blow," for which she was arrested.[23]

Throughout the time of occupation, however, it was primarily whites using violence to intimidate blacks into submission. A military court found that civilian Edward Hughes "did commit an assault with intent to kill" a black woman in New Bern "by shooting at her twice with a pistol, both shots taking effect upon her person." Union soldiers guarding the approaches to New Bern reported that Confederate army pickets would shoot at blacks whenever they had an opportunity. In 1864, several blacks who tried to cultivate land outside of Union lines were captured or killed by rebels. In March 1865 former slave Toby Williams was "accosted by a man with a double-barreled gun, who after asking him some questions, deliberately killed him."[24] The most illustrative example of violent confrontation in the wake of Emancipation was the story that opened this chapter, when Joel Henry Davis and Henry Rieger tied up and mercilessly beat a former slave woman for demanding that Davis release her daughter from bondage. Violence was native whites' response to their disenchantment with a Federal policy that prevented the maintenance of the antebellum social status quo.

Unlike local whites, who simply wanted the prewar Union restored, some Federal officials desired a much greater change. Foremost among them was Horace James, who, as early as June 1862, asserted: "It is not enough to bring back this country to its position just before the breaking out of the rebellion. The 'Union as it was' is not what I want to see restored. Let us rather have it purified and perfected, coming out holier and freer from this dreadful ordeal, sanctified by the baptism of blood." A soldier agreed: "The more we learn of the despicable social condition of the South, the stronger appears the need of the purification which, in the Providence of God, comes of the fire and the sword."[25]

DESPITE WHITE PROTESTS, blacks hastened such efforts to "purify" the southern social system. They sought employment, especially work that would give them the opportunity to own land—a foundational piece of autonomy. The desire to be independent and autonomous drove some African Americans to risky lengths. Horace James declared that, with little land available on which to settle freedpeople, "some of the more fearless among them did indeed venture to hire tracts of land a little out of the towns, or on the 'debatable territory' along the railroad and the Neuse, and attempt the culture of cotton or corn, or the making of turpentine." James admitted that those who sought such independence took their chances with Confederate raiders or secessionist sympathizers and often forfeited their freedom or their lives. Though some tried to maintain their independence from all whites, many others took advantage of the Union army's demand for labor.[26]

Escaped slaves began working for Union authorities from the moment the army first arrived in the region. In April 1862, just a month after the capture of New Bern, one Union soldier noted that over seven hundred able-bodied black men had arrived in town looking for work. "They all find employment," he wrote. "Some work on the fortifications, some unloading ships — more are really needed to perform the labor to be done here." When Mary Washington brought her family of eight to New Bern in December 1862, her two oldest boys went to work in the quartermaster department; each son earned ten dollars a month, which Mary used to support the family. In fact, the government employed many freedmen in the quartermaster department as teamsters and manual laborers, while some regiments put them to work as cooks. Some freedmen were assigned more specialized roles. In New Bern, Willis M. Lewis served at different times as a guide and scout for Federal troops, as well as a nurse at regimental hospitals. Jacob Grimes, an escaped slave, "was employed by the U.S. government as a detective," presumably to monitor illicit trading activities or treasonous actions against the government.[27]

Other escaped slaves served in much more dangerous roles as spies and scouts for the Union army. Vincent Colyer stated that many black slaves "visited within the Rebel lines, Kinston, Goldsboro, Trenton, Onslow, Swansboro, Tarboro, and points on the Roanoke River: often on these errands barely escaping with their lives." He admitted that they were paid far too little for this risky service. Nonetheless, the former slaves appeared satisfied: "They seemed to think their lives were well spent, if necessary, in giving rest, security and success to the Union troops, whom they regarded as their deliverers." One scholar has argued that slaves went as far as three hundred miles into southern territory to gather important information about Confederate troop strength, positions, and intentions. Union soldiers respected the efforts of these black spies who were so familiar with the native landscape and terrain.[28]

Union soldiers also appreciated the willingness of blacks to serve them personally; soldiers hired black men as servants, which angered local whites. In April 1862 James Rumley complained that officers employed them in various capacities and "promised to pay *them* and not their owners, for their services." One soldier stated that even the youngest black refugees knew the value of money: "The black boys want to hire out as servants, and at such low rates that many of the men in the ranks have one to run errands, draw water, wash their tin dishes." The hiring of servants became such a nuisance and so disruptive to army discipline that on December 4, 1862, Colonel Horace Lee of the 44th Massachusetts Regiment ordered all blacks, except servants to commissioned officers, out of the camp.[29]

While black men worked for the army as manual laborers or servants, black women used their domestic skills to earn money. They provided meals, mended uniforms, and washed clothes for the Union soldiers. Others baked goods and sold them in the army camps for quite a profit. In November 1862 one soldier wrote, "Some are very intelligent and charge reasonable prices for things while the whites ask four times what they are worth." Another commented, "The Negro women are round every day selling ginger-bread[,] cakes[,] pies and other things[,] and it is remarkable how they know all about money and are so ignorant in every respect." Some women established legendary reputations as cooks. One soldier told a friend that he and some companions had gone down to dinner at "Jane's" place, where they enjoyed a savory meal of pork steak, fried liver, baked sweet potatoes, hoecake, and coffee. "She was cook for one of the first families," he wrote, "& now drives quite a business on her own account." Unable to make any money as a slave, Jane drew on her culinary skills to build up a lucrative business after gaining her freedom.[30]

Slave craftsmen also took maximum advantage of their skills. In early 1865, Horace James reported, slaves "have come in, and among them many mechanics and skilled laborers, so that New Berne has now a good supply of tradesmen, in nearly all the different branches essential to social prosperity." Captain Josiah Pender's former slaves Eliza Garner and John Pender were carpenters who constructed buildings and repaired ships for the Union army. The ex-slave Pender, whose wife "was badly whipped" by secessionist sympathizers "on account of his loyalty to the government," found himself having to work with Union authorities who could also be unsympathetic and heavy-handed. Pender complained when a Union surgeon confiscated his personal chest of carpenter's tools in order to repair the hospital; the officer "[threatened] to have me put in the guard house if I did not give them up." After the war Pender and a fellow black carpenter filed a claim with the Federal government for their loss. Though the arbitrators ultimately rejected their claim, the men had continued asserting their right to privileges they deserved as free men — assertions that had been honed during wartime occupation.[31]

Likewise, slave mariners converted their skills into service for the Union authorities. Caesar Manson, who had been publicly humiliated when Josiah Pender shaved his head at Fort Macon in 1861, worked as a boatman carrying the U.S. mail, while other seamen shuttled goods and passengers between Fort Macon, Beaufort, and Morehead City. Another former slave, whom the Union soldiers called "Cuff," sailed across the harbor every morning from Beaufort to Fort Macon to ferry over any soldiers who wished to visit the town, undoubtedly for a small fee. James noted the preponderance of black watermen in the region, musing: "The Negro is here an aquatic animal, and takes to the water almost as readily as the sea fowl that abound in this vicinity." "Not less than one hundred men are constantly employed in boating, this business being wholly in the hands of the Negroes," James wrote in early 1865. "And a remunerative calling it proves to be, indeed." In fact, some amassed enough wealth to purchase important material possessions. Andrew Ward, a former slave who lived in Beaufort, saved up his earnings and purchased his own boat in 1863 "for the convenience of visiting his wife," whose home was on Bogue Island across the harbor. These male and female former slaves who resided in the region did not merely wait for government largesse; rather, they actively sought to supply the northerners' demand for their skills in order to gain employment and improve their material condition.[32]

In addition to providing valuable services to Union personnel and securing financial freedom, employment allowed the building of a robust free black community. Many freedpeople lived in temporary camps outside of Beaufort and New Bern. One of the largest and longest-lasting of these camps was the Trent River Settlement, which would be named James City in honor of Horace James. While serving as superintendent for Negro affairs, James helped create a number of refugee camps on abandoned lands confiscated by the Federal government. Only days after taking office, he established the Trent River Settlement about a mile and a half south of

Headquarters of Vincent Colyer, Superintendent of the Poor, in New Bern, 1862. From *Frank Leslie's Illustrated Newspaper*, June 14, 1862. (Courtesy of North Carolina Collection, University of North Carolina at Chapel Hill)

New Bern on the southern end of the confluence of the Trent and Neuse rivers. The land had once belonged to Richard Dobbs Spaight, a former governor of North Carolina, and had most recently been owned by Peter G. Evans, who was serving as colonel of a Confederate cavalry unit. The tents or makeshift shacks of the future James City and other camps were arranged in neat rows like regimental camps, and allowed for intermingling and community building among its residents. In these camps, freedpeople engaged in their own political development and community organization. Blacks established their own churches, schools, relief societies, and self-help associations, which became centers of their political life.[33]

One of the most influential black leaders in the New Bern camps was Abraham Galloway, whom historian David Cecelski describes as "arguably the most important leader in North Carolina during the Civil War and Reconstruction." The native-born Galloway, who remained prominent until his untimely death in 1870, was an energetic Union agent who organized black military outfits, wrangled concessions from Union authorities regarding black enlistments, and led relief efforts for freedpeople in the region. In pursuit of the latter, he developed strong relationships with black women in the camps to offer relief to the incoming refugees. He established a particularly close relationship with Mary Ann Starkey, who used her home as a political meetinghouse, school, and church. As Cecelski points out, the industrious Starkey "also led a black women's relief society that solicited funds, and supplies among both the former slaves and northern abolitionists for refugee families, and, later, for black soldiers." Instead of merely waiting for the northern benevolent societies to provide supplies and support, Galloway, Starkey, and hundreds of other freedpeople were actively trying to improve their own situations, exhibiting a remarkable degree of steely self-reliance that had been forged during the heat of slavery.[34]

One of the strongest centers of social engagement was the local barbershop. After his carpentry tools had been taken from him, John Pender opened a barbershop in Beaufort where freedmen met to discuss the progress of the war. In 1863 David Parker, a literate freedman, also opened a barbershop, which served as a nexus of freedmen's activities. "Many times in my shop we talked about the war," Parker recalled. "Sometimes I received papers and could read them and tell them colored people what battles had been fought and who were victorious and all about the reports of the battles and the movements of troops. My shop was sort of general head quarters for the colored people to come to for news." Not only was the barbershop an important social center, but it also exemplified one of the most lucrative types of employment. When Horace James listed the highest-grossing occupations among freedpeople in 1864, barbers were near the top of the list, earning an average annual income of $675 (compared to an enlisted man, who made $13 a month, for a yearly income of $156).[35]

James further observed that many freedpeople, not just barbers, were prospering under occupation. "Some of these people are becoming rich; all are doing well for themselves, even in these times," he wrote. Grocers ($678), carpenters ($510), blacksmiths ($468), turpentine farmers ($446), coopers ($418), and masons ($402) all made handsome average annual incomes. Some individual freedmen and freedwomen, primarily those engaging in the turpentine business, earned more than $3,000 in one year, while over a dozen from assorted other occupations grossed more than $1,000 in 1864. When James called on freedpeople in New Bern who worked independently to report their income for 1864, he tallied 305 men and women reporting a total gross income of $150,562, an average of nearly $500 a person. James was greatly impressed by the freedpeople's innate business acumen: "They evince a capacity for business, and exhibit a degree of thrift and shrewdness, which are ample security for their future progress, if they are allowed an equal chance with their fellow-men."[36]

MANY BLACK MEN FELT that enlisting in the U.S. armed forces allowed them the greatest opportunity to earn that equal chance with their fellow whites. Some local freedmen served as sailors and seaman on military and commercial Union vessels, while others enlisted in the black infantry regiments. Few things upset local whites more. The sailors, who as James Rumley reported, were "often fugitive slaves whose masters reside [in Beaufort]," engendered a mixture of outrage and fear among the citizenry for, as Rumley noted in August 1862, "Some of the rascals are armed." Seeing black sailors walk the streets prompted Rumley to envision the apocalyptic day when "armies of black negroes may yet be turned upon us to complete the ruin and desolation that Yankee vandalism has begun." Old antebellum fears of slave insurrections, fueled by memories of Santo Domingo, Nat Turner, and John Brown created such an intense negrophobia that by March 1863, Rumley anxiously declared: "Visions of armed and infuriated bands of these black traitors, like imps of darkness, rise before us and darken the future."[37]

Whites became even more disturbed later in the spring of 1863, when African Americans demonstrated their commitment to the Union cause and exhibited their personal self-worth by enlisting in black infantry regiments. "A recruiting office has been opened today by the Yankees for negro volunteers on Front Street," the fiery Rumley wrote from Beaufort on June 1, 1863, "where the black traitors are gathering in considerable numbers." In spite of white outrage, African Americans desired to demonstrate their equality as men. In a speech to a Beaufort audience, Abraham Galloway invoked the themes represented in enlistment and independence, arguing that "their race would have not only their personal freedom, but political equality, and if this should be refused them at the ballot box they would have it at the cartridge box!"[38]

African American enlistment practices became politicized to represent both manhood and the privileges that rightfully accompanied freedom. Teachers from the American Missionary Association recognized the importance of enlistment to African American psychology: "The action of the government in incorporating the colored people into the army creates a new era in their history; it recognizes their manhood, gives them a status in the nation, and is open acknowledgment of their value to the country in the time of its peril." A northern missionary noticed how the attitudes of black men changed when they donned the Union blue: "I could see a stern determination, an instinctive longing to cope with battle & death, to bequeath these blessings to the long oppressed millions of their race." Enlistment also brought many practical benefits for the soldiers' families. Mary Washington was able to draw rations from the commissary for herself and her six remaining children after her oldest son Lewis joined a Union cavalry regiment in 1863.[39]

Many African Americans had been waiting for the opportunity to enlist from the moment Union troops arrived. William Henry Singleton, a former slave from Craven County, claimed that over one hundred black refugees had been drilling on their own as early as the spring of 1862, anticipating the time when the Lincoln administration would allow African Americans to join the army. In January 1863 one Massachusetts soldier wrote: "I think there could be here in Newbern one thousand who formally were slaves, but who are now free, enlisted in the Union army, who would fight like Tigers to defend their rights as they now enjoy them." Indeed, when the Federal government finally authorized the enlistment of black soldiers in the region a month later, volunteers flocked to the enlistment office, but only after negotiating for certain rights.[40]

Massachusetts soldier and recruiting agent Edward W. Kinsley related an encounter he had with New Bern's Abraham Galloway in early 1863 regarding black enlistments. Kinsley claimed that Galloway had persuaded the blacks not to sign up right away. "So great was his influence among the colored people that all matters of importance concerning them were left to his decision." Kinsley may have exaggerated Galloway's power in making decisions, but his statement does reveal that blacks had bonded together to negotiate suitable terms with Union authorities before they enlisted in the army. When Kinsley agreed to meet with Galloway to discuss enlistment demands, he was blindfolded and carried to a secret attic room, where his blindfold was removed; he found himself surrounded by many blacks, while "right in front of him stood Abraham Galloway and another huge negro, both armed with revolvers." With this display of intimidating negotiating tactics, Galloway, whom Union authorities also valued as a skilled spy, was able to extract the concessions that freedpeople demanded from the Federal government. They insisted not only that North Carolina blacks should be paid the same as black soldiers in Massachusetts (where the 54th

Abraham Galloway
(Courtesy of State
Archives, Division
of Archives and
History, Raleigh)

Massachusetts Regiment had just been formed), but also that "their families should be provided for; their children should be taught to read; and if they should be taken prisoners, the government should see to it that they were treated as prisoners of war." Kinsley, on his own authority, pledged that the government would meet all these demands (though there was no way he could guarantee them). As a result, he reported, "The next day the word went forth, and the blacks came to the recruiting station by [the] hundreds and a brigade was soon formed." Even allowing for some exaggeration of the timetable, the spirit of enlistment did become quite vigorous within the black community in early 1863.[41]

In the first muster in February 1863, a Union officer reported that 413 African Americans already had answered the roll. In April a Union soldier noted, "They are enlisting Negroes here at a grate [sic] rate[.] Two hundred nearly enlisted in about two days." On May 24 a Union officer reported that over four hundred had enlisted in that week alone. Opportunities to enlist were even more plentiful after General Edward Wild's arrival in New Bern on May 17 to recruit from the local black populations in order to fill up his "African Brigade." At the urging of Massachusetts governor John Andrew, Secretary of War Stanton had authorized Wild to raise a brigade of black troops in eastern North Carolina. Wild began mustering men into the 1st North Carolina Colored Volunteer Regiment as soon as he arrived in New Bern. Within one month, over five hundred men had enlisted in Wild's brigade.[42]

The pride and satisfaction that black men enjoyed from enlisting became apparent to outside observers. One Union soldier who had feared that freedmen could not "be converted into serviceable recruits" was amazed to see their transformation on donning the Union bluecoats. "The National uniform was as a magic robe to them and they straightened up and stood erect in it, at once men and soldiers," he remarked. "The touch of the rifle as their hands clasped it seemed to fill their veins with electric life." In fact, the act of enlisting served as a major source of empowerment for black men throughout the region, and the prospect of martially participating in winning their own independence prompted thousands to enlist before the war ended. Though accurate numbers of black enlistments from Carteret and Craven counties are difficult to ascertain, over five thousand blacks joined the Union army from North Carolina; almost all of them came from the occupied region of the state.[43]

Black enlistment efforts met plenty of resistance from local whites as well as Union soldiers. Many white soldiers — even liberal, antislavery ones — maintained decidedly racist views after their arrival. For instance, whereas General John G. Foster, the department commander in May 1863 zealously supported General Wild's recruitment efforts, his successor in August, Major General John J. Peck, did not share this enthusiasm and discontinued the practice as a matter of policy. As a result, the vast majority of black enlistments in the region occurred before August 1863. Peck discouraged the use of black troops in North Carolina and quickly ordered all of them to Fort Monroe, Virginia, on August 28. He also provided no assistance to those regiments still in the process of recruiting to fill out the African Brigade, and the officers of these unfilled regiments had to scramble to outfit their regiments in Virginia.[44]

While sentiment was divided among Union soldiers as to the propriety or desirability of enlisting black soldiers, most eventually accepted the fact as a practical measure if nothing else. Some soldiers grew to appreciate the fighting qualities of the black troops. Henry Clapp, of the 44th Massachusetts Regiment, wrote home in April 1863 from New Bern that his regiment placed the local black troops "as sort of night-picket in half-defiance of the directions from head-quarters, and [they] perform their duties splendidly. It is absolutely impossible for any one to get either in or out of the lines, when they are on guard." Clapp gave positive endorsements of their mettle, saying: "They are in respect models of courage, vigilance and trustworthiness, and the bands of rebel guerrillas who infest the out skirts and who caused almost constant alarms by night, before these men were put on, stand in the greatest dread of them." Revealing his own adherence to prejudicial stereotypes, Clapp further praised their "unique" skills: "They all know every forest path and have eyesight like cats so that at night while their color will let them be perfectly hid in the shadow of a tree they themselves see everything." Some soldiers, though certainly not all, overcame their initial hostility toward black enlistment and recognized it as good for the war effort. As Massachusetts soldier Edward J. Bartlett wrote to his sister in 1863, "I think that enlisting Negroes is going to be the saving of the country, and I am glad that they have come to it at last."[45]

WHETHER ASSERTING THEIR manhood as soldiers or simply trying to advance their material conditions within Union lines, African Americans demonstrated their fervent desire to assert their independence and improve their lives. Nearly all former slaves viewed education as the crucial determinant of their personal autonomy. The inability to read or write represented a tangible symbol of slavery; in fact, bondspeople had been punished severely for attempting to learn to read. North Carolina slave testimony recorded during the Works Progress Administration interviews of the 1930s reveals the taboo whites placed on black education. "You better not be found trying to learn to read," recalled Hannah Crasson. "Our marster was harder down on that than anything else." Patsy Michner confirmed this: "You better not be caught with no paper in your hand; if you was, you got the cowhide."[46]

Supporting testimony also came from more contemporary informants than octogenarian freedwomen trying to remember their childhood. Horace James heard slaves decry their masters' restrictions: "If any of them saw us with a spelling-book trying to learn to read, they would take it away from us and punish us." William Henry Singleton recounted how his master "whipped me very severely" just for opening a book. Even the hint of a slave seeking some reading knowledge would bring instant retribution from concerned masters. Nonetheless, many slaves still sought education because of its empowering virtues. As one clandestinely educated slave noted, "I felt at night, as I went to my rest, that I was really beginning to be a *man*, preparing myself for a condition in life better and higher and happier than could belong to the ignorant *slave*."[47]

Many slaves sought, primarily through surreptitious means, to acquire some education. These efforts were surprisingly successful. Historians have suggested that between 5 and 10 percent of southern slaves had at least a rudimentary degree of literacy by 1860. Union soldiers confirmed these suspicions in the New Bern–Beaufort region. In 1863 Henry Clapp wrote: "I should say that about one in fifteen of the men, women, and children could read. We find that many learned or began to learn before they were freed by our army—taking their instruction mostly 'on the sly' and indeed in the face of considerable danger." Therefore, it is not surprising that former slaves, whether refugees or enlisted men, embraced the educational opportunities offered by Union soldiers and members of freedmen's aid societies that entered the region. Of course, Union attempts to educate blacks, which began immediately after occupation in 1862, angered local whites and created conflict between Union officers and military governor Edward Stanly. When Vincent Colyer set up the two evening schools for blacks in New Bern, it rankled Governor Stanly, who ordered Colyer to close the schools on the grounds that teaching blacks to read was against North Carolina law. Colyer closed the schools and went to Washington to protest.[48]

Closing the schools had the most pronounced impact on the black population that had benefited from them. As many as eight hundred African Americans attended the schools from April, when they opened, until June 1862, when they closed, demonstrating the intense desire among ex-slaves to improve their condition. A correspondent for the AMA wrote that "the old people dropped their heads upon their breast and wept in silence; the young looked at each other with mute surprise and grief at this sudden termination of their bright hopes." Their hopes were soon rekindled, however, as President Lincoln informed Colyer that Stanly had no authority to close the schools; furthermore, "he had given Gov. Stanly no such instructions as would justify him in these acts." Colyer returned, and the schools reopened in July 1862 over Stanly's protest.[49]

Union soldiers in the region realized that the escaped slaves had the capacity for learning. While a Union officer in New Bern wrote the editor of the *New York Tribune* stating that he could not "think the negro is capable of immediate cultivation equal to that of the white race," he nevertheless admitted that "they are capable of a much higher cultivation than is generally believed, I am convinced. They have a strong desire to learn, which will sometimes surmount the greatest obstacles." The officer noted blacks' clever way of gaining knowledge, bred in the dependence of slavery: "They keep eyes and ears open to all that is going on around them, and in this way often learn much that is not intended for them to know."[50]

Union soldiers began conducting impromptu schools wherever they could, but it was too large a task for the military to undertake alone, especially given the transitory nature of the soldiers in the region. However, help soon appeared when the first agents of northern benevolent societies, led by the AMA, began to arrive in the region in 1863. But before the AMA brought the full weight of its resources to bear in North Carolina, individual officers, soldiers, and benevolent society teachers had been operating makeshift schools wherever there was room. Throughout the wartime occupation, teachers held class in churches, army barracks, barns, abandoned plantation buildings, basements, or deserted jails, and one officer taught his pupils "in the rear of the Quartermaster's office." One instructor commented, "We teach in a barn fitted up with seats for nearly four hundred persons," which during the winter "is heated by only one Sibley stove, and having no sash in the windows." Students still attended despite the fact that it was so cold that the teacher "taught every day so far in a hood, blanket shawl, and thick gloves."[51]

Instructors also improvised teaching supplies. One soldier related that in May 1862, "As primers were not at hand, an olive green window shutter served for a blackboard, the instruction being mainly oral." Teachers used Bibles as standard texts. Yet Union agents improved the situation as quickly as possible, constructing new schools and recruiting supplies and teachers from northern benevolent societies. Horace James, who had spent many years fostering education in New England, reported in May 1863 on his efforts to get good teachers. For former slaves, he said, "nothing short of 'yankee school ma'am's' will answer for their children." He energetically and largely successfully pursued such teachers and pushed for expanding the number of schools.[52]

The northern agents noticed the determination and joy that local blacks showed while attending school. Massachusetts soldier Henry Wellington wrote his sister about the freedpeople's enthusiastic reaction to learning: "You would think there was a thunder shower coming if you could see them coming out of the school." Horace James observed, "The children learn just as rapidly as children at the north." Nevertheless, young Miss Carrie Getchell of the AMA, stationed in Beaufort, remarked in February 1864 that teaching middle-class northern white children was a far different experience from teaching poor southern black children, whose enthusiasm and energy in the classroom called for harnessing. "There are a very many things which will require much patience and perseverance to correct," Getchell reported. "They are very pugilistic in their tendencies. I am at a loss to know why it is so."[53]

Determined freedpeople used every spare minute to study. A soldier in the 23rd Massachusetts pointed out: "Grown men, employed in 'dug outs' to catch and raft logs, brought, on their way to the saw mill . . . [their] spelling book[s] which [were] speedily whipped out and zealously studied at every break, however short, in their onerous task." An officer's wife, visiting her husband at New Bern in February 1863, told a friend: "I have frequently seen in the street the Negro teamster[s], poring over their primers and spelling books, while waiting for something or other." AMA missionary William Briggs observed: "After a hard day's work, they return to their homes, take their frugal meal, change their dress when they can make a change — come to the school & devote an hour and a half to earnest study." Some adults sought individual arrangements for education, bartering practical goods for instruction. One Union soldier recounted: "Aunty Southwhite gave me a quilt tonight on condition that 'I learn her how to read.'" Freedpeople also used their hard-earned money to provide opportunities for their further enhancement. When Yale-educated Rhode Island minister George N. Greene arrived in Beaufort from New York in October 1863 to open a school, he collected $84.88 from local blacks to defray operating expenses. Residents of the Pine Grove Settlement, one of several camps outside of town, raised $95.00 and told Greene they would raise "another hundred if necessary in order to educate their children."[54]

These missionaries began to establish schools throughout the region and brought their own civilian teachers to instruct the freedpeople. With their arrival, freedpeople found yet another way to gain the education that many northerners perceived as their most desired form of empowerment. With

another northern institution, however, came another set of Yankee preconceptions of, and expectations for, southern blacks. Local African Americans
had to negotiate with these new agents as well to carve out the autonomy
they desired, while the northern civilians, primarily female teachers, had to
learn to adapt to the foreign local environment, while they tried to impose
their own brand of civilization and refinement on the freedpeople.

CHAPTER 5

The Experience of Northern
Benevolent Societies during Occupation

When northerners arrived in coastal North Carolina during the Civil War, they discovered that the African Americans there, as elsewhere in the South, shared an overwhelming desire to acquire literacy. Susan A. Hosmer, one of the first New England teachers to appear in New Bern, wrote in September 1863 that, for local blacks, learning to read "seems to be the height of their ambition." Freedpeople held a deep, abiding resentment toward their former masters who systematically prevented them from obtaining this measure of enlightenment. Among the many evils perpetrated on blacks under the peculiar institution, one former slave specifically identified what he considered the most egregious. "There is one sin that slavery committed against me, which I will never forgive," he declared. "It robbed me of my education."[1]

Northern missionaries and teachers — the majority of them from New England — began arriving in coastal North Carolina in 1863 to teach those former slaves who had been denied an education. The American Missionary Association (AMA), the first organization to send teachers to the region, issued an "Appeal for the Freedmen" in its monthly publication in January 1863, calling on Christian soldiers to come forward to help in the great education crusade. While acknowledging that the freedmen had physical needs, the "Appeal" also proclaimed: "They need intelligent friends and counselors, to guard them against the insults, impositions, immoralities and various abuses of those who hate them, and are interested to prove that the Negroes are an improvident race, unfit to take care of themselves." The AMA felt it could provide the intellectual, spiritual, and moral education necessary to make the freedpeople independent. Over the next two years, dozens of northern teachers — a majority of them women — traveled to North Carolina to provide enlightenment for the previously benighted people.[2]

The freedpeople generally appreciated their efforts. One woman told her teacher, Susan Hosmer, how she had sought to become literate even as a slave. "When mistress was in good humor, I used to cry," she related, "and then she would let me take a lesson, so I learned to read a little. In my ignorance, I promised the Lord, if he would please let me learn enough, so that I could read the Bible, I would ask no more." But the drop of knowledge simply led to a greater thirst for more. "Now my desire is, to get more knowledge," the former bondswoman said, "and I bless God that he has sent you out here. I want to do all that I can for you, now that you have come so far to teach us."[3]

These teachers faced many dangers — primarily from the threat of Confederate attack, hostile local whites, and disease — as well as difficult working conditions, including inadequate materials, classroom space, and living quarters. Despite the hardships, northern teachers undoubtedly felt some sense of accomplishment. Letters like the one from freedman George W. Jenkins in New Bern to his former instructor, Sarah, who had returned north on vacation, undoubtedly vindicated the time and strenuous efforts she expended in the South. In June 1864 Jenkins wrote her: "We will never forget the kind teachers for bringing light to our land, when she was Dark as night. They came in spite of rebs. Their reward is not in this world, but a world to come."[4]

Though the interaction between northern missionaries, teachers, and local black and white inhabitants had its share of success stories like the newly literate Mr. Jenkins, it also revealed many tensions. Local whites often resented the arrival of these emissaries, who sought to uplift the blacks in their midst. The freedpeople also challenged their northern benefactors, disputing control over churches and schools, the message or curriculum taught in each, as well as who would do the preaching or teaching. Not all teachers had been bona fide abolitionists before the war and did not identify with black rhetoric to use the school for societal transformation. Most white teachers tended to concentrate on uplifting degraded blacks, who would then be trained to survive and perhaps thrive in a northerner's version of a free labor society. In addition, conflicts emerged between teachers over petty grievances; rifts developed between the competing benevolent societies over leadership positions, school locations, and fund-raising;

and sectarian strife pervaded the region as rival denominations disputed the "proper" spiritual message.[5]

The New England missionaries and teachers came with certain preconceptions of helpless and puerile freedpeople, and a blind confidence that installing a New England system — with a properly paternalistic attitude — would be the best way to lift up the downtrodden former slaves. Indeed, as historian Nina Silber has argued, female teachers helped shape the emancipation process — teaching literacy and important labor skills — but simultaneously helped perpetuate the notion that African Americans were second-class citizens.[6] Meanwhile, freedpeople, infused with a strong sense of self-reliance, sought autonomy over their social institutions. They had definite ideas about the nature of the education they required and wished to establish independent schools free from white control. As a result, whites and blacks were constantly negotiating social, political, and cultural boundaries in the region. Ultimately, blacks were frustrated in many of their efforts to achieve autonomy, as the Federal government withdrew its wartime level of support, reneged on promises, and allowed former Confederates to repossess their abandoned lands. Nonetheless, the strong spirit of independence acquired by blacks could not be eradicated by the actions of hostile whites after the war. Much of their newfound power emanated not only from the efforts of the secular soldiers of the Federal government, but also from the well-intentioned work of the Christian soldiers of benevolent societies to help the freedpeople "take care of themselves."[7]

UNION AGENTS PROFESSED an earnest desire to educate the slaves in coastal North Carolina as well as throughout the South. In a sermon printed in William Lloyd Garrison's antislavery Boston-based newspaper, *The Liberator*, in June 1862, Henry Ward Beecher, the outspoken abolitionist minister from Massachusetts, declared: "I feel that if this struggle is to inaugurate the policy, not only of emancipation, but of teaching, the auspices of the future are blessed." The AMA and other northern benevolent societies entered eastern North Carolina to ensure that blessing. Though Union officers and even some barely literate local blacks had begun teaching in makeshift schools in the spring of 1862, the AMA opened its first two formal schools in New Bern on July 23, 1863; the pupils were taught in two black churches by four ladies from Massachusetts. The AMA became the largest aid organization not just in coastal North Carolina, but across the South, ultimately contributing over $5 million to assist freedpeople during and after the war. Formed in 1846 in Albany, New York, the association became an abolitionist and educational society with its primary goals being to instruct and support former slaves. It began sending missionaries to the occupied portions of the South in 1861 (initially to Fort Monroe, Virginia) and emissaries to North Carolina in the summer of 1863.[8]

The AMA, like most northern missionary societies, tried to institute stringent requirements for those women who wanted to go south as teachers. Not every woman who volunteered was selected. First, a prospective teacher had to apply to the society, outlining her qualifications and explaining her desire for the position, then get recommendations from a minister and her former school's principal attesting to her spiritual assets and practical skills. AMA chief secretary George Whipple once rejected three applicants because he doubted "very much whether they have the view of the importance of the work that we have, and whether their hearts are in it." However, though the AMA had established strict rules—to avoid poor reflection on its organization should the teacher fail—such regulations served more as suggestions and were frequently ignored. In one instance, Mary S. Williams was hired despite her admission that she had no teaching experience, was in poor physical health, and had never been away from home. She taught in Wilmington and Beaufort from 1868 to 1870.[9]

Reverend Horace James, who, as superintendent for Negro affairs for the Department of North Carolina, was instrumental in getting teachers for the New Bern–Beaufort region, could not help but admire the poetic justice of some of his efforts. After an AMA agent had established a school at remote Clubfoot Creek in Carteret County, the first teacher sent to instruct the former slaves was "a cultured lady" from West Newton, Massachusetts, by the name of Caroline E. Croome. James related: "The rebels had slain her noble husband while in command of his battery at South Mountain [on September 14, 1862], and she would avenge his untimely death by teaching ignorant Negroes how to throw off the yoke which those dastardly rebels had put upon their necks." He mused, perhaps with a quiet smile at the workings of divine providence, "This was the sublime retaliation of the gospel." Indeed, Croome served steadfastly as a teacher in the region, despite repeated threats against her by disgruntled white citizens.[10]

Dedicated teachers like Croome—who taught in the New Bern–Beaufort region until 1872—made an immediate difference in eastern North Carolina. By the end of March 1864, New Bern boasted eleven schools for freedpeople; Beaufort had three, and there were nine more in other occu-

House occupied by "Yankee school ma'ams" on Broad Street, New Bern, 1863. The building no longer exists. (Courtesy of North Carolina Collection, University of North Carolina at Chapel Hill)

pied parts of North Carolina. Typically these were one-room schools, where adults and children were taught separately whenever possible; frequently there was only one teacher per school. The demand for teachers soon became acute as the number of students grew exponentially. July 1864 found three thousand black students enrolled in classes. Though the schools closed temporarily because of a yellow fever outbreak, they reopened in December. By 1865 James could proudly report that there were nineteen day schools and eight night schools operating in the region.[11]

Many northerners were aware that African Americans were not the only ignorant, impoverished population in eastern North Carolina in need of uplifting. "This place has many families of the poor whites, who are as destitute of all the advantages of Education, as the Negroes themselves," AMA agent H. S. Beals, a former teacher and principal in New York and Massachusetts, wrote from nearby Plymouth, North Carolina, in August 1863. "I do not doubt, that a careful, prudent man would secure the attendance of their children to a Col[ored] school, if it was desirable." The AMA's Susan Hosmer discovered that some lower-class whites in New Bern were even willing to ask for help. "Being earnestly requested by a mother, a white child was permitted to become a member of our school," she wrote in September 1863. "Since then several others have come in without permission and as we come to work for all, they have not been turned away."[12]

Yet integrated schools were rare, as most whites refused to join blacks in the classroom. Reverend George N. Greene reported in October 1863 that he had succeeded in getting more than four hundred poor white children to enroll in segregated schools yet to be established. Greene warned, however, that "[I] have met in my labors among them some very rabid Secesh. Indeed, I was told when I first came here a white school would not go at all." He was uncertain that such a school would be allowed to thrive, for the stigma of whites being taught by the same people who had come to the region to instruct former slaves was very powerful. After the war such sentiments only increased throughout the state. Few whites consented to permit their children to attend the same schools as black students or be instructed by the same teachers. Thus, in the course of Union occupation, few schools were opened for whites. Not only were northern benevolent societies more interested in elevating the poor, ignorant, former slaves, but also they determined that the native white hostility to black education would prohibit a full welcome of those same whites to the privileges of education.[13]

Some local whites tried to intimidate northern teachers and discourage black students from attending schools. In 1864, for example, three white men torched a black schoolhouse and threatened the female teacher with violence unless she promised to "never again teach the niggers to read." Perhaps more than employment and enlistment, local whites feared the empowerment that education granted to freedpeople, because it reached even the youngest members of black society. This instruction held dangerous implications, as the northern teachers introduced ideas that transcended spiritual lessons and charitable efforts to teach reading, writing, and arithmetic.[14]

African American students and their white teachers persevered in spite of these hostile conditions. In addition to threats of violence and bad weather, the exigencies of wartime often halted classes. When a rebel army under General George Pickett threatened New Bern in February 1864, Union officials forced a black school out of Fort Totten, and a school near the Trent River had to close for a week because the incessant cannonading made it too difficult to hold class. From New Bern in early 1865, one teacher commented: "We are in hourly expectation of an order for the opening of our churches for hospital purposes." Despite the hardships that teachers had faced from the beginning, Horace James praised their perseverance, proclaiming them to be "both capital stuff, and true as steel. They are happy in the work & winning the favor of the community."[15]

NOTWITHSTANDING JAMES'S OPTIMISM, the dangers of the region started to take their toll on some teachers, who questioned the wisdom of traveling to a war zone to teach the freedpeople. "However light a matter the Northern papers may make of it, we were in great danger of being captured that first week of February [1864], as New Berne was defended by an insufficient number of troops," Emily Gill informed the secretary of the AMA. A week later she concluded: "The unsettled military state of this part of the country, and the consequent hasty and frequent changes submitted to by ourselves and our people have made me feel somewhat of 'a poor soldier.'" The constant tension "subjected me to headaches . . . and strengthened a growing desire to come home and feel more at rest." Gill went north in April 1864 and did not return to North Carolina. Like Gill, several teachers left in frustration over the difficult living and working conditions; others were discouraged that former slaves were not as receptive to northern moral and spiritual instruction as they were to education.[16]

Nonmilitary enemies also took their toll on students and teachers alike. In the summer of 1864, a yellow fever epidemic hit New Bern and Beaufort, killing hundreds of blacks and whites, and forcing many to flee or quarantine themselves in the city. As a result the freedmen schools shut down in July but reopened in December when the epidemic had passed. Carrie M. Getchell, a dedicated young AMA teacher, who had taught extra classes to cover other teachers who had taken ill, contracted a violent cold herself in March 1864; she died rather suddenly from severe tonsillitis, but only after an emergency and very painful laryngotomy had been performed. When informed of her plight only moments before the end, the twenty-four-year-old Getchell bemoaned in disbelief: "Have I come down here to die?"[17]

Getchell, having grown frustrated by the slowness of the military bureaucracy in building her a room near the Morehead City wharf to put her closer to her soon-to-open school, had insisted on walking several miles from her lodging to the railroad depot. "It will be a long walk to the depot," she wrote George Whipple, "but I much rather do it than delay longer." Her death caused loved ones at home to castigate the administration of the schools in the region. A "display of energetic promptness on the part of those whose business it was to do the outdoor labor & provide easy & convenient boarding places for lady teachers might have retained Carrie much longer in her earthly labors," commented one bitter correspondent to Horace James. The writer had heard more complaints from other teachers, telling James: "They talked of unpardonable inefficiency on the part of those men at Beaufort placed there just for the purpose of doing these things which they did not do & which the ladies must do or see their time wasting away without accomplishing their desired work." Getchell was certainly not the only female teacher to suffer from a severe illness, nor was she the only one to die during her service. But the excoriations of the authorities after her death illuminate the undercurrent of tension, questionable competence, and spitefulness that also characterized the northern agents' work.[18]

Occasionally, missionaries and teachers complained about the assignments they received. For some, such as Miss Antoinette L. Etheridge, the designated location was not primitive enough. On learning that she was to teach at Clubfoot Creek, twenty miles from Beaufort, she asserted: "The people [there] are self-sustaining, have never been slaves. This takes a little from the interest. I mean we can not feel that tender sympathy that we would have were they recently bondsmen." Teaching those merely destitute of knowledge was not nearly as motivating to her as teaching those former slaves whom, she presumed, needed to be nurtured and uplifted from their disadvantaged condition.[19]

Other northerners felt that their assigned destination was far too primitive. When Congregationalist minister Timothy Lyman and his wife arrived at Hatteras Inlet in August 1864, they balked, finding the outpost "too crude." Mrs. Lyman remarked that she did not know "people could live as they do here, so few comforts." Horace James, disdainful of their lack of commitment, commented that the Lymans "appear to be thoroughly disgusted with Hatteras Inlet, without having so much as introduced themselves to the people with whom they proposed to labor." James continued: "Feeling as *she* does, I have strongly advised them not to go there, for it would be a sin against the people and against God for them to enter upon their labors with so little faith as they have." While upset by the Lymans' lack of conviction, James seemed to have forgotten his own first impression of Hatteras. When there with Burnside's expedition in February 1862, he had concluded: "It is the most forlorn, forsaken, barren, wretched sand hole I ever looked upon." The Lymans merely agreed.[20]

Such mordant observations were relatively common among the northern aid workers, all of whom were in the region ostensibly for the same purpose. Conflicts surfaced, personalities clashed, and complaints about fellow missionaries or teachers flowed freely both to local administrators and to northern friends at home. Some female teachers grumbled at the intense scrutiny they were under and how the actions of a few could tarnish the virtue of all. Nellie Stearns, who shared a house with seven other young women, told a friend about the social stigmas they faced. Though she was writing from New Bern in November 1865, the societal rules she described applied from the moment northern women set foot in the region in 1862. "We have to be so careful how we behave here," she began. "We are very closely watched by the Southerners and others too." Stearns denounced the sexual indiscretions of a colleague, candidly reporting that a young northern soldier "came in the other night and had a regular romp with one of the girls. They made a great noise and I have just heard there have been remarks about it by people who passed. This young lady is very lively and rather coarse and rude, and I suspect she will get us all into trouble." Stearns was well aware that any hint of sexual promiscuity by one risked besmirching the reputations of all the young women teachers in the region. With this foremost on her mind, Nellie complained: "A few thoughtless girls bring scandal on all the rest of us, and I declare it makes me provoked. There are abominable stories about the teachers circulated and believed too even by sensible Northern people."[21]

Nellie Stearns was one of many missionaries who found fault with their compatriots. In a letter of December 1864 to Secretary Whipple, Reverend William Briggs, an AMA superintendent in Beaufort, wrote: "I learn Miss Howe has written you unfavorable things in regard to Miss Spalding. I would suggest that if teachers are allowed to begin this game, the Lord only knows where it will end." Two months before she died, Carrie Getchell apologized to Whipple for her negative comments about her fellow teachers: "I hasten to write you fearing that in my last I used language which conveyed more than I really intended it should. Your rebuke I acknowledge as just, and thank you for it." She attempted to calm Whipple's fears, declaring: "I assure you that there has no 'root of bitterness' sprung up among us. We are interested in each other's welfare, and entertain the kindest feelings towards each other."[22]

Other letters from northern aid workers belied Getchell's sense of amity. At the same time that Whipple read her penitent pledge, he would have received Horace James's less-than-compassionate appraisal of the AMA's Beaufort agent, Reverend George N. Greene. "Mr. Greene is fast lapsing into utter imbecility and chronic nothingness," began the disparaging missive. "He does not *preach*, nor *teach*, nor do anything but *fuss* and laze around to the annoyance and contempt of all." Other AMA workers were also disappointed in Greene's work. According to one agent, Greene "was strangely inefficient in regard to the preparation of schoolhouses for the teachers and that he had drawn upon himself and to some extent on the whole establishment the wrath of the Army officers." William Briggs, who had earlier cautioned about teachers reproaching each other, could not refrain from informing Whipple that Greene "has been a great annoyance to me not so much from what he has done but from what he has *not* done." A few months after the war, the superintendent of the North Carolina branch of the Freedmen's Bureau would complain to the AMA home office that the inefficient and indolent Greene was "embarrassing the work in which we are engaged."[23]

Even the dogged and determined Horace James was not spared censure by other agents. The first time that visiting AMA emissary Reverend William Hamilton spoke of meeting James in mid-January 1864, he was effusive in his praise, claiming: "I could not but admire the untiring energy and perseverance with which this noble servant of Christ pursues his work of emancipation and enlightenment." But only six days later, Hamilton's tone had changed entirely. "To say that Mr. James received me coldly would not fully express the idea of my reception," Hamilton wrote to the home office. "His manner was freezing—many degrees below zero." Hamilton also had unkind words for James's wife: Her "manner was invariably distant and forbidding" and she was once "grossly insulting" to him. He even went so far as to say: "I have been told that Mrs. James whose conduct was so strange towards me has been at times insane, but I fear she has infected Mr. James also with her antipathy."[24]

Hamilton's caustic comments reveal more about the strain James was under than it does about his poor social skills. Besides his own probable personal unhappiness at having an AMA informant come to investigate how the superintendent was running his operation, James was aloof to Hamilton for a variety of other reasons. News had just arrived that a large Confederate force was marching toward New Bern, threatening invasion of the town, which forced James to cancel a planned trip to Roanoke Island just as Hamilton arrived. Beyond the military dangers, James was constantly deal-

Horace James, chaplain and superintendent for Negro
affairs in New Bern (Courtesy of State Archives, Division
of Archives and History, Raleigh)

ing with black demands for the redress of grievances. Hamilton observed that on January 19 "a succession of contrabands, male and female, presented themselves. One desired to have a grant of the use of some land near one of the forts confirmed. Several were making claims for unpaid accounts against the government contractors. Others were threatened with ejection from the houses they occupied. Each case was noted down and the claimant dismissed with assurances that his rights would be secured to him."[25]

While trying to address each person's claim, James was engaged in a months-long campaign to get quality teachers. Though many freedpeople had made it known that they would like to have black teachers — and as the war went on, they actively sought black teachers themselves, often out of the pool of black soldiers in the region — James had a strong preference for white teachers over black ones. When the home office informed him that it was recruiting black teachers, James demurred. "As to *colored teachers* from the north," he wrote, "I do not see the way clear for them coming among us as yet." He believed black teachers to be less skilled than white ones, explaining: "I want to bring to the system all the influence of efficiency and even e'clat which *white* teachers can give it, so as to accomplish the most in a short time." He similarly rebuffed a black minister from Boston who desired to send African American preachers to the region.[26]

James had been continually distressed by the scarcity of teachers and the low quality of several who came. Only two weeks before Hamilton arrived to observe his operations, James had written Secretary Whipple, "I entreat you not to send any more except A No. 1 Teachers. *Privately*, while the first two you sent us possess a lovely & sweet christian character, they lack the promptness, energy . . . [and] force, which are highly desirable." In addition to his frustration over the dearth of teachers, James was faced with the challenge posed by the ineffective George Greene, a problem he resolved on January 20 by ordering Greene to go preach and teach at Clubfoot Creek — as much to get him out of everyone's way in Beaufort as to help the black population in Clubfoot Creek.[27]

His dealings with Greene revealed yet another task that James had to address delicately — that of coordinating and placating the various benevolent societies, many of which had extremely sectarian views. For instance, Greene was a Baptist, and James, himself a Congregationalist like most members of the AMA, wrote wearily to Whipple on January 16: "If the Baptist[s] will only send a man who is smart, and wide awake and *knows* something, we would welcome him. But if you were to withdraw [Greene], they would make a poor show of crying persecution." Indeed, balancing the numer-ous societies that contributed to the freedpeoples' relief could be a tricky business. In addition to the AMA, the National Freedmen's Relief Associa-tion, the New England Freedmen's Aid Society, the Education Commis-sion of Boston (also known as the Boston Society), and many other private organizations furnished goods, money, and teachers to the relief efforts in North Carolina. All donations ultimately flowed through James's office, as he determined where to disperse money, clothes, teachers, books, and other supplies. These societies collectively provided an enormous amount of relief to freedpeople in the region. In the first four months of 1864, for example, benevolent societies contributed so much clothing that James distributed nearly 13,000 items of clothing—worth over $7,500—contributed by be-nevolent societies.[28]

The different organizations, though sharing similar goals, did not always get along or agree on how to implement those goals. While Greene had pro-fessed, "I am not so Sectarian that I cannot work with *any christian*," James still made a strenuous effort to send only Baptists who would cooperate with him, a prospect Greene admitted he found "pleasant and agreeable." William Briggs gave voice to one of the rifts, claiming, in early January 1865, "The cause of the Boston Soc. in ignoring the other societies and the Super-intendent is unaccountable unless we imputed to them the most unworthy motives." Of the Baptist organization, he proclaimed, "I have yet to find a class or clique more intolerant," though "I have taken unwearied pains, knowing their jealousy, to avoid the *appearance* of sectarianism."[29]

REGARDLESS OF DENOMINATION, those with ministerial proclivities had ample opportunity to aid the local freedpeople. Beaufort and New Bern became centers of black religious resurgence during the Union oc-cupation. On the last Sunday in August 1863, fifty people were baptized. Susan Hosmer wrote, "A good old colored lady said there never was such a day in Newbern, and she blessed God that she ever saw a Yankee." Previ-ously, whites had forced African Americans to observe their own expressive mode of religious worship, led by black preachers, clandestinely. Slaves had told Horace James they had never enjoyed preaching by white ministers under slavery. "The ministers we used to hear would always be telling us to be obedient to our masters on earth and then we should be accepted by our masters in heaven," he recounted. "They never told us we had any rights." As historian David Cecelski has aptly deduced, however, slaves must have kept up their own practices before the war given how rapidly they were able to establish their own churches during the occupation.[30]

New Bern housed thousands of freedpeople eager for the establishment of churches as well. In early June 1863, James informed the AMA that "a good man would find full employment and a grand field in the colored camps about the city." He had already met one: Edward S. Fitz, a private in the 43rd Massachusetts and a strong Methodist, "had been preaching in the largest colored church here ever since last December." Fitz had decided that when his nine-month regiment was decommissioned in the summer of 1863, he would return to New Bern to continue his work. Fitz did return and served as a Freedmen's Bureau agent through 1866. "They wish to have him, and have already pledged him ample supports," James wrote. He further opined, "This is better than any other way I think, and as the people have chosen their own minister, so let it be. It is their right."[31]

Other northern ministers disagreed with James's democratic principles when it came to a church's leadership and message. In August 1864 Congregationalist Reverend Timothy Lyman complained: "I am in no wise a sectarian in my feelings. . . . But I claim that the greatest and most immediate demand of this people (the Blacks) is the *correction of some great errors and evils* in their modes of worship." These errors could be remedied only by instituting a Congregationalist solution, which meant opening new churches with northern white-educated ministers. Six months later, Lyman was still outraged at the resistance of black churches to white preachers. He lamented, "We seem to be driven to the policy of organizing new churches from the *difficulty* if not *impossibility* of white missionaries gaining access to their pulpits as teachers." Lyman blamed this development on the greedy "*ambition* of their leading men." Lyman, as well as many other reformers, denounced what he saw as the ignorance of black preachers: "It is principally *one thing* that they strive to effect in their hearers and that is *a kind of happy personal experience.*" He further deplored that "they carry the idea that religion consists chiefly in a kind of joyful exhilaration," instead of a dark denunciation of deathly sin. Lyman favored individual reflection on sins, emotional detachment, and denial of temptations. However, he misunderstood the nature of the black communal experience. Slave religion had been focused on the expressions of joy and hope for a better future for the slave community. Black ministers did not undertake the program of preaching that dour Congregationalists like Lyman thought absolutely necessary for the morally degraded former slaves: "They do not much preach against the evil habits of their people — as lying, thieving and unfaithfulness in their domestic vows to which they are prone."[32]

Lyman's pointed remark reveals another unsightly truth about benevolent society members in eastern North Carolina: northern missionaries and teachers had strong, preconceived ideas about what was best for the freedpeople, ideas that often conflicted with what the freedpeople believed. In offering their aid, northern benevolent societies expected blacks to bend to their wishes, especially when it came to the content and methods of pedagogy and preaching. In their experience, freedpeople found that these insistent, well-meaning missionaries and teachers rarely viewed them as equals. For instance, many northerners dismissed the highly emotional religious tradition of African Americans as "ludicrous and saddening," and full of "strange, wild ideas." Lyman contemptuously described a service he had attended: "When anything *powerful*, as they say, comes from the preacher they begin drumming with their feet, like a kind of suppressed applause, so when they have their 'mourners,' for through all the first prayer and sermon time they keep up a *moaning* sound." At the conclusion of the formal sermon, when the minister issued his invitation to the altar — a practice itself that Congregationalists disapproved of — Lyman declared that the ensuing scene "beggars description." Others found it more amusing than disheartening. Charles Hubbard, of the 45th Massachusetts, described his response to a black religious meeting he had witnessed in early 1863: "It was sad to think these poor creatures could hope to win salvation in such a manner, yet at the same time, the absurdity and comicality of the whole affair was irresistible and showed a phase of Negro character both strange and amusing."[33]

Generally, the staid northerners were more astounded by the blacks' physical reactions to, rather than their verbal recitations of, the gospel. "When I was going to dinner from guard last Sunday," related another Massachusetts soldier, "I heard the greatest hollering ever." When he investigated the black church from which it came, he saw "some [people] on the floor, some jumping up and down, some waving their hands. . . . It sounding as much like a pack of wild animals as anything I can think of." Still another amazed soldier wrote that "it would be impossible for me to undertake to describe" a black religious meeting. Members of the congregation jumped up and rolled on the floor with the spirit, and "one went so far that she tore almost what clothing [she wore] off and the minister could not hold her. He had to tie her and then let her kick." The unsympathetic Reverend Lyman deplored such lack of restraint: "My spirit sinks within me in sorrow to think of their noisy extravagance around the altar of my beloved Lord, who is the Lord of *order* not confusion."[34] Missionaries, like the order-worshipping Lyman, sought to educate former slaves in order to reform their moral character, which many considered despoiled or dissolute, and try to give them a sense of social responsibility and stability in the tumultuous times. In other words, they hoped to remake them in an idealized northern middle-class Christian image, ignoring the freedpeople's cultural mores. These self-righteous teachers were blinded by their own cultural values and their innate sense of superiority. Shortly after the war Horace James proclaimed, "The only manner in which the South is to be regenerated and its society rejuvenated and made what it ought to be, and hence the country saved, is by reproducing New England and its institutions" throughout the backward region.[35]

African Americans, on the other hand, were quite practical, accepting a certain amount of northern proselytizing while using the benevolent society members to garner the material possessions as well as intellectual lessons they needed to achieve autonomy. One northern missionary in New Bern, who had hoped to convert ignorant former slaves, learned that "greater good might be done by holding a pair of shoes, or a new frock in one hand, and the Bible in the other." In January 1864 she exulted, "It is wonderful how much more influence you can have over those who do not believe, by doing something for their souls and bodies at the same time." The young woman did not understand that most likely this was part of the freedpeople's plan. Many former bondsmen recognized the value of playing to northern stereotypes of their ignorance to help address their insufficient material possessions, just as they had acted the part of Sambo in slavery times to gain concessions from whites. Slowly the northern agents began to realize how they were being used. From Roanoke Island in December 1863, one agent wrote: "Yesterday a woman came asking for a flannel for her sick babe. She seemed honest, but there is so much wrongdoing that I am compelled to ascertain always."[36]

While missionaries and teachers were trying to redeem former slaves' spiritual souls and elevate their intellect, respectively, they were actually heightening freedpeople's awareness of their political bodies and the rights inherent in being a free person—offering visions of a promising future in which African Americans could control their own destinies without being beholden to whites. A black soldier's comment to an AMA agent reveals that African Americans heartily imbibed from this hopeful fount. "Do you know how responsible your situation is?" the soldier asked. "We listen to every word that you utter to us, so that nothing that you utter is lost to any of us. If we do just as you instruct us to do, and we lose our souls, whose fault will it be?" Though this soldier perhaps feared going to hell, his quotation serves as an effective metaphor for those who did not dread their eternal damnation as much as a potential worldly one. If freedpeople diligently followed the advice of their northern deliverers and the promised land of respect, economic independence, and personal autonomy did not emerge, their betrayal would be devastating.[37]

CHAPTER 6

The Effects of Occupation on Union Soldiers

On the oppressively hot afternoon of July 11, 1862, Captain William Augustus Walker of the 27th Massachusetts Infantry Regiment, an avowed abolitionist, sat inside a house in downtown New Bern and witnessed a "great buck nigger, very black and very fragrant," with "bare feet, tattered shirt and knotted hair," fanning the flies away from a lieutenant as he wrote. Though Walker agreed that "the flies are really tormenting and the heat is intolerable," he declared: "I had rather endure both, than to have one of those confounded dirty niggers anywhere within twenty feet of me." He believed that "as a class they are lazy, filthy, ragged, dishonest and confounded stupid." Ironically, Walker had strong convictions against slavery. Though he was devoted to "destroy[ing] from off the face of the country every vestige of this enormous crime," and would sacrifice his life for it at the battle of Cold Harbor on June 3, 1864, he still could not abide the actual physical beings who personified the abstract institution of slavery.[1]

General Ambrose E. Burnside's personal secretary, Daniel Read Larned, who was also in New Bern, shared the captain's antipathy. He remarked to a friend, "The negroes are niggers all over. They are ignorant, lazy, [and] thievish." Larned told Burnside's wife that "they are the laziest, and the most degraded set of beings I ever saw." To his sister, he admitted: "It seems as if all my letters have been 'nigger, nigger' since I came here, but if you could see them you would not wonder. They are amusing, yet disgusting." Even U.S. Treasury agent John A. Hedrick, an antislavery Unionist as well as a native North Carolinian, held a low opinion of blacks in general. On his way to Beaufort, Hedrick described one of the contrabands on board his steamer as being of "the pure Guinea nigger style, full of talk and I think a little impudent." These attitudes reveal that even well-meaning Yankees had a difficult time coming to grips with the massive influx of African Americans who sought refuge within the safety of Union lines. Many of those who welcomed freedom for the slaves could not get beyond their own preconceived ideas of slaves as filthy, simple-minded, dissembling dependents.[2]

The majority of Union soldiers in the region were volunteers who sought to preserve the republic their founding fathers had created. However, their experience along the coast of North Carolina exposed them not only to the petty tyrannies of army life, but also to a foreign environment, one whose climate, inhabitants, and culture shocked their sensibilities. Their unhappiness led to much grumbling about the weather, the land, the people, army rations, fellow soldiers, and officers. Ultimately, the experience of occupation tested their convictions — weakening some while strengthening others. Union troops serving in the occupied region suffered from sagging morale caused both by military defeats elsewhere and by their own sense that their government was not using them in the most efficient manner to end the war. But despite their personal denunciations of their own particular circumstances and even the policies of the Federal government, the majority of soldiers remained motivated to accomplish their mission — sustain the war effort until its conclusion. Their letters reveal that most Union troops managed to suppress their inward despair in order to fulfill their strong sense of duty.[3]

DURING THE COURSE OF the Federal occupation of New Bern and Beaufort, soldiers from more than four dozen regiments served in the region for varying periods. These men came from the northeastern states — fifteen regiments were from Massachusetts, while several hailed from Pennsylvania, Rhode Island, Connecticut, New York, and New Jersey. When they enlisted, they answered no specific call to go to the North Carolina coast to work with refugee slaves and local Unionists. Instead, they answered the same siren song that attracted hundreds of thousands of their brothers in arms in the spring and summer of 1861. Many of these men appreciated the privileges that came with enlistment. Private Henry White, of the 21st Massachusetts Infantry, who enlisted on July 5, 1861, was struck by the deference shown to the troops by political officials. When Massachusetts governor John Andrew, Secretary of War Simon Cameron, Secretary of State William Henry Seward, and Secretary of the Navy Gideon Welles reviewed his regiment outside the nation's capital in November 1861, "with head[s] bared," this hardscrabble, thirty-five-year-old shoemaker and father of four remarked proudly: "I never expected to be placed where such men would take off their hats to me."[4]

Many of those who signed up for military service professed a desire to preserve the integrity of the Union. Samuel Storrow, a private in the 44th Massachusetts, explained to his father why he interrupted his studies at Harvard to join the army. "What is the worth of this man's life or that man's education," Storrow argued, "if this great and glorious fabric of our Union, raised with such toil and labor by our forefathers and transmitted to us in value increased tenfold, is to be shattered to pieces by traitorous hands and allowed to fall crumbling into the dust." Though his father had all but begged him not to go to war, Storrow remained firm in his conviction. "What shame, what mortification would it cause me years hence to be obliged to confess that in the great struggle for our national existence I stood aloof, an idle spectator, without any peculiar ties to retain me at home and yet not caring or daring do anything in the defense of my country." Storrow ultimately gave his life in his nation's defense. After serving nine months in New Bern, he reenlisted in the 2nd Massachusetts Regiment, which was attached to General William Sherman's army. Storrow was killed on March 16, 1865, at Averasboro, North Carolina.[5]

Private Charles Duren, of the 24th Massachusetts Infantry Regiment, debated with his merchant father, who wanted Charles to stay in his job clerking for a mercantile firm in Cambridge. At the beginning of July 1861 from Boston, Duren wrote his father: "I *can not* if I would resist. It is no sudden and exciting burst of patriotism, from the first I have been willing & desirous, of giving my life (if *God wills*) to my country's cause." Benjamin Day, who enlisted in 1862, was going to fight "to protect our flag against the menaces of a traitorous foe, to fight for that liberty which was bought by the blood of our forefathers." Theodore Parkman's father tried to get him a commission, only to learn that it would take months to come through. Parkman decided to enlist as a private. When his father attempted to dissuade him, naming the menial chores that a private would have to engage in, Parkman bemusedly remarked: "Well you know, father, I am not going for the fun of the thing." These soldiers would take part in one of the war's first offensives to capture southern ports.[6]

In December 1861, Lincoln authorized General Ambrose Burnside to lead an expeditionary force to seize the ports and sounds of coastal North Carolina.[7] Burnside set about drafting his plan of attack for an expedition that would shove off from its northern staging ports in January 1862. He intended to capture Roanoke Island, which controlled waterborne access to Albemarle Sound, as well as New Bern and Beaufort, two important ports at the southern edge of the Outer Banks. New Bern would provide an excellent base for staging raids into the Confederate hinterland, while Beaufort's deep harbor not only offered the perfect refuge from the unpredictable Atlantic storms, but also would serve as a prime refueling and repair station for ships on blockade duty. The expedition proved successful, as the general achieved his three objectives in less than two months with relatively little loss of life.[8]

Though Burnside had brought these men to North Carolina, he did not remain long to share their trials. In early July 1862, the War Department ordered him to sail for Virginia to provide relief to General George McClellan's distressed Army of the Potomac. Burnside departed the New Bern–Beaufort region with seven thousand men on July 6. He left behind three brigades, numbering about nine thousand men, under the command of General John G. Foster. These remaining brigades would serve as the backbone of the occupying force in North Carolina. Burnside's success on the coast made him very popular with his army. After he left the state, many soldiers spoke of their attachment to him. A Rhode Island soldier later remembered that despite Burnside's mixed record during the war, he "was loved by the troops in North Carolina."[9]

THE TROOPS MAY HAVE loved their bewhiskered commander, but they did not adore the region to which he brought them. North Carolina might as well have been a foreign country, for that is how many northern soldiers viewed the climate, landscape, and inhabitants. After eating possum meat for the first time, one urban soldier commented: "I feel I am seeing strange countries, perhaps following in the footsteps of Lord Bateman as well as of Raleigh." Most soldiers were predisposed to think poorly of the southern landscape and culture, based on what they had read about the South in travel accounts written before the war. One soldier wrote to his sister, "If you want to know how these N.C. swamps appear, just look up a sketch by Porte Crayon of the eastern part of North Carolina in an old number of Harper's that will show you exactly."[10] Their exposure to eastern North Carolina's natural environment did not change their impressions greatly. Private Edward J. Bartlett of the 44th Massachusetts marveled at the dense woods, which were "so different from northern forests." Instead of the many varieties of chestnut, beech, maple, walnut, hickory, birch, poplar,

General Ambrose Burnside (Courtesy of State Archives,
Division of Archives and History, Raleigh)

and elm trees that infused the forests surrounding his native Concord, eastern North Carolina was covered with "great pines and oaks . . . hanging down with long grey moss . . . all overgrown with a thick underbrush of briers." Another Massachusetts soldier opined, "All of us felt, I believe, that if we were fighting for soil and not for ideas, there was nothing in that first view worth conquering or holding. One drop of Northern blood was too large a price for a million acres."[11]

The ubiquitous pocosins not only were difficult to navigate, but also concealed many unusual antagonists. On April 12, 1862, as his regiment marched up to Bachelor Creek to set up an outpost north of New Bern, Dexter B. Ladd, a private in the 23rd Massachusetts, wrote: "We have frequent skirmishes with the Enemy—nothing but Swamps, Snakes, Rebels & Lizards round here." The aggressiveness of the insects that plagued the region also astounded the soldiers. Connecticut resident Oliver Case noted that annoying New England insects had nothing on the sandy hills of the North Carolina coast, "where sand flies and fleas seemed as if to foreclose mortgages upon your carcass." Then, of course, there were the omnipresent mosquitoes. One species proved a very dangerous enemy in the summer of 1864. The *Aëdes aegypti* mosquito, carrier of the dreaded yellow fever, made its presence felt beginning in July, causing an outbreak of yellow fever that killed nearly one thousand civilians and soldiers.[12]

In addition to the ferocious insects, northern soldiers were struck by the unusual duration and intensity of the southern summer, producing a heat for which they were not acclimated. "Thermometer standing 108 degrees in the shade," wrote John E. Bassett on July 8, 1862. In fact, Bassett, a native of Southbridge, Massachusetts, opened nearly every diary entry for July and August with a comment about how unbelievably hot it was. Isaac Newton Parker, from Rodman, New York, wrote his sister: "It is so awful and mighty hot for the last few days that it seems almost impossible for man or beast to move about in the sun." Of the diabolical heat that radiated out of the miasmatic swamps, Sergeant George Jewett of the 17th Massachusetts exclaimed one hot July day: "I don't believe the devil would live here if he wasn't obliged to."[13]

WHILE THE NATURAL environment seemed foreign to Union troops, the local inhabitants also left a distinctly unfavorable impression on many. Soldiers had heard much about the supposedly degraded poor whites of the South, and exposure to them did little to alter their negative opinions. Of the Confederate troops who fled to Union lines after the capture of New Bern, one Federal soldier wrote: "I pity them from my heart; the most of them are not intelligent[,] not half of them can read[,] so one of them told me they are just the men to be led by the nose by political leaders." Others were less sympathetic. Daniel Larned asserted that the poor whites of New Bern "are a most forlorn and miserable set of people." The next day he described their "contemptible" appearance, saying "They are white a[s] chalk, long, lean, a[nd] lanky with long yellow hair."[14]

The coarseness that characterized some southern white women particularly disturbed the young men serving in the Union army. One soldier proclaimed that he would never be seduced by a southern woman. "You spoke about falling in love with some of these southern girls," Alfred Otis Chamberlin wrote his sister in October 1862. "Do not worry yourself about that fore thare is not a woman in all North Carolina that I would snap my finger for." Northern soldiers also excoriated the peculiar southern female practice of taking snuff, which northern soldiers found revolting and horribly unrefined. "The women here, both white and black, 'dig' snuff like thunder," declared Sergeant Jewett. He described the process to a friend: "They put the snuff on a piece of pine, and stick it up in their gums, and then smack their lips as though they were eating something peculiarly nice. It will do for niggers but white women, faugh!" Massachusetts soldier Henry Clapp professed that he would scorn a local white woman over any alternative. "I don't imagine that I shall ever be put to the proof," Clapp wrote, "but I believe that were I forced to the horrible alternative of choosing a bride from these whites or from the negroe women, I should prefer the darkest Ethiop that ever made midnight blacker, rather than one of these wretched, forlorn, poor white women."[15]

Not all soldiers found the southern women to be so unrefined. Dexter Ladd kept a diary, where he recorded his amorous adventures while on duty. In June 1863 he wrote, "Sgt. Bragston and I went scouting and got acquainted with some good looking girls." They went to see them twice more, and at each visit Ladd commented that they "had a gay old time." Some soldiers' libidos drove them to mingle with the opposite sex even if the women's loyalties were somewhat ambiguous. In March 1863, to his sister Martha, Private Bartlett described one of his more memorable encounters: "About a mile from camp there lives a man (poor white) named Hardison. They have Union protection but are secesh enough. Well! He has two very pretty daughters." Bartlett and a friend went to their house on the pretext of looking for eggs. "They then asked us to come in. We were very glad to accept! The two young ladies were at home alone. . . . We sat down and had a very pleasant half hour call. They were very pretty, modest and polite girls. Cassie the younger is the handsomest but her sister Lizzie is the smartest and brightest. They are about 16 or 18 years old. They have not left the house for a year, have not been to New berne since the capture. They used to go every day to school." Bartlett admitted that part of his socializing took on the air of a traditional chaperoned courting ritual: "Cassy was spinning and I handed her her shreads of cotton, and [played] the gallant." Cassandra and Eliza Hardison (age twelve and fifteen respectively in the 1860 census) lived in the household of their father, the modest farmer Isom Hardison, north of New Bern. Their twenty-three-year-old brother, Elijah, who joined Captain Hugh Cole's company in May 1861, was killed at the battle of Antietam on September 17, 1862. The sisters' hospitality toward young Bartlett and his friend revealed that the sense of loneliness and isolation created by military occupation could lead to surprising interactions between inhabitants and soldiers.[16]

More surprises were in store, as other soldiers carried out the courtship ritual to its sanctification. In May 1863 Corporal Charles W. Lawrence in the 44th Massachusetts Regiment married "a lovely young secesh damsel," the daughter (most likely eighteen-year-old Jane) of New Bern banker Israel Disosway. The New York–born Disosway had been a prosperous slaveholder before the war, with real estate and personal wealth valued at nearly $27,000. On the marriage, Disosway transferred his remaining property (obviously exempting the slaves) to Lawrence, while he, for unknown reasons, refused to take the oath and left town with other secessionists. Lawrence's was the most discussed, but not the only, wartime wedding, as several Union soldiers found their wives in the occupied towns of eastern North Carolina. From Washington in February 1864, one New York soldier wrote: "Marrying is very popular here. The soldiers are going it strong. I could be married to 5 or 6 in two weeks if I had a mind to," though he personally chose not to succumb to the temptation.[17]

WHILE SOLDIERS WERE EITHER disgusted or entranced by the appearance and habits of the local whites, they were shocked by the overwhelming numbers of African Americans in the region. Though the Union army ended up freeing the slaves, the majority of soldiers did not consider the abolition of slavery to be a primary motivation for their enlistment. Many

carried strong racist feelings to war with them, and their subsequent expo-
sures reinforced their preconceived notions of blacks as inferior beings. Few
of these soldiers had had any interaction with African Americans before
the conflict, and now they were forced into a crucible of racial adjustment.
William Walker's comment in the first paragraph of this chapter — "they
are lazy, filthy, ragged, dishonest and confounded stupid" — encapsulated
the soldiers' beliefs regarding slaves. A common stereotype that the soldiers
repeated was that blacks preferred a filthy existence and seemed immune
to the sweltering heat. In the summer of 1863 Private Alfred Holcomb of
the 27th Massachusetts commented to his sister: "The little nigs are lying
around in the sun and sand as thick as toads after a shower but we have to
keep in out of the sun to feel comfortable." He further emphasized their
lack of regard for personal cleanliness: "If a nigger goes to set down he will
go out of his way to get in the sand before he will sit on the grass. The nas-
tier they get the better they feel." Soldiers also believed that blacks were
naturally too indolent to work without compulsion. Captain William G.
Leonard of the 46th Massachusetts asserted: "Many of them are too lazy
to work well, & they need the restraint of the soldier & the discipline of
Courts Martial to make them profitable laborers." He proposed to enlist
blacks in work battalions, set up like regiments.[18]

Many soldiers took advantage of local blacks whenever possible, exploit-
ing their friendliness, playing dangerous pranks on them, and using them
as exotic toys. Edward Bartlett related, "The boys are having great sport trying to make 'Long' the nig who washes our dishes dance. I wish you could
see a darkey dance. It is a kind of a shuffle like the Irish dance." In December 1862, while on an expedition toward Goldsboro, Dexter Ladd "seized
my nigger" whom he amusedly dubbed "Gutta percha." On one cold night,
Ladd "woke up and found Gutta Percha lying between me and the fire. I
immediately roll[ed] him into the fire and he did not move until one of his
boots burnt off when he thought he kinder smelt some nigger's foot burning and such a Howling I never heard before."[19] In late 1862 Nathan G.
Newton wrote his mother: "The other day we had some fun with them.
Our regiment would give one of them 5 cents and they would put them in
a blanket and toss them up and down[,] some times their feet would be in
the air and their head, sometime they will but[t] their heads to geather."
Ladd recorded on the back lining of his diary an example of the impromptu
and humiliating "oaths" the soldiers would require the escaping slaves to
take: "I, Junius Long, or any other man do Solemnly Swear to Support the

Constitution of these United States and Black yer Boots, get a Pail of water and shine up your Brasses and Bear True allegiance to the Pope of Rome, John Brown and Brigham Young, So help me General Burnside or any other man."[20]

Obviously, these comments reveal a profound disrespect for African Americans' intelligence and manhood. These images of them as inferior beings were rooted in the eighteenth-century development of racial ideology, in which whites justified their exploitation of blacks by creating negative racial images. Theories of racial inferiority stemmed from a form of biological determinism, which affirmed that blacks were intellectually and socially inferior largely because they did not share "civilized" European cultural traits. On the other hand, many northerners were also steeped in Free Soil ideology, which denounced the institution of slavery as antagonistic to free enterprise and detrimental to the white working class. Northern soldiers grew up loathing slavery but rarely distinguishing the institution from its workforce. As a result, they found they could simultaneously hate slavery and slaves. The first year of exposure often brought out the worst in soldiers' racial prejudices.[21]

Some of this antagonism stemmed from ordinary soldiers' perception that blacks received more favorable treatment from Union officers. In August 1863 Private Holcomb complained to his sister, "A nigar is thought more of here than a private." Another soldier believed that blacks had more freedom than the troops, as the former slaves were able to come and go at will while soldiers had to have signed passes to leave their camps.[22] Many black women, who came into camp ostensibly to sell pies and cakes, often ended up dispensing sexual favors. Sexual interaction began immediately after the troops arrived. In May 1862 James Rumley commented ruefully: "Some of [the soldiers] have been seen promenading the streets with Negro wenches." Edwin Fish of the 3rd New York Artillery assured his young wife that he would remain faithful to her despite the temptations that surrounded him. "I do not think as much of the darkies as I did," he wrote. "About half of them are regular prostitutes and I am sorry to say a good many of the first boys that came out are degraded enough to run with them." Isaac N. Roberts was disgusted by the scandalous lack of virtue some officers displayed. "Some of the Captains in a regiment I know of . . . will not permit a private to enter their quarters, without first having a sergent [sic] go in, and ask permission for an interview," he protested. "Yet Nigger wenches are seen to go out and in 2 or 3 times a day, and even to stay all night. And all of this has to be endured for the love of country or for glory. And for one I must confess I am tired of it."[23]

Their sour experiences in North Carolina caused several soldiers to denounce home-front liberals who proselytized about black rights. "I would like to have that ace cousin of mine drafted and see how he likes the land of dixey and the black greasy niggars," Alfred Holcomb declared in August 1862. "He would not think to mutch of them as I have." Hale Wesson of the 25th Massachusetts was much more vehement in his condemnation of the ubiquitous presence of African Americans. In September 1863 he told his father: "As for Niggers I am disgusted with their infernal Black harts now. They are set on the same barrel with a white man. There is no being where they are. . . . They are master now and we are slaves. . . . I say dam the nigger."[24]

Wesson's bitterness stemmed partly from government efforts to enlist black men in the armed forces. While Union authorities in New Bern began raising black troops in February 1863, the process did not start in Beaufort until May 30. At the beginning of July, James Rumley happily noted in his diary: "Mutterings of discontent which are heard from officers and soldiers plainly indicates [*sic*] that this Negro which has been introduced among them stings their pride, quenches their ambition, and is actually disintegrating the already broken fragments of the once massive and powerful army of the Union." Though the army was not in danger of collapsing, as Rumley hoped, it did show signs of discontent. Mary Peabody, while visiting her husband in New Bern in March 1863, had written: "This question of Negro regiments is going I hope to be fairly tried, but the feeling against them is doubtless very strong and it seems to me strangely puerile." Typically, resentment was hierarchical. "As a rule it seems to grow stronger as you descend in rank, the privates having more feeling than the officers," Peabody continued. Yet this was not always true. Over dinner one day in 1863, Commodore H. K. Davenport, commander of the Union gunboat squadrons, asked Mary's husband, Captain Oliver Peabody, "'What should you do, sir, if you were to meet a Nigger Colonel, Should you salute him?'" "'Certainly, I should,'" replied the captain, adding that rank outweighed skin color. Mary related, "The commodore looked at him with horror and getting up from his chair gesticulated violently exclaiming in his indignation, 'My blood boils at the thought.'"[25]

The presence of black troops caused heated discussions between officers as well as enlisted men. Long after the war, Charles Codman of the

45th Massachusetts Regiment remembered the officers' reactions when the first black troops arrived in 1863. "Many of the officers — especially the New York clubmen on General Foster's staff — were much opposed to the levying of Negro troops and said so," he recalled, "but the general himself was much too wise to do this." Codman tried to overcome this prejudice by deliberately exposing his staff to a black soldier:

> General Wilde had a colored surgeon on his staff, a Cuban by birth, but educated in France — a very modest & quiet man. The opponents of Negro troops thought it bad enough that enlisted men should be Negroes, but that an officer should be of that color was beyond words. I asked Wilde . . . to bring his colored surgeon with him some day. . . . Major Jack Anderson appeared on this occasion with some other officers. As they had often said that they would not recognize a Negro officer socially, I wondered what would happen — but they behaved perfectly well, as I felt certain they would.[26]

As Codman's story reveals, Union soldiers adapted to the presence of black soldiers and eventually accepted them as, if nothing else, a means to help end the war. When the 55th Massachusetts (Colored) Regiment arrived in July 1863, a Union surgeon declared: "We were very glad to see them, even if they are black, for our garrison has been quite small. . . . I do not object to black soldiers, but rather, think they should do some of the fighting." A naval officer was impressed with the black troops he had watched drill in June: "There is a firmness & determination in their looks & in the way in which they handle a musket that I like." The officer admitted his misconception of them: "I never have believed that a common plantation negro could be brought to face a white man. I supposed that everything in the shape of spirit & self-respect had been crushed out of them generations back, but am glad to find myself mistaken."[27]

These comments suggest not only that constant interaction with African Americans changed the white soldiers' preconceived ideas, creating more complex racial models, but also that the military occupation's intense exposure to seemingly foreign groups had the potential to lead to a reappraisal of ingrained attitudes. Such cultural exchanges could be positive instead of consistently negative. Yet much depended on the individual's sense of empathy or heightened consciousness. In eastern North Carolina, several northern soldiers helped African Americans try to acquire land, obtain employment, and gain some education, while others abused and inflicted terror and violence on the former slaves whenever possible. For the next several years, the Federal government and its army would grapple with the dilemma of what to do with the freedpeople in the region.[28]

THEIR EXPOSURE TO African Americans and the unrefined habits of local whites could disgust northern soldiers, but it primarily just served to remind them that they were in a foreign environment. However, their frequently hostile encounters with white residents often weakened their morale. In addition to verbal insults from the fairer sex, the hit-and-run attacks perpetrated by Confederate military units and civilian sympathizers tried the patience of occupying troops. Soldiers occasionally witnessed guerrilla violence practiced on local Unionists. In June 1862, a New Jersey soldier told of a "party of Confederates (farmers by day and soldiers at night)" who evaded Union pickets and kidnapped a local minister. The victim "had refused to identify himself with the cause of rebellion," according to the soldier, "and having committed the crime of addressing a Union meeting, composed of his neighbors, incurred the mortal hate of secessionists, who embraced this opportunity of wreaking vengeance upon him." Mary Peabody, while visiting her husband in February 1863, reported: "Just across the river here from New berne [sic], the Secesh are hunting down the Union people, men women and children with the greatest inhumanity and barbarity."[29]

Local Confederate sympathizers also actively sought to impair the Union infrastructure. Rebels torched an important steam sawmill outside of Beaufort in May 1863, often sabotaged the railroad track between New Bern and Beaufort, and burned the printing office of the Union-controlled *New Bern Daily Progress* in December 1864. In perhaps their most impressive destructive feat of the coastal war, rebels burned Cape Lookout Lighthouse on April 3, 1864, increasing the difficulty of navigation for Union transports and blockading vessels at the southern tip of the Outer Banks. The inability to prevent these outrages increased the soldiers' sense of military impotence and heightened their resentment.[30]

Union soldiers were annoyed that they could rarely bring the rebel fighters to a full battle. Hale Wesson informed his father: "There is not much fighting here except bush whacking with Guirillas, nine of our regiment has been shot as yet." The Yankees felt far too vulnerable in the face of guerrillas who intimately knew the local terrain. About 3:00 one morning in November 1862, some mounted Confederate guerrillas attacked the guard of a Union encampment outside of New Bern before fleeing through the woods. At daylight, the northern captain noted: "By the tracks they appeared to be well mounted and acquainted with the by roads — and were around us in several directions during the night."[31] Guerrillas seemed to be hiding everywhere in the woods and along the rivers around New Bern. One night as John M. Spear, a surgeon with the 24th Massachusetts, traveled by canoe from Portsmouth to New Bern with two black assistants, he became aware that "the banks of the Neuse River swarmed with guerrillas. . . . We could see their fires and hear them talking, and there would be an occasional shot." After the war, one Connecticut soldier recalled a Confederate guerrilla in the New Bern area named O'Connor whose "infernal gang continually hovered about our lines, sometimes mounted and sometimes not, shooting our pickets, capturing outposts, raiding weak defenses and terrorizing things generally." The frequency of these clandestine raids on Union lines set the northern troops on edge. A Rhode Island soldier later described his experience on picket duty one night in a dense pine forest: "Everything appeared to assume a weird and strange appearance. Our imaginations would see in every stump a rebel, and the hogs that run at large through the forest of North Carolina, appeared in the darkness like men coming towards us." Undoubtedly, many a porcine adversary paid the last full measure of devotion that night.[32]

Clandestine violence occurred within the city limits as well. A rebel shot and wounded a Union sentry in New Bern on the night of July 25, 1862. After one such incident, an angry Massachusetts soldier suggested that "they had ought to take everyone else they catch and shoot them. That would stop it as quick as anything." On August 14, sentries caught a guerrilla who fired at them. The captured conspirator was a Confederate prisoner who had been paroled at Fort Macon back in April. "You see how much principall they have," Hale Wesson remarked to his father. "They are men whose daily walk on earth [is] an insult and disgrace to the sun that shines on them." Another soldier claimed that the guerrillas who plagued his unit "dressed in citizen's clothes, and shot our men in cold blood, whenever opportunity offered." Identification was difficult because "when they saw a considerable body of our men approaching, they were unionists, neutrals, or 'know nothings,' as they chose." Rowland M. Hall, of the 3rd New York Cavalry, declared local whites to be "the falsest creatures imaginable." The region was plagued with "guerrillas who will waylay and shoot you going home, curse Jeff Davis & profess Union sentiments with the greatest imaginable zeal."

Occupying soldiers like Bartlett and Hall greatly resented their inability to distinguish friend from foe in this new kind of war.[33]

The guerrillas practiced terror tactics as well. In August 1862, one soldier's regiment found two Union cavalrymen who had been "all Shot two pieces" by Confederate guerrillas. The men had been stripped and robbed of their money and possessions; one of the victims "had his stabbed heart cut in half with a knife." New York's Isaac Parker told of Union troops who had been killed and left out in the open in humiliating positions, stripped down to their undergarments. Parker felt he would rather die than be captured by the rebels, informing his sister that he knew a similar fate awaited him if he were "captured whole."[34] The decision to make a public spectacle of these degraded and humiliated corpses, leaving them where Union soldiers on patrol would find them, imparted a symbolic message. Rebels, too militarily weak to conquer their former geographic possessions, could at least momentarily demonstrate their power, through an exercise of terror— demonstrating that Union soldiers occupied a hostile land and that venturing outside the safety of their garrisons could bring gruesome results. In February 1864, after capturing a detachment of the 2nd North Carolina (Union) Infantry Regiment in an isolated outpost near New Bern, Confederates executed twenty-two of these native North Carolinians who had previously deserted from the Confederate army. In the eyes of the Confederates, those men who had forsaken their country's cause and joined that of the enemy had insulted their sovereign nation. Confederate spectacles of corpse mutilation and executions were acts of state-sanctioned terror intended to cow both Union soldiers and Unionists. Moreover, such deeds spoke to an elevated sense of retributive violence, to a drifting away from a gentleman's code of warfare, and to a quickening of "the hard hand of war."[35]

These acts of violence only heightened the desire for retribution among the disgruntled occupiers. The ambiguity of southern allegiances led to increasingly punitive measures by Union soldiers, including the confiscation and destruction of property and an increased number of arrests of suspicious white residents. As has been true of conflicts throughout U.S. history, when the occupying American soldier no longer is able to clearly distinguish combatant from noncombatant, the scale of reprisals grows. Once troops reach the point of considering every civilian to be a potential enemy, they justify engaging in harsher actions against those civilians, which often leads to a moral degeneration among the combatants themselves. Reflecting the escalating sense of retaliation, Union soldiers took out their vengeance on suspicious locals. They methodically destroyed houses from which snipers fired at their sentries. They imprisoned those who spoke out against the Federal authorities in any way. Mrs. Haney Smith implored the department commander, General John G. Foster, to free her husband, who had been jailed for cursing a provost guard. Owen Sempler begged for his own release from prison, where he had been sent for six months for "drinking and keeping bad company." When James Williams deserted the Confederate army and turned himself in to Union pickets outside of New Bern on May 1, 1863, the pickets immediately suspected that he might be a spy and imprisoned him. After three months in jail, Williams complained to the provost marshal: "I have [been] treated very unjustly. I come heare to be protected under Baner that I was born under and to fight if is required or do any other thing that is required."[36]

Union soldiers took particular delight in roughing up suspected guerrillas. While his unit was patrolling farms where Confederate cavalry had recently been active, William Lind captured an armed male civilian. Lind "took him by the throat" and marched him out to the road. There, Lind said, his captain "told me to take him out there and shoot him [if] the devil would not give up his arms to us. I told him to hand them over or I would run my bayonet through him." Lind admitted, "I did stick it into [him] a little." The man "[shook] like a leaf" and "begged so hard for his life." They spared him but plundered all the valuables from his house as payback for aiding the guerrillas. The chance of catching guerrillas and exacting retribution was a strong motivation for many soldiers. Alfred Holcomb admitted to his brother, "I would go twenty miles enny day to get a squint across my old musket at one of the cowardly devils." The problem was that guerrillas blended into the countryside so well that twenty-mile marches to catch them seemed necessary. As one Union soldier sardonically commented, "The Rebels youst to say that it took 5 yankees to whip one of them, but it is the other way[;] it takes 5 yankees to catch one of them." Having to endure this peculiar form of warfare was just one of the many complaints of Union soldiers occupying eastern North Carolina.[37]

TIED TO A LIMITED geographic region with little prospect of a major battle and subjected to constant annoyance by small rebel units, the Union soldiers on occupation duty had ample reasons to voice their displeasure. Regional pride caused divisions within the army, as New England soldiers showed their disdain for their mid-Atlantic counterparts. Captain Oliver Peabody, of the 45th Massachusetts, wrote his wife Mary: "Those about us are mostly New York or Penn. and do not compare favorably with our men in discipline or appearance." George H. Weston averred that non–New England regiments presented "a very unfavorable comparison both as regard morality & general intelligence." He quipped, "The feelings of patriotism must indeed be strong that would lead one to enlist as a private in one of those regiments."[38]

Several units were nine months' regiments from Massachusetts, organized in August 1862, one month after the Federal government authorized the Militia Act. These regiments were formed from a class of well-educated young men, many fresh from Harvard College, who endured taunts from the others. These men also received substantial bounties to entice them to fill out the quotas required of the state governments. Naturally, these belated inducements angered those already in the field. These "bounty men" received much harassment from older regiments that had volunteered before such enticements were offered. Many veterans mocked the newcomers with questions like "What did you do with your hundred dollars?" and called them "nine month 'well-to-does.'" Other men were compelled into service through the Federal Enrollment Act of March 1863. Massachusetts soldier Joseph Barlow, who had expended much ink complaining about his time in the army, wrote his wife in August 1863: "I thank god that I was not bought or drafted to fight for my country." Soldiers maintained a certain code of respectability; those who would not voluntarily sacrifice their time and services for the cause, but must be lured in by money or coerced by force of arms, were beneath their contempt.[39]

Coupled with regional pride and the rivalries among volunteers, bounty men, and conscripts was the average soldier's general dislike of the rigors, drudgery, and perceived injustices of army life, which were exacerbated in the unbroken tedium of occupation. Joseph Barlow likened army service in an occupation zone to "being shut up in the State Prison." Those not complaining about being inmates grumbled about being the guards, as all found the daily grind of guard duty disagreeable. Edward Bartlett, whose regiment was assigned to provost duty in New Bern in April 1863, wrote: "I don't fancy it much. . . . The chief duty is to arrest drunken soldiers, salute officers, and make privates show there [sic] passes — in short a sort of policeman." Three weeks later Bartlett underscored his disappointment: "Provost duty is horrible. The whole regiment despises it." Private Alfred Holcomb

Rear of quarters of Company A, 45th Massachusetts Infantry Regiment, while on provost duty in New Bern, ca. 1863 (Courtesy of North Carolina Collection, University of North Carolina at Chapel Hill)

agreed: "This is the hardest duty that we [have] ever done." The hardship stemmed from the unrelenting monotony more than the threat of physical danger.[40]

Monotony led many soldiers to drown their loneliness and boredom in the bottle, occasionally with disastrous results. John Hedrick informed his brother that twenty-five-year-old Lieutenant William Pollock of the 3rd New York Artillery "committed suicide by blowing his brains out with a pistol" on the sweltering night of Monday, August 4, 1863. Though Hedrick did not know specifically what inner demons tormented the lieutenant, he surmised that liquor braced him to perform the task, acknowledging that Pollock "had been in the habit of drinking excessively for some time past." Other soldiers fortified themselves with enough liquid courage to make known their true feelings about the service and those under whom they served. On Thanksgiving Day, 1862, several soldiers became intoxicated and delivered impromptu speeches on the rebellion and their military service. "One remarked in his speech that he did not enlist for no $2000[;] he enlisted because he was a d-m [sic] fool." Observing the axiom of *in vino veritas*, Private Dexter Ladd remarked that the statement was "pretty near the Truth." The abuse of liquor led occupation soldiers to commit a host of petty crimes "prejudicial to good order and military discipline," such as theft, larceny, and battery. Some actions were downright surreal. On April 9, 1862, Charles Walcott related that the previous night, "a private in the 11th Conn. regiment, so drunk that he could hardly walk, even with the aid of a Negro who accompanied him, carrying an ancient copper coffin, was arrested by our guard as he passed our camp. The coffin bore the name of Richard D. Spaight, a distinguished Revolutionary patriot, and governor of North Carolina from 1792 to 1795." Union authorities promptly returned Spaight's coffin to its burial place.[41]

Several soldiers longed for combat to relieve the boredom of occupation duty. Dr. Samuel C. Hunt remarked that the men in his regiment gave three hearty cheers when they heard they were preparing to go on an expedition into the countryside: "Anything to break the monotony of camp life. The soldier even welcomes the fatigues of the march & the dangers of the battlefield as a change." Indeed, soldiers' letters reveal an alacrity and exhilaration when they recount expeditions they took into the countryside, while letters from those stuck in provost guard duty frequently display petulance and melancholy. Stephen Driver, from the 23rd Massachusetts, complained of his regiment's occupation duty in New Bern in July 1862, four months after the city was captured. "Although not exposed to [the] same dangers and hardships as when on the march or in the battle," Driver stated, "I am heartily tired of it. Life is, with me, a dull, monotonous routine, spiced with but little of excitement." His sentiments exemplified a Union officer's acknowledgment that, although guard duty was not as dangerous as battle, "long continued duty in a city was not, however, desirable for a soldier. Its effect was very disastrous to a wholesome esprit du corps."[42]

Occupation duty also heightened enlisted men's anger at officers, which stemmed from the latter's exercise of tyranny over the former. Life in the occupied zone offered little on which to focus officers' martial attention, so they often more closely scrutinized their men for petty grievances and sought various avenues for their own amusement. The net effect of these actions was to weaken morale among the fighting men. Soldiers resented the officers' privileges, including access to liquor, comfortable quarters (usually in local homes while soldiers lived in encampments), and a seemingly endless amount of free time. Enlisted men believed a double standard existed in the punishment of crimes. Alfred Holcomb confirmed that some officers behaved badly, writing in June 1862: "We see them drunk and carousing about the streets every day sometimes half a dozen at a time, but if a private gets a little down he is turned over to the provost marshal and his pay taken away." In January 1863 William Augustus Willoughby wrote of his disgust with the officers in his regiment: "I have just been out for Regimental Inspection by our beautiful Colonel who was beautifully drunk and who had a beautiful fight last night with one Captain Quinn of Company G over three or 4 w[omen] who they got to quarter in their barracks through the night." Colonel James McChesney of the 1st North Carolina (Union) Regiment condemned the conduct of his former adjutant, J. A. Chenery, who had disgraced himself in Beaufort in 1864 by associating too freely with lewd women. On June 10, 1864, Chenery married Lizzie Snowdon, "a notorious prostitute who has followed her calling before and since the several towns in this State were occupied by our forces." McChesney lamented that Chenery's behavior became "a cause of general remark and public scandal" in the town and the army.[43]

THE DISGRUNTLEMENT WITH army life under occupation indicated a growing sense of demoralization among some of the volunteers. From the summer of 1862 through the spring of 1863, Union armies suffered a string of humiliating defeats, especially in the eastern theater. Many soldiers became despondent about the lack of battlefield success and their own inability to participate in the war's climactic fights. The events of 1862 and 1863 certainly tested the conviction of many Union soldiers who were engaged in the seemingly thankless task of occupation and trying to preserve a Union that many local inhabitants seemed ambivalent about securing. Their letters to loved ones and friends at home showed the depths to which many men sank during this year and coincides with the scholarly consensus that the winter of 1862–63 was the lowest ebb of morale among the northern soldiers and on the home front.[44]

Repeated military disasters in Virginia in 1862 led many soldiers to conclude that letting the South go its own way was the prudent measure. On September 12, after the defeat at Second Manassas and the subsequent Confederate invasion of Maryland, William Lind wrote: "I believe . . . that the rebels [are] going to whip the north yet." On the same day, Isaac N. Roberts told Dr. Ebenezer Hunt back home in Danvers, Massachusetts: "I have come to the conclusion that we can never whip the rebels." After the Union army stopped the Army of Northern Virginia's advance at the battle of Antietam in September 1862, morale revived, but only briefly.[45] By November, the despondency had returned for many. "I will be heartily glad when this infernal war is ended," wrote one soldier. "It seems as if one was to be kept from one's friends forever and all for want of proper management at Headquarters." Roberts, whose correspondence with Dr. Hunt revealed him to be a decided pessimist, wrote after the Republicans' poor showing in the 1862 elections (in which they lost thirty-five seats in the U.S. House of Representatives): "Now my last hope is almost gone. I am now ready to give up, and Dr., you have no idea of the growing dissatisfaction among the troops." After hearing of Burnside's overwhelming defeat at Fredericksburg in December 1862, Edward Bartlett wrote his sister: "All this fighting and killing men does not seem to amount to anything. We have pretty much come to the conclusion that fighting will never end the war." Joseph Barlow agreed, enlightening his wife in a Christmas letter: "I tell you we are all getting sick of this war. It never will be settled by fighting; the way things are going on it never will be over."[46]

A few soldiers had determined to get out of the war by refusing to re-enlist when their original terms of service expired. On New Year's Day, 1863, the traditional day of new resolutions, David P. Reynolds of the 3rd Massachusetts noted: "There is one resolve most of the soldiers will firmly make, that is, Should they ever return they never will enlist a second time." Eben Thomas Hale, a nine-month volunteer with the 45th Massachusetts, told his mother: "It will take more money than there is in this country to make me enter the service again." Besides, he sardonically quipped, he wanted others to have their chance: "I feel that it is a great privilege to fight for one's country and not wishing to monopolize all the glory of putting down the rebellion I shall stand aside and allow those immortal patriots who have been advocating a vigorous prosecution of the war, getting up loyal leagues and joining home guards to try a little actual service and see how they like it."[47]

These sentiments speak to the larger problem of weakened morale among Union troops in occupation zones. Perhaps surprisingly to modern sensibilities, no soldiers in North Carolina recorded their experience away from the major bloody battlefields as a fortunate break or something to be desired; instead, their spirits sagged as their likelihood of fighting diminished. Quite simply, soldiers stuck in occupation duty questioned the legitimacy of their usage. They had volunteered to help preserve the Union but could not see how their service in a secondary field helped further that aim.[48] Morale is a broad, rather amorphous concept, with many characteristics and many factors influencing it, but every scholarly definition supports the notion that a soldier has to feel he is being used in the most efficacious manner toward achieving victory. Hence, those soldiers who are removed from the possibility of combat, or any similar action they perceive as integral to the cause or the maintenance of their country, tend to suffer a lagging morale.[49]

The occupation troops in New Bern and Beaufort during the Civil War began exhibiting three primary emotions: frustration, depression and resentment. While frustrated by their inability to engage in combat and depressed by the monotony of occupation duty, they most commonly exhibited resentment, which led to the traditional response of "griping," in which the soldiers revealed their hostility toward their duty. These emotions led Joseph Barlow to denounce the administration's handling of the war, indifference to its troops, and those who seemed to be profiting on the backs of the soldiers: "What does the infernal traitor and contractors care about my life or any Soldier's life? This is a war for to make money with our blood." Connecticut soldier William H. Jackson, resenting his experience of occupation in New Bern, acknowledged: "I am sorry to say . . . that I am not so patriotic as I was once."[50]

Studies have shown that morale is often lowest among those soldiers stationed in secondary arenas, while morale of those in the armies on the front lines is often higher. The chance to engage in decisive battle, to contribute something tangible toward ultimate victory, boosts their spirits. "In defining morale," wrote British military historian John Baynes, "there is no better tonic for soldiers than to win a battle." Soldiers on occupation duty in North Carolina faced little prospect of engaging in battle, much less winning one. This demoralization reached its zenith in 1863. Though such disenchantment did not completely cease after that pivotal year, fewer soldiers were so candid in their letters about it. Perhaps many had simply tired of repeating the same laments to their loved ones, but more likely, as the prospect of ultimate victory became more probable, their outlook improved.[51]

SOLDIERS' PATRIOTISM MAY lose its initial incandescence; they may become despondent; they may, at times, doubt their chances of success, especially in the wake of military defeats. Despite these feelings of despair, a major theme that emerges from the Civil War letters of occupying soldiers is one of *steadfastness*.[52] Though many complained about army life and their usage, they still had a strong sense of obligation to see their service through to its ultimate and, they hoped, successful conclusion. Charles B. Quick, of the 3rd New York Artillery, wrote his sister: "I have often thought that I was sorry that I ever enlisted but now I am glad that I did enlist when I did, for now I feel as if I had done part of my duty toward my Country." Though badly burned in a tent accident, Quick reaffirmed his sense of duty to support the cause: "As long as the Regiment stays I want to stay with them, and I feel it my duty to do so." He reasoned, "It does not seem right for me to go home until we are shure of Victory."[53]

Even in some of their darkest moments, soldiers found reason to hope. After hearing of the Union defeat at Chancellorsville in May 1863, Josiah Wood of the 27th Massachusetts penned a stirring lament: "O how I long to sie this rebellion chrushed that there may not be any more such cenes of blood and suffering but peace and prosperity again smile on an undivided and happy country." He followed this requiem with an earnest call for greater sacrifice: "But we must make up our minds to work." Wood was confident of a final triumph, remarking: "It is hard to guess how long this war may last . . . [yet] I have no fears for the final result." Henry Clapp also grieved over the loss at Chancellorsville: "Today we are all profo[u]ndly in the dumps on account of the news from Hooker. I am by turns hopelessly depressed, decidedly elated, furiously indignant." Like Wood, however, Clapp testily declared: "I am wild with every body, also, for talking as if this defeat — if it is one — were going to ruin our cause."[54]

While many civilians in the North called for an end to the war, soldiers refused to follow suit. In fact, those who issued increasingly louder demands for peace in the wake of Union military defeats — such as Peace Democrats, or Copperheads — greatly angered Federal troops in the occupied region of North Carolina. In April 1863 New York soldier Herbert Cooley, writing from New Bern, asked his father to warn his friends that "they must not join the Copperheads and resist the draft[,] for a division of the people of the North at the present would be disastrous to our arms." Cooley had once told his father that he often felt he wanted to "quit the army forever," but he contained his unhappiness and in July 1863 was not only no longer interested in leaving the army, but also was incensed that his fellow New Yorkers were revolting against the draft and not volunteering to join the army instead. "Why do they not come up manfully to the support of those already in the field and who (if I must say it myself) are making almost Superhuman efforts to crush and root [out] the rebellion?"[55]

Other soldiers also revealed their disgust with the dissenters at home. In his final letter from the front, written on May 18, 1863, four days before he was killed outside of New Bern in a skirmish with Confederates, Colonel John Richter Jones of the 58th Pennsylvania Regiment shared his earnest conviction that the war must not be stopped until victory was achieved. "It is better for the great interests of man to expend the whole present generation at the North, than to consent to the separation of the American nation," Jones wrote. "We are not ready for peace yet. If it were patched up by nominal restoration of the Union, it would be but a hollow truce. We must whip the South into proper respect for us." Jones then turned his anger on those who called for an immediate cessation of hostilities. "The men who cry peace before the time for peace will stand historically with the men of the Hartford Convention," referring to the ill-fated antiwar Federalist conference of 1814.[56]

After the military successes in 1863, few soldiers' letters addressed the issue of peace before ultimate victory. Most soldiers rededicated themselves to the cause. By March 1864, when explaining to his wife why a majority of the men in his regiment reenlisted after their original three-year term of service had expired, New York officer Nelson Chapin summed up the sentiments of the troops in the occupied region. "It is a very great mistake to suppose the soldier does not think," he wrote. "Our soldiers are closer thinkers and reasoners than the people at home. It is the soldiers who have educated the people at home to a true knowledge of objects the rebels had in view and to a just perception of our great duties in this contest." Even while dissenters were "crying out that the government was crushing out Liberty, every soldier knew he was fighting not for his own liberty but for the liberty of these same croaking ravens, and more for the liberty of the human race for all time to come." Mary Peabody observed the same thoughtful tendencies among the soldiers, asserting: "I think the men in the army are much more hopeful and patient than the thinking people at home." Indeed, the large number of Federal troops who likely voted for Abraham Lincoln in November 1864 helped propel the president to his reelection victory. These soldiers voted in favor of continuing to prosecute the war to its ultimately successful conclusion.[57]

Thinking soldiers also recognized the root cause of the war and the need to eradicate it. Despite their personal distaste for African Americans, many Union troops pragmatically embraced emancipation. Joseph Barlow had stated in June 1862 that he opposed emancipation because he feared it would prompt the South to fight on indefinitely. But by October 23, 1862,

Barlow had reevaluated his position, announcing to his wife: "I do like the President's Proclamation. I back him up in anything to put down this rebellion." Other soldiers welcomed emancipation as the war's new moral imperative for tearing down the divisive institution of slavery. Charles Duren declared that he was committed "to help in not only restoring [the Union] to what it was before but more, to cleanse it from *the* curse of slavery *forever*." Most soldiers realized that the sectional conflict would never end as long as slavery remained intact. Surgeon John Spear admitted that "the President's Proclamation is pretty rough on the South, but I am very glad he has got up the courage to issue it, for Slavery is certainly the cause of this war, and just so long as it exists, just so long will there be trouble between the North and the South."[58]

This belief helped fortify the men who were fulfilling their dreary duty in North Carolina. In January 1863 Massachusetts soldier Benjamin Day proclaimed his resolve, which was shared by many of his compatriots: "Let us if necessary fight anew the battles of the revolution[;] let us spill our blood if necessary to protect that liberty unsullied for our children." That same month, John Spear somberly reflected on the enormous costs of the war but did not surrender to despair. "I do not have the least inclination to give up," he vowed, "but will fight it out even if it should take ten years, yes, or twenty, for before we are through I want to see the curse of slavery, which is the real cause of the war, wiped from the land." Nelson Chapin was just as dedicated as Spear: "We had better carry on this war twenty years longer than to yield one iota of our rights. The Rebels have forfeited all theirs, and now we have but one thing to do, make one vigorous effort and the rebels must yield, and then with universal emancipation we shall have lasting peace and prosperity."[59]

The dull experience of occupation, the psychological lack of satisfaction in their military endeavors, the enforcement of often distasteful Federal policies, and the emerging hostility of local whites all turned idealistic Union enlistees into more cynical veterans. Their extended contact with both the agents of the Federal government and the southern citizens who challenged that government's legitimacy altered their perceptions of the nation for which they fought. A prolonged exposure to the petty tyrannies of army life, the monotony of occupation, unpopular Federal policies, degraded southern inhabitants, and the natural and cultural environments of coastal North Carolina, so dissimilar to their own, occasionally tempered their patriotic convictions and led to the demoralization of many of them. Yet, despite the hardships and tedium they suffered, soldiers remained steadfast in their dedication to putting down the rebellion. Union soldiers relegated to the monotony of occupation duty proved remarkably capable of containing their inward despair in order to fulfill their strong sense of duty.

CHAPTER 7

White Rejection of Union Occupation

On the morning after the capture of Beaufort in late March 1862, Major George H. Allen of the 4th Rhode Island Regiment recorded: "A few Union people were found here, who, to the great disgust of the rebel element, freely mingled with our boys, shaking them by the hand." Several residents, however, were hesitant to embrace the Federal forces at first. When Allen tried to use a five-dollar U.S. Treasury note to purchase some items from a store, the proprietor snapped "We don't take such stuff here," implying that only Confederate currency was acceptable. Yet after April 26, when Fort Macon had been subdued and the port reopened for trade, bringing northern merchandise and the prospect of profitable commerce to the town, Allen noticed a change in the local population's attitude. "They at last acknowledged that we had wrought a very great and acceptable change in their affairs," he wrote. With the apparent likelihood of financial gain, previously aloof residents "were now quite sociable." After the war Allen, whose regiment departed for Virginia on June 30, 1862, fondly remembered: "We can never forget our life in Beaufort, or the pleasant relations sustained with its inhabitants."[1]

Not every relation was as pleasant as Allen recalled. In postwar memoirs soldiers could portray their tours affectionately, but in contemporary letters home, they mentioned some recalcitrant individuals and growing hostility to the occupation. By 1863, northern troops had completely changed their tune in regard to the locals. After nearly a year of occupation, one soldier complained: "I doubt very much the union feeling in North Carolina." Another declared in March, "There is plenty of professed union men who will shote [*sic*] you out of the window if they get a chance." Even Treasury agent John Hedrick, who believed he encountered much Unionism in 1862, asserted in August 1863: "The great loyalty, which is said to exist in some parts of this State, I think, exists in the minds of the news writers rather than in reality." After spending ten months in the region, a disillusioned Massachusetts soldier offered a particularly acerbic appraisal: "A year ago.... I supposed we were going to help a poor oppressed people who were forced into the rebellion by a minority — now I have learned that the whole south is united. They can continue the war forever if necessary." He further bemoaned, "They hate the old flag — they hate free government — they hate every principal of right — they are not worthy to be called Americans — our nation would be stronger and better without them."[2]

This shift in tone occurred primarily because white citizens had become increasingly hostile. Many whites became disillusioned with both the tactics of the Union army locally and the larger Federal policies implemented by the occupying force. Residents, seeking to take advantage of new economic opportunities while simultaneously maintaining the social status quo, had wedded themselves to the Union. Yet, just a few months into the honeymoon, many apparent Unionists were rejecting their occupiers, primarily over perceived arbitrary uses of Federal power and serious disagreements over racial policies. In Carteret and Craven counties, local whites demonstrated that racial supremacy was more important than economic interests. Contrary to President Lincoln's earnest hope, the experience of Union occupation would ultimately drive residents more firmly into the Confederate camp than they probably would have been otherwise. During wartime occupation, local whites reacted against what they perceived as proscriptions of their trade, Federal destruction of private property, negligence toward Union supporters, and, most importantly, a far too radical racial policy.[3]

GEORGE ALLEN NOTED THAT when the port of Beaufort reopened in April 1862, "Business of various kinds began to be renewed with cheerfulness and profit." Many residents in New Bern, Beaufort, and the surrounding countryside found the opportunities for trade too enticing to resist. Farmers and fishermen engaged in a lucrative trade and barter with the Union soldiers and northern merchants. In New Bern, Wednesday was designated as "Trading Day," when people living outside the picket lines could go to the city market to exchange their farm products for the necessities and luxuries provided by northern merchants — all under the supervision of the provost marshal. Some used this occasion for nefarious reasons. Also in April the soldier-editors of the *New Bern Daily Progress* warned "all

Union men to watch closely the boatmen who come here to market," many of whom may appear "for other purposes than the legitimate purposes of honest traffic." Some unscrupulous Union officers took advantage of trading days for personal gain, furnishing army supplies to Confederate agents posing as farmers in exchange for gold.[4]

Profiteering was a universal vice that tempted soldiers in every theater of the war. It plagued occupied areas of Mississippi, Tennessee, and the South Carolina Sea Islands, where cotton was the tool of corruption. In New Bern and Beaufort, it was the naval stores industries that offered the promise of great wealth. As late as October 1863, John Hedrick said that naval officials charged only twelve dollars a barrel for turpentine, while it sold for thirty-five dollars in New York. Unprincipled officers could reap huge profits from such maneuvering. Because of this type of abuse and because the navy needed large quantities for its own use, the Treasury Department prohibited private purchases of naval stores and regulated trade among soldiers.[5]

Residents who profited from the presence of the Union soldiers and traders were content as long as they enjoyed relatively uninhibited trade. Yet, as the war progressed, the Federal government began regulating trade among them as well, which caused considerable discontent. Because of the rampant abuse of alcohol by soldiers, Union authorities forbade local merchants from selling this potentially profitable item to the troops. Of course, many attempted to do so anyway. George W. Taylor, owner of the Ocean House Hotel, undoubtedly brightened many a soldier's Christmas in 1862 by dispensing liquor behind the provost's back. The provost complained that on Christmas Eve Taylor had "sold liquor to many persons in violation of privileges heretofore granted him & through his means the night was riotous & disorderly." The provost marshal had to order him twice to close his bar.[6]

Residents and northern merchants found clever ways to bring illicit beverages into the occupied zone. In Morehead City in November 1862, the provost reported: "I have seized three boxes of contraband stuff, marked 'Horse Medicine.' It turns out on a minute examination to be genuine Bourbon Whiskey." Hedrick and his assistants cited several ship captains for smuggling liquor into the port. In December 1864, an aide to the provost marshal in Beaufort caught three residents selling liquor to a soldier — in the rear of the provost's office, no less. The provost fined the men twenty dollars each and sentenced them to forty days in jail.[7]

In addition to prohibiting the sale of "demon rum," the authorities regulated trade by granting passes to transact business only to those who had taken the oath of allegiance to the United States. However, some canny residents applied directly to military governor Edward Stanly for special dispensation. Beginning in May 1862, Stanly granted several passes without requiring the oath, which assuaged the concerns of some locals who no doubt feared the retribution they would suffer if the Confederates ever recaptured the coastal region. Stanly's generosity irritated Federal military authorities who were trying to enforce the War Department's directives. As the *New York Times*'s New Bern correspondent pointed out in the late summer of 1862, Stanly displayed "manifest favoritism toward men whose antecedents, as well as their present line of conduct, are such as to inspire doubt of their friendliness to the Union." In January 1863 he announced, "There are several good citizens in this town, who have always been loyal & for good & sufficient reasons [are] excused from taking the oath of allegiance for the present." Stanly specifically granted four Beaufort men this trading exemption status — Isaac Ramsey, Benjamin L. Perry, Thomas Duncan, and James Rumley. Ramsey, Perry, and Duncan were three of the most successful businessmen in the county before the war and jointly owned the county's largest steam sawmill, while Rumley, the clerk of the county court, was decidedly secessionist.[8]

The provost marshal, Captain William B. Fowle Jr., had only been in Beaufort for three months, but that was long enough to recognize the allegiance of these four men. "None of these gentlemen have taken the oath of allegiance, in my opinion none of them are loyal men, this opinion is formed upon information obtained from truly loyal citizens, also from my personal observations," he decried. "I have seen joy plainly depicted upon their faces when news was received of the reverse at Fredricksburg & grief at the Murfreesboro news. These facts & many others of similar nature convince me that their sympathies are with the Rebels." Fowle surmised that the four men used their passes to illicitly trade salt and other necessities up the rivers to Confederate lines, and sought to deny them passes. Other officers joined Fowle in denouncing Stanly's liberality with passes.[9]

Stanly seemed too willing to accept declarations of loyalty. He granted many passes to residents whom he perceived as Unionists so they could travel and take goods through Union lines without being molested by the soldiers. However, some passes ended up in the hands of known Confederates. Mary Peabody stated that in March 1863, when Union cavalry captured some Confederate bushwhackers, "One of the guerrillas they took had in his pocket a pass and protection from Gov. Stanly and at the same time a lieutenant's commission from Jeff Davis." Another soldier confirmed Peabody's story; he also claimed that several of the captured bandits "were recognized as having been in the city only a few days previous and as trading under a permit from Governor Stanly." Stanly frequently engaged in heated arguments over the dispensation of passes with the army provost marshals, as well as the naval officers who patrolled the rivers and resented the fact that he granted passes on the waterways. Ultimately, U.S. naval authorities refused to recognize any passes given out by Stanly, and the War Department revoked his power in the matter.[10]

Even residents who had dutifully taken the oath of allegiance found their trade prospects diminished in 1863. Expeditions into the country-side and occasional Confederate threats of attack forced military authorities to frequently suspend all trade outside of the town limits of New Bern and Beaufort. Treasury agent John Hedrick, who supported an unfettered trade because he received a percentage of the custom duties collected at the port of Beaufort, complained in January 1863 of General John G. Foster's latest order prohibiting trade. "I am getting tired of being blockaded here," Hedrick wrote. "Besides I somewhat doubt the propriety of stopping all communication with the north. If he thinks that he will prevent the Rebels from knowing what is going on here by that means, he is certainly mistaken." As the spring came, Union officials enacted further proscriptions on local trade. On March 31 President Lincoln proclaimed all northern trade with occupied regions of the South illegal, except under the supervision of the Treasury Department. In April 1863 Hedrick observed that "business is very dull in my line and I expect it to be still duller." As a result of Lincoln's proclamation, Hedrick asserted, "all commerce between here and Newbern will be shut off." Local businessmen also felt the effects of the ban. On May 3 Hedrick complained, "If a man buys a pound of coffee or a paper or pins, he must go to the Provost and get a permit to take it from the wharf with him."[11]

Not surprisingly, some residents who chafed under these restrictions resorted to illicit means to make a profit. Solomon Witherington, a Craven County farmer who lived outside of New Bern, enjoyed the privilege of trading between the lines, though many people debated his scruples. One postwar informant recalled that Witherington was "loyal to the U.S. Govt, that as such he went in and out of the lines of the U.S. Army at New Bern at will & unquestioned, selling the products of his farm to the Government & U.S. troops & purchasing needed supplies as required, and that all this would not have been allowed had he been disloyal." But another citizen remembered Witherington's activities differently: not only was he "a strong secessionist and in favor of the war," but also "it was reported and believed in his neighborhood that [Witherington] was engaged in trading between the lines" illegally. Other witnesses testified that the farmer's sympathies were ambiguous. His friend Elijah Ellis boasted of Witherington's equal treatment of southern and northern soldiers who visited his farm: "When the Southern troops came to his house he treated them as gentlemen and when the Northern troops came he treated them the same." Many residents undoubtedly shared Witherington's willingness to trade with anyone who offered them payment.[12]

Active trading between the lines occurred on the waterways surrounding Beaufort as well. On June 1, 1863, a company of the 9th New Jersey Regiment was ordered to Bogue Island to interdict illegal trade between that place and neighboring Swansboro. While doing so, the soldiers entered the cabin of a known Unionist — Horatio Frost, a fifty-four-year-old illiterate fisherman, widower, and father of seven — and captured three Confederates having lunch with him. Frost had found his ability to market his wares along the coast curtailed by the new Union regulations. This Unionist, whose loyalty had never been questioned before, likely made an economic alliance with Confederate soldiers in the region in order to provide for his large family. The New Jersey soldier does not record what punishment, if any, Frost received as a result.[13]

By late 1863, many residents had learned how to work within the Union regulations. But John Hedrick noted that local traders acted more out of self-interest than any ideological motivation. On September 27 he wrote, "In making shipments to the interior, the owner of the goods has to swear that 'he is in all respects loyal and true to the government of the United States and that he has never given voluntary aid to the rebels in arms nor in any other manner encouraged the rebellion.'" According to Hedrick, the people had no qualms taking the oath. "They reason thus, 'When the Southern forces were in possession here I would bring my corn, flour, fish and potatoes to market and would sell to any one who would give me the most money. Or if a soldier should come to my house and wish to buy potatoes I would sell them to him, not because he was in the Rebel service but because I must have money.'" Such was the case for most locals who relied on trade for their livelihood. The color of his uniform was less important than the color of the money that the buyer offered. The Federal restrictions would remain in place until May 15, 1865, when Union officials lifted martial law and no longer issued licenses to trade. Though economic enticements had wooed many locals to the Union side soon after the Yankees arrived, the restraints placed on trade during the occupation caused many to ponder the depth of their attachment to the Union.[14]

NOT ONLY DID LOCAL whites resent the trade restrictions, but also they believed that Union soldiers were becoming increasingly undisciplined, especially on expeditions into the countryside. Those who had taken the oath of allegiance, but lived outside of the occupied towns, complained to Governor Stanly of ill treatment. Stanly relayed to the Department of North Carolina's military commander, General John G. Foster, that "in numerous instances, well authenticated, [Union soldiers] entered and robbed the houses of loyal men, destroyed furniture, insulted women, and treated with scorn the protections, which by your advice I had given them." Similarly, when residents rebuked soldiers for their actions, retaliations became more destructive. In late 1862 Stanly fumed that to one Union officer in particular, "House-burning seems becoming, not an extreme medicine of war, but a matter of amusement, to the men he is supposed to command."[15]

Occasionally physical assault supplanted house burning. In November 1862, Corporal Zenas T. Haines of the 45th Massachusetts Regiment reported that when a private in his company was searching a suspected "rebel's" house for firearms, the homeowner "forcibly resisted" the soldier's efforts to secure a weapon. The private "used the butt of a fowling piece over the head of secesh with such good effect that all resistance ceased." In December 1862, as a Union expeditionary force marched toward Kinston, Haines's compatriots concentrated on foraging from the local populace. On that cold, windy day, Haines said, his regiment encountered "a spunky secesh female, who, with a heavy wooden rake, stood guard over her winter's store of sweet potatoes. Her eyes flashed defiance, but so long as she stood upon the defensive no molestation was offered her." Being December, one can see why the woman fought so tenaciously for one of her subsistence crops that might sustain her family through the winter. "When, however, she concluded to change her tactics, and slapped a cavalry officer in the face," Haines noted with amusement, "gone were her sweet potatoes and other stores in the twinkling of an eye."[16]

Locals interpreted such actions as indiscriminate persecution by an undisciplined army. Such persecution included the arrest of any citizen suspected of being disloyal. One memorable encounter described by Haines illustrates the fear spread by the army: "In the house of one poor miserable paralytic wretch we found a double-barrelled gun, loaded & capped. 'This is what picks off our men of nights,' said a sgt. of cavalry," who eventually "satisfied himself that the sick rebel was not playing possum." Haines mused, "The scared & forlorn expression on the yellow and haggard face of his wife was a study for an artist." Of course, one must question how Haines knew which locals were "secesh." A desire to defend private property was a normal act of self-preservation, not one directed solely at Union armies. Confederate troops wreaked as much havoc on southern citizens as Union troops. In fact, Confederate depredations in eastern North Carolina became so unbearable that, in a December 1863 letter to Jefferson Davis's secretary of war, James Seddon, Governor Zebulon Vance asserted sardonically: "If God Almighty had yet in store another plague worse than all others which he intended to have let loose on the Egyptians in case Pharaoh still hardened his heart, I am sure it must have been a regiment or so of half-armed, half-disciplined Confederate cavalry."[17]

Some Union authorities recognized the difficult plight of people living in no-man's-land — the area outside of direct Union control but subject to raids by both sides. In March 1863 Edward Stanly asked General Foster: "Can I give to people whose loyalty is not & has never been questioned any assurance that you can see them protected? As matters now stand, the loyal men & women, aged & infirm, outside of our lines, are the most unfortunate & oppressed in our country. Both sides pillage and rob them." Thomas Kirwan of the 17th Massachusetts Regiment understood the residents' dilemma:

> It can be judged what a hardship it was to planters and dwellers in that section. They naturally sympathized with their own people, but if they held intercourse with the Union forces, they were suspected by the Confederates of giving information as to their movements, while the Union troops not only suspected that they gave information of army movements, but when picketing or bushwhacking was indulged in, at night, it was believed that it was these professed noncombatants who did the shooting.

Indeed, both sides suspected those living outside of Union lines of disreputable activities. As Kirwan aptly noted, "They were thus between the upper and nether millstones, and suffered accordingly," particularly from pillaging.[18]

Union soldiers prided themselves on their pillaging prowess, especially on the periodic raids into the countryside. "If you could see the ruin, devastation and utter abandonment of villages, Plantations and farms, which but a short time ago was peopled, fenced, and stocked," one soldier wrote his wife, "no cows, horses, mules, sheep, or poultry to be seen where ever the Union army advances." The soldier concluded, "This whole country for all purposes of maintenance for man or beast for the next twelve months is a desert as hopeless as Sahara itself." Agnes Paton, a young woman who lived just outside Union lines, remembered these raids by Union soldiers as a constant cause for concern: "When you live near the lines, there is no rest or quietness, [there was] always something to worry. Just as soon as things would get quieted down, here would come a Regiment or two singing."[19]

Occasionally, pillaging led to fantastic images like the one described by an amused Massachusetts soldier. On one foray a fellow infantryman "had looted a medical office and found a skeleton. He was marching off, the skeleton hanging over his shoulder, with a bayonet through his mouth and his heels clattering on the ground." Desperate to prevent plundering by Union forces, those civilians who had taken the oath of allegiance would place white flags on their houses to signify that they had Union protection. Another soldier was entertained by the plea of a barely literate Unionist, whose house northern troops used as a picket outpost. The turpentine distiller had scrawled over his mantle: "This is my Howze i is for the younion Plesse don't tare up my Pain [pine] treezes I have a protexion from the Ginerl. [Signed] Riley Wetherington."[20]

These raids were not the actions of a wayward few. Deliberately destructive expeditions sent into the countryside from occupied coastal North Carolina towns were intended to deprive the Confederacy not only of the cotton crop, but also of grazing lands for southern cavalry and foodstuffs for the rebel army. Though Stanly and the region's white inhabitants deeply resented them, these new, harsher measures were part and parcel of a formal Federal policy — indicative of the retreat from conciliation — that was being implemented in many areas of the South, not just North Carolina. Judging from Confederate reactions, the Union soldiers enforced this policy effectively. Leonidas L. Polk, a lieutenant in General Daniel Harvey Hill's North Carolina army and future leader of the Farmer's Alliance in the 1880s, marched with his troops through sections of eastern North Carolina that had been visited by the Union troops in March 1863. "We went 30 miles through as fine and rich lands as in the state and I saw only about 4 acres preparing for a crop," Polk told his wife. "Large and rich plantations [were] entirely deserted and the only marks left of their recently prosperous and happy owners and tenants was the lonely chimneys of their fine and beautiful residences. Everything was burnt and destroyed that could be."[21]

In addition to using stronger measures against local property, the Federal government established stricter policies regarding suspected disloyal civilians. Officials in Carteret and Craven counties evicted those who refused to take, or reneged on, the oath of allegiance to the United States. The first eviction notice came in October 1862, when Massachusetts soldier James Glazier wrote his wife: "The white people of this city have had their choice—to take the oath, or leave." Glazier reflected ruefully: "I pity those who went away for many of them were honest people and loved us as their own sons and brothers, but we cannot know the trials of persons in their circumstances." Another was less empathetic, stating: "I am glad they have gone for they were a nusence."[22]

The second eviction order came in the spring of 1863. On April 20 a Massachusetts soldier informed his wife, "This causes great rejoicing among the soldiers for they were getting pretty saucy." He added, "It is what ought to have [been] don [sic] one year ago." John Hedrick noted that by June 1863, the threat of eviction had created much anxiety in Beaufort. "A great many of the citizens are frightened," he wrote. "Some are afraid of being drafted [into the Union army] and others of being sent out of the lines." Such attempts to suppress disloyalty severely damaged the relationship between Union forces and the civil society they were trying to support. In a letter to Massachusetts senator Charles Sumner after the war, Edward Stanly condemned the actions of Union soldiers: "Had the war in North Carolina been conducted by soldiers who were Christians and gentlemen, the state would long ago have rebelled against rebellion." Instead, "Thousands and thousands of dollars worth of property were conveyed North. Libraries, pianos, carpets, mirrors, family portraits, everything in short that could be removed was stolen by men abusing flagitious slaveholders and preaching liberty, justice and civilization."[23]

Some local Unionists assailed the Federal occupiers in retaliation for their treatment. When surgeon John Spear commandeered a boat, he found himself under attack by the vessel's owner, an avowed Unionist from Portsmouth named Robert Wallace. Wallace recounted how Spear had come to take Wallace's skiff, claiming that it had been left in the charge of a local black boy. "I remarked that if the boy said the skiff was left in his charge, that he told a damn lie, and if I caught him in her I would kill him." When Spear replied "No you won't," Wallace threatened Spear. "I said I would serve you so too," he related. "I then forbid him coming in the yard, told him if he did I would kill him." Spear later returned with soldiers and arrested Wallace, who grudgingly admitted his error and promised, "I will neither by word, deed, or action do anything against the U.S. in any form whatever."[24]

Among other angry reactions, in January 1863 some Portsmouth residents seized the U.S. flag from a revenue cutter and hid it. Spear and his black employees recaptured the banner. Spear commented: "The question I would like to ask some of these professedly strong Union people is, If you are such good friends of the Union, why did you want to secrete the Union flag?" Obviously, the actions of the government had spurred some citizens to take subtle measures of resistance and rebellion. Others' actions were more overt. On May 8, 1863, the surgeon wrote: "I have been at the Provost Marshal's office the most of the day, as witness in a case in which a professedly strong Union man is charged with disloyalty and using treasonable language." Spear did not identify the defendant, but apparently his anger had boiled over and led to the arrest. This dissenter was not the only one vocalizing disdain for the Union forces. Similar expressions of disdain for the Union forces prompted another Union soldier to remark, "There is no Union sentiment here. About all are either silent or growling most of the time because we are taking away their rights."[25]

Local white women also participated in treasonable activities. One early February afternoon in 1865, Union soldiers arrested Emeline Pigott as a spy and imprisoned her in Beaufort. Living just north of Morehead City, Pigott had engaged in several clandestine actions to aid the Confederate army, and she often carried mail between the lines illegally. She admitted that she frequently fed Confederate scouts, carrying meals to them in the woods: "Some time Yankeys would be in the house while the Confederates [were in the woods, and] were both fed from the same table." On February 8 she enlisted the aid of her brother-in-law, Rufus W. Bell, to assist her in her latest mission. Underneath her apparently enormous hoop skirt she wore two pairs of Confederate pants and a pair of boots and, remarkably, carried a shirt, a cap, a dozen linen collars, and pocket handkerchiefs; fifty skeins of silk, spools of cotton, needles, toothbrushes, combs, knives, razors, gloves;

and several letters addressed to Confederates. About 4:00 P.M. Union soldiers arrested the pair and discovered Pigott's hidden contraband. A Union newspaper in Beaufort reported, "On being arrested, with consummate impudence, she blustered about the arrest of high-toned *Southern* ladies as though *they* could do nothing wrong." Union soldiers confined her in the Beaufort jail before moving her to a New Bern jail, where she was held for a couple of weeks before being released for unspecified reasons. To protest her arrest, some residents caused such a disturbance at a local store that the provost marshal apprehended a number of them, closed the store, and fined each agitator ten dollars. Union authorities then rigorously enforced the oath of allegiance, especially among women. A northern soldier took satisfaction in stating, "A great many of the 'little dears of Beaufort' swallowed the bitter Yankee pill and took the oath of allegiance this morning."[26]

In addition to arresting citizens or seizing their property in retribution for disloyalty, Union forces often confiscated or destroyed residents' property either out of military necessity or caprice. In the spring of 1862 Union officers from the 9th New Jersey Regiment commandeered the *Annie Grey*, owned by Benjamin L. Roberson, a fifty-year-old Beaufort mariner and father of five. In June, Roberson, who had voluntarily taken the oath of allegiance, appealed to Governor Stanly for the return of his boat. His request was granted. Roberson repaired minor damages to the vessel, only to have the provost marshal demand it again a month later. Appealing to Stanly in July, he "protested against his taking my boat on the grounds that I was a man of family and without my boat I should be deprived of the means of obtaining a living for my family & further that my boat has been taken out of my possession by the officer on a former occasion." Stanly referred him to the department commander and endorsed his request. Writing to the commander in November, Roberson asked for either compensation or the return of the *Annie Grey*, claiming that the loss of the boat, which he valued at five hundred dollars, "has injured me very seriously as it was the only source of income I had." Despite repeated pleas Roberson never received compensation or saw his boat again. Several years after the war, through the auspices of what became known as the Southern Claims Commission, southern civilians could apply to the Federal government for compensation for property taken or damaged by Union forces, provided they could sufficiently demonstrate their loyalty during the war. Roberson filed such a claim for his boat, only to have it disallowed because he had had a son in

Emeline Pigott (Courtesy of Carteret County Historical Society, Morehead City)

the Confederate army; therefore, in the eyes of the commissioners, he had shown insufficient loyalty.[27]

Military authorities confiscated property from many other people who considered themselves loyal to the Union. Reuben Fulcher of Beaufort helplessly watched naval officials commandeer his $1,200 schooner in July 1862. An agent of the Commissary Department took Daniel Bell's eighteen-foot sailboat, *Carrie*, on June 11, 1863, at Morehead City. Desperate for raw materials to build barracks, erect fortifications, and improve port facilities,

Union authorities took 50 tons of timber from Daniel Dickinson's farm on Core Creek and another 125 tons from his relative and neighbor, William H. Dickinson. They also tore down David W. Bell's two-story house outside of Carolina City in the summer of 1863, David S. Quinn's small farmhouse near Morehead City in January 1864, and Jesse Fulcher's fish house. Like the other residents, Fulcher and Quinn were upset because they believed they had demonstrated their loyalty as well as they could, often feeding the Union officers and men, for which they "made no charge and received no pay."[28]

After the war, each of these men applied to the Southern Claims Commission for compensation for their lost property. All of their claims were denied because postwar arbiters found their loyalty suspect. Union authorities now had difficulty accepting Unionism in a region that had become known for its hostility. Taking the oath of allegiance and offering succor to Union soldiers no longer was enough to demonstrate one's loyalty. In rejecting William Dickinson's claim, the commissioners stated: "He took the oath of allegiance to U.S. after our Army occupied that section, but that is far from conclusive on the subject." Even more telling, they asserted, "He did not suffer for the Union cause. He was not threatened or molested by the Rebels."[29]

David S. Quinn received similar treatment. Though he proved that he had often given food to the Union soldiers, the commissioners declared: "We are not told the circumstances under which the Union soldiers were fed or the sick soldiers nursed — whether it was done for pay — under compulsion — from motives of humanity or from patriotic motives." More damaging was that Quinn did not appear to have endured violence because of his Unionism: "The rebels never molested him & he was never even threatened on account of his union sentiments & he did nothing whatever for the Union cause." Though he had receipts from the Union provost for his house and a sworn deposition dated February 1, 1864, affirming that he had taken the oath of allegiance, the commissioners rejected his claim, primarily because he, like Dickinson, did not *suffer* for his loyalty, at least not from Confederate persecution. But Quinn and many other residents became increasingly displeased with the suffering they endured at the hands of the Union occupation forces, especially the confiscation of their property.[30]

MANY LOCAL WHITES found their bodies as well as their belongings subject to a form of confiscation by Union forces. Beginning in 1863, Federal soldiers and recruiting agents started coercing Carteret men, as well as Confederate deserters and refugees who fled to Union lines, into joining the 1st or 2nd North Carolina (Union) Regiment. Charles Henry Foster, a lieutenant colonel and recruiting officer, did not assuage any fears in April 1863 when he told residents of Carteret County "that if they did not volunteer, . . . they would be conscripted before long." Other officers advocated filling up regular military units with men from the local populace. As Beaufort's provost marshal in November 1863, Colonel James Jourdan dealt with Confederate deserters who fled to his lines. Having initially claimed that these men voluntarily signed up, Jourdan was later embarrassed to learn that some of his recruiting agents "have by display of firearms, threats of personal violence, imprisonment as rebels, spies &c, attempted to compel men to enlist."[31]

John Hedrick mentioned other coercive tactics used on the potential recruits: "The way the deserters and refugees are treated, is to put them into prison until they are willing to volunteer in the Union army." Though he was unsure how long they were confined in jail, Hedrick said that "they always let them out when they do volunteer." He further commented that material destitution combined with peer pressure often persuaded refugees to enlist. "There are a great many things brought to bear upon them to induce them to join the army," he wrote. "Most of them come in a destitute condition. Some of them have their families with them and when they arrive, they have no place to go for shelter and subsistence except . . . to the military. They are promised large bounties, a place for their families to live in and an outfit of clothing if they will volunteer." Comparing it to a sort of freshman hazing, Hedrick related: "When a refugee comes in. . . . All the Buffaloes get after him and before he knows what he is about he has joined the regiment." Yet he did not see anything untoward in these coercive tactics. James Rumley, who was not so forgiving, condemned them: "[Refugees] come in squads of four or five, and as soon as they set foot upon the place are besieged by Buffalo recruiting officers (who are swarming over the county) and are wheedled or frightened into the Federal service." Rumley viewed these men with a mixture of indignation and pity: "Some poor deluded wretches enter there, and are induced by false representations to sell themselves to the public enemies of their country."[32]

Many locals who had voluntarily joined the army believed the Federal government provided insufficient monetary compensation. A captain in the 1st North Carolina (Union) Regiment complained to Governor Stanly:

"Some of the volunteers in our Regiment are unable to provide for their families from the wages they receive as soldiers, on account of the very high cost of provisions & the dependence in many cases of a large family upon such earnings." He suggested a supplemental pay increase, claiming: "The loyal states with very few exceptions afford pecuniary aid to the families of their volunteers. Everything the North Carolina soldier buys for his family to live upon or to wear costs perhaps double or treble its former price, while there is no corresponding increase in his pay." Stanly forwarded his request to General Foster, but there is no record of a response. A Union officer noted in March 1864 that the 1st North Carolina was due four months' pay; he urged the paymaster at Fort Monroe, Virginia, to expedite it, "as very many of the families of its soldiers have to rely upon the monthly pay for their principal subsistence." As Charles Henry Foster pleaded when payroll was several months behind, "Mere personal persuasion and influence are not sufficient, without at least some money, to hold a large number of men together." Indeed, lack of pay was one reason for several desertions.[33]

More locals fled the Union army after Confederates captured several dozen members of the 2nd North Carolina (Union) Regiment outside of New Bern in February 1864. On February 2, after being constantly "menaced by the enemy," most of Company F of the 2nd North Carolina, which had been defending Beech Grove on the Neuse River north of New Bern, surrendered to a small Confederate army commanded by General George Pickett. Confederates tried and hanged twenty-two members of the company between February 5 and 22, near Kinston. Some of the Confederates tormented the imprisoned "buffaloes," denying them food for several days. Confederates also simultaneously hung thirteen of these men from one gallows, stripped them of their clothes, and, according to some accounts, harassed and robbed the victims' widows who tried to tend to the mutilated bodies. In justification, the rebels indicated that they executed only men who had been deserters from the Confederate service, though Union officials disagreed. One Confederate witness declared: "I think such an example ought to learn our men better" about the dangers of deserting and joining the enemy.[34]

The example was effective, as many native soldiers fled to quieter sectors or deserted the Union army, believing that it was not doing enough to protect them. In March 1864, twenty-eight men deserted their Federal company, and many of them made their way from the front lines at New Bern to the more protected Beaufort, where they were arrested by the provost marshal. Their colonel tried to excuse their conduct, claiming: "Several of them had brothers or other near relations who were hung at Kinston; all of them acquaintances and old neighbors or comrades, who thus expiated the crime of loyalty upon the gallows; and the news of the horrid and bloody massacre was fresh when they were, as they supposed, ordered to the front." The new department commander, General Innis Palmer, noted the stark change in attitude among the North Carolina soldiers. In May 1864 Palmer complained to Secretary of War Edwin Stanton, "The North Carolina troops I consider useless . . . as the execution of the Carolina troops at Kinston had very much demoralized the whole of them."[35]

The families of these native Union soldiers also felt neglected by Federal authorities, who often failed to follow through on promises of money or provisions. In April 1864 the colonel of the 1st North Carolina wrote that when the theater's commander, General Benjamin F. Butler, visited the region, "I called his attention to the many cases of destitution among the families of the men of my regiment, the majority of whom had been driven from their homes by the enemy and in many cases not allowed to bring a change of clothing with them." The colonel appealed for rations and money to be sent without delay, noting: "These people are worthy of it, their husbands are good soldiers and have comparatively been of little expence to the government." Six months later there were still bureaucratic delays in doling out the pensions due to the family members of the men executed at Kinston. Several applications had been sent back for lack of proper documentation, prompting General Palmer to implore the Treasury Department auditor to accept the claims without requiring further proof. Many times the required documents simply did not exist. "For instance a marriage certificate is required: many of these people were perhaps married years ago by some ignorant country justice and a record or certificate of the fact was perhaps never made at all," Palmer said. "I believe the claims have been prepared as fully as is possible with the means now at hand." Furthermore, the general was moved by their destitution and demanded their claims be processed quickly: "As a matter of humanity if nothing more, they should at once receive the pittance that is due them."[36]

Many Unionists, both enlisted men and civilians, frantically fled to Beaufort in the spring of 1864, after the Confederate military successes. Rumley characterized the fleeing "buffaloes" as "wretched victims of Yankee lying and trickery," who "with their squalid and destitute women and children are flocking to Beaufort, as their last place of refuge on the soil of their outraged and insulted state." Undoubtedly many of these refugee soldiers, like George W. Jones, a twenty-four-year-old painter whose brother had been executed at Kinston, felt they had been "fooled into [enlistment] . . . with the promises of protection" by the Yankees. Seeking a discharge after only three months of service, Jones complained in April that he was "looked upon as a traitor and a coward by the majority of the North as well as the South and neither feel willing to protect me." He gloomily asserted, "I feel like a prisoner [whose] sentence is death awaiting the day of execution." His lugubrious lament indicates that even Unionists felt betrayed by Federal action, or inaction, as the case may be.[37]

BUT *NOTHING* ANGERED white residents more than the perceived gracious treatment northerners gave to the local African American population. The flash point of white anger came when Lincoln issued his Emancipation Proclamation, which did not exempt North Carolina though it did excuse many other occupied regions. Although most scholars agree that the Federal government's policy of emancipation did not include any real desire to provide complete independence or equality—and therefore, its revolutionary nature was quite limited—that reality is less important than what local whites perceived at the time. White North Carolinians saw only radical policies of social equality and the dreaded fear of all white supremacists: eventual amalgamation. As Massachusetts soldier Zenas Haines noted on October 31, 1862, "There was a right smart of Union here before the proclamation, but now it is the other way."[38]

Native son James West Bryan, a prominent antebellum Whig politician and Carteret County representative, had articulated the views of the region's residents in an 1835 speech in which he proclaimed: "This is a nation of white people, its offices, honors, dignities, and privileges are alone open to, and to be enjoyed by, white people." Furthermore, "The God of Nature has made this marked and distinctive difference between us, for some wise purpose, and assigned to each color their proper and appropriate part of the Globe; and I can never consent to [their] equality." Twenty-eight years had not altered those beliefs from the minds of coastal white residents, who feared that Lincoln's Proclamation was the first step toward such equality. They had accepted occupation as a means of returning to the prewar Union but found that the Federal government had different ideas. By 1863, this new Union—embodied in the Emancipation Proclamation and the educational and uplifting goals of arriving northern benevolent societies — represented radicalism that southern whites, even many Unionists, rejected. This included Governor Stanly. Stanly had warned the Lincoln administration in June 1862 that unless he could give North Carolinians "some assurance that this is a war of restoration and not of abolition and destruction, no peace can be restored here for many years to come."[39]

Hoping to exempt North Carolina from the Proclamation by having an elected representative in the U.S. Congress, Stanly called for a vote in December 1862. The governor personally backed Jennings Pigott, a Unionist from Carteret County (though he had been living in Washington, D.C., for several years), who opposed emancipation. Pigott's main challenger, Charles Henry Foster, had organized a local party, the Free Labor Association, which advocated compliance with the president's Proclamation and expected to draw on this support to win the election. Foster, an opportunist who had emigrated from Maine in the 1850s and edited a secessionist newspaper in Murfreesboro, North Carolina, before the war, had many detractors (especially John Hedrick, who aggressively campaigned against him). The *New Bern Daily Progress* also backed Pigott, proclaiming that the war was fought to restore the Union, not "to establish Free Labor in North Carolina."[40]

In the January 1, 1863, election, in which only white males who had taken the oath of allegiance were allowed to vote, Pigott won overwhelmingly, amassing 594 votes to Foster's 157. The election totals indicate that local white Unionists opposed emancipation, as they voted against Foster and his Free Labor Association ideals. Nevertheless, Foster protested the outcome on the grounds that Pigott lacked the requisite residency status to be a legitimate candidate, and Congress ultimately refused to seat him. In the meantime, eastern North Carolina was not exempted from the Emancipation Proclamation, despite the earnest wishes of its white residents. Later Stanly condemned the Proclamation, declaring that it "crushes all hope of making peace by conciliatory measures. . . . It will fill the hearts of Union men with despair . . . strengthen the hands of detestable traitors . . . [and] to the negros . . . bring the most direful calamities." Detesting the radical turn the war had taken, Stanly resigned the governorship in protest over the Emancipation Proclamation in January 1863 and left the state in late March, ending his association with the occupation forces. Stanly may have also departed so that he would not be deemed guilty by association. On Christmas

Day, 1862, in Beaufort, a crowd had hung him in effigy, believing that despite his professed beliefs, he was actually allied with the antislavery administration.[41]

FROM THE FIRST MOMENTS of the Union occupation, whites resented the fact that northerners allowed former slaves a multitude of previously forbidden freedoms. Disapproving whites saw blacks attend school, confiscate white property, and be disrespectful to their former masters. Furthermore, Federal authorities employed blacks and paid them directly for their labor. Union officials also granted legal rights to freedpeople, an act that appalled white residents. In late May 1862 James Rumley complained that Union officials used slaves as informants, "get[ting] information from them as to the political opinions and conduct of their owners." Moreover, "A Negro, who in our civil courts could not be heard except through his master can appear [before the provost marshal] as the accuser of any white citizen, and cause the citizen to be arrested." Northern soldiers also seemed to allow blacks more privileges than whites. When a New Bern farmer went to the market to purchase fish, his daughter recalled that he "was ordered by a Federal officer to 'stand back, soldiers first, negroes next, and rebels last.'" As John Hedrick maintained in late July 1862, "The slaves are about as free as their masters, or a little more so now because the niggs can go without passes, while the whites have to have them." Undoubtedly, Union officials granted these freedoms because there was little doubt about the loyalty of blacks — unlike that of whites.[42]

Conflicts also occurred on several occasions over housing for black and white refugees. In November 1862 Charles Henry Foster, while recruiting for the 1st North Carolina (Union) Regiment, proposed to the department commander that all blacks currently living in Beaufort be removed from their houses to the contraband camps developing outside of town, "so that the loyal men who enlist from exposed situations in the county may move into [the houses] with their families." Foster assured the commander that he could enroll one hundred men in a few weeks. Governor Stanly, he said, approved of the plan. Without hearing any firm comment from the department commander, Stanly authorized Foster to begin implementing the policy. Provost Marshal William Fowle Jr. reacted angrily and wrote his own letter to the department commander. Foster had been taking charge of all abandoned buildings, and "in case the buildings are occupied by negroes, he is to demand rent of them & if they don't pay eject them. The negroes in question are the very contrabands to whom the Government is issuing rations," Fowle fumed. "Of course if they cannot pay for food, they cannot pay rent & I suppose shelter must be provided for them." To local whites, Stanly appeared to be sympathetic to their desires while Fowle represented the Federal government's prerogative to elevate blacks over whites.[43]

Whites also became enraged at Federal efforts to enlist African American soldiers in the region. Rumley complained on May 30, 1863, that a Beaufort church had been "prostituted to the most unholy and damnable work of raising Negro volunteers for the armed service of the Yankee government." Soon authorities moved the recruitment to the symbol of county justice, the courthouse. "Nothing during our captivity has shocked the feelings of our people more," claimed Rumley. Though the use of the courthouse probably offended the clerk of the county court more than others, Rumley was not alone in his indignation. Even John Hedrick, the antislavery Unionist, admitted that he "would much rather see a hundred negroes sent from than one into the State." Hostility toward the empowerment of blacks, and the social chaos that it caused, became so palpable that Hedrick informed his brother in July that most Beaufort whites "wish to get rid of slavery and negroes, and if they can not dispose of the latter any other way, they wish to kill them." Private Charles Duren of the 24th Massachusetts sensed the same reaction. "They say if you free the slaves don't leave them here, we can not or will not live with [them]," he wrote his parents. "They never will repeal those laws. The[y] hate a negro, talk about them[,] regarding them as no better than a beast." Whites felt the traditional social order had been inverted by the Union occupation, which Rumley scathingly indicted as a "reign of niggerism."[44]

The frequent interactions between freedpeople and Union soldiers, whom Rumley believed actually preferred blacks to whites, exacerbated white resentment. Federal troops did have open, sometime intimate, relations with blacks, but the majority of northern soldiers in the area, including the antislavery ones from New England, maintained decidedly racist views. Simultaneously, however, many northern officials compared African Americans favorably to poor whites of the same economic condition. "The Negroes are not so helpless and dependent as the poor whites," proclaimed Horace James, superintendent for Negro affairs in New Bern. "They are more fertile in expedients, more industrious, more religious, and more active and vigorous in body and mind." Dr. Jesse William Page, of the U.S. Sanitary Commission, who operated a hospital in New Bern, agreed

James Rumley, secessionist diarist of Beaufort (Courtesy of
State Archives, Division of Archives and History, Raleigh)

with James; it was Page's opinion that the poor whites were "a more helpless
and spiritless race than the Negroes in the same section. . . . They have more
pride, but less activity." In refugee camps, industrious freedpeople grew
vegetables for subsistence and the market, while local poor whites seemed
far less active. James concluded, "Of those who are equally poor and equally
destitute, the white person will be the one to sit down in forlorn and lan-
guid helplessness, and eat the bread of charity, while the negro will be tin-
kering at something, in his rude way, to hammer out a living."[45]

Union authorities showed a preference for employing industrious freedmen over poor whites, perhaps because many officials deemed poor whites to be inferior to blacks "in intelligence, energy, and every thing else that makes up a noble character." Edward Bartlett of the 44th Massachusetts compared the two lower-class groups: "The poor whites, what a miserable class they are. . . . The blacks are far ahead of them." Poor whites discerned this condescension from their occupiers and considered it to be an insult to their honor. They had fled to Union lines expecting opportunities for economic and perhaps social advancement. When it became apparent that some white northerners held them in lower esteem than blacks, poor whites reacted angrily and sometimes violently. A few took covert action against their occupiers in retaliation. "There are a set of poor whites around here," wrote Bartlett, "who are Union-looking citizens in the day time and 'guerrillas' at night, who raise hogs and sweet potatoes by day and in the night shoot our pickets."[46]

Poor whites also publicly rejected the attempts of northern benevolent societies to improve the lot of African Americans. In November 1864, poor whites caused a panic in a black church in Beaufort by threatening to blow it up with the congregants inside. Three white men torched a freedpeople's schoolhouse in Beaufort and threatened the female teacher with violence unless she refused to ever teach freedpeople again. Ultimately, whites feared that their occupiers were going to convert blacks into Radical Republicans who could potentially undermine conservative white power. It did not help that once the war ended, several Union authorities advocated granting blacks the right to vote. Regarding black enfranchisement, Joseph Barlow admitted in June 1865: "I do not think they should vote now, not until they have become more enlightened," which he thought would take about ten years. "But at any rate," he declared, "I had rather they would vote than a Rebel."[47]

This attitude hints at the sentiments of the northern troops by the end of the war. Over the three years of occupation, the soldiers became fed up with the hostility they encountered from residents, as well as the drudgery of daily duty. They looked forward to returning home. On April 11, 1865, news arrived in New Bern that Robert E. Lee had surrendered his army at Appomattox two days earlier. Thomas Carey of the 15th Connecticut rejoiced: "Such news as this awakens the liveliest emotions in camp. We talk of home with bright anticipations tonight." Union troops wished to leave this unappreciative sandy stretch of North Carolina as soon as possible. White residents heartily wished to see them go. The apparently heavy-handed tactics of the army had angered many locals. Years later, Elizabeth Oakes Smith described the locals' attitudes in Beaufort: "They were for the Union mostly, but an army is an army, and with the best intentions commanders could not fully protect neutrals," implying that the army's prolonged presence and the assorted acts of plunder associated with it would naturally engender resentment.[48]

By the war's end, Carteret residents had become extremely recalcitrant under Union occupation, creating a suspicious uneasiness among Federal authorities. Even after the Union suspended martial law in favor of civil government in July 1865, allowing for a civilian mayor, town commissioners, and police force, Federal officers were skeptical about the qualifications of the residents who would fill these positions. One official told New Bern's military liaison in charge of shifting to civil government that he must appoint only truly loyal men. "The mere taking the oath of allegiance will not be held conclusive of loyalty," the official wrote, foreshadowing the judgments of the postwar Southern Claims Commission arbiters, "for it is not unreasonable to suppose that a man who has been guilty of treason may be willing to commit perjury." The official wanted to make sure that only the proper sort of men attained positions of police authority, because "to arm and give more power to traitors is worse than doing nothing."[49]

Despite these warnings, Federal officials, who distrusted the strength and depth of white loyalty, were unable to completely impose their political preferences over the region. Local whites would not allow such control. Just over a month after Lee surrendered, coastal resident Dehlia Mabrey rejected the idea of whites acquiescing to Federal rule. When pondering whether the South would submit to Yankee control, she emphatically answered "No! Our spirits are not subdued, neither can they make us love them." She spoke prophetically of future white resistance to Reconstruction in the region when she declared that "discord and strife are and will be the watchword of the Union." Most whites in eastern North Carolina shared Mabrey's antipathy. Given the destruction of their property, the regulation of their economy, the insults to local white women, and, most trenchantly, the empowerment of their former slaves, local whites perceived that the policies of the Federal government were simply too humiliating to abide.[50]

IN EASTERN NORTH CAROLINA, a man's actions during the war served as a litmus test for his postwar success. Those who stood by the Union often found themselves ostracized from the community. Elijah S. Smith, a native of nearby Beaufort County who served in the 1st North Carolina (Union) Regiment, epitomized such social exclusion. "Since the close of the War of the South," he wrote Benjamin Butler in February 1869, "I have had a hard time of it, for the fact that we were doubed with the title of Buffalows, and that the Cessionist got temporarily in power, in my Section of the Country, consiquently we have been very much oppressed." Men who served in the North Carolina Union regiments faced even greater dangers than just social isolation. Oscar Eastmond, a northern officer of the 1st North Carolina, pleaded for Federal protection in June 1865, when local soldiers were scheduled to be mustered out: "Surely the government will not now send them to their home defenseless, leaving them to the mercy of those from whom both themselves & families have suffered taunts, & violence during the rebellion." Eastmond recognized that for local whites who detested the military occupation, "the humiliation of defeat & subjugation can never eradicate unprincipled hatred from their bosom nor prevent secret plots of midnight violence & highway murders." For whites in eastern North Carolina, as one Union officer explained later, "It cost something to be loyal to the Union."[51]

White residents made certain that their fellow whites who had allied too closely with the Union occupiers during the war were held accountable afterward. This denouement can be traced most clearly in the postwar fate of Carteret County merchants.[52] Former Beaufort hotel owner Benjamin A. Ensley had navigated the shoals of Unionism in Beaufort, only to find himself shipwrecked on a newly Confederate shore. Though he initially avoided taking the oath of allegiance in 1862 and 1863, Ensley finally relented in 1864 in order to continue managing his store in Beaufort and negotiated regularly with Union officials. But after the war he could not escape his creditors, many of whom undoubtedly were annoyed by his caving in to Union authorities. Ensley was "being sued freely and frequently." By July 1867, "very badly broke in fortune," he moved to neighboring Hyde County, an area known for its wartime Unionism, to try to carve out an existence.[53]

Encumbered by large debts before the war, George Taylor, proprietor of the Ocean House hotel, was barely making ends meet. The war solved his immediate financial woes when his establishment became the hub of Union activity, garnering him sizable profits. In December 1865, the boost from Federal contracts had righted him, and he was "worth 10 or 15 thousand [dollars] . . . [and] doing good business." Yet citizens had a long memory, and their rejection of his wartime choices propelled him back into debt. In May 1868, he sold all of his property to his brother, for whom he worked as an agent. In December 1871, however, the local credit agent still commented harshly that Taylor was "worth nothing."[54]

Similarly, German-born baker John B. Wolf had lived and practiced his skills in Beaufort for fifteen years before the war. He remained there through the conflict and worked for the Union army, providing bread for Federal hospitals. Wolf recalled that he "was threatened by the secessionists of this place in case the Confederate troops ever came to Beaufort to be reported on account of my union feeling." The government employment during the war had proved economically beneficial to Wolf. In January 1861 a national credit agency had indicated that he was "worth very little"; indeed, he claimed to be worth only three hundred dollars in the 1860 census. By December 1865, the same credit agency declared Wolf to be worth as much as three thousand dollars. But his business steadily declined over the next five years; in June 1870 an agent pronounced him "broke" and recommended not extending him credit.[55]

Anson Davis enlisted in Josiah Pender's company on May 13, 1861, while two of his brothers joined other Confederate units. Davis served faithfully until captured at Fort Macon in April 1862. Like many others, Davis (along with one of his brothers) chose not to return to his company after he had been formally exchanged in August 1862. Instead, he opened a small grocery and liquor store in Beaufort. During the war he achieved modest success catering to Union soldiers and officers, and by December 1865 was deemed to be worth nearly three thousand dollars by the local credit agent. Yet less than a year later, Davis was no longer in business. Thomas Canaday, a grocer and confectioner, was another young man who chose not to leave Beaufort when the Union army arrived. In 1865, the credit agent noted that Canaday had "made money during the war"—about ten thousand dollars. By 1868, however, Canaday's windfall was gone. The agent declared that he was "broke and [had] gone to Kansas."[56]

Joel Henry Davis, who had played a prominent role in his community as a Unionist, ran a successful dry goods store. After the war he formed a partnership with his son-in-law Henry Rieger, the man who had helped him whip his freed slave (in the story that opened Chapter 4), and their business was "moderately successful." But Davis's defense of white honor was not enough to remove the stain of Unionism from his family. By June 1871, the partnership's store had "been burnt out & [had] not resumed business."

David W. Morton, a grocer, was the first to greet Union troops entering Morehead City in March 1862; he had even convinced a nephew to desert the Confederate army. Local whites never forgave him. While the credit agent claimed that Morton was "doing very well" just before the war, in the ledger's first postwar entry, Morton was out of business. When a postwar commissioner asked his nephew if he knew "if Mr. D. W. Morton was ever persecuted for his Union sentiments," the nephew replied: "I think he sold out and went away from here on that account."[57]

Conversely, those who had steadfastly maintained their Confederate allegiance during the Civil War found postwar Beaufort to be a friendly place. Stephen Decatur Pool had led the effort to organize a Confederate militia company as much to salvage his personal reputation as for patriotic reasons. Yet once he embraced the Confederate cause as his own, Pool never looked back. He distinguished himself under fire during the siege of Fort Macon in 1862, he brazenly taunted Union officers outside New Bern in 1863, and he edited a "rebel" newspaper in New Bern after the war.[58] James Rumley, the secessionist diarist, returned to his old post as clerk of the county court without complication, as residents knew his true sentiments even though he had grudgingly dealt with Union authorities. James L. Manney had served as lieutenant and then captain of the company raised by Josiah Pender in 1861. Manney was captured at Fort Macon but reported for Confederate duty when exchanged. After the war, he returned to Beaufort and practiced medicine. Though he never attained dazzling wealth, Manney owned a comfortable home and enjoyed a spotless professional reputation; he was universally acknowledged by the locals and credit agents to have a good character and to be "in very good standing." Similarly, hundreds of former Confederate soldiers regained their property in Craven and Carteret counties and often became community and political leaders.[59]

Isaac Ramsey is another example of a Beaufort native who remained in Union lines during the war, but whose secessionist actions maintained his reputation. Ramsey enjoyed wealth and good community standing before the war and retained it after. Though he had to satisfy his prewar creditors and lost the value of his eighteen slaves, which helped reduce his personal value from over thirty thousand dollars in 1860 to fifteen thousand dollars in 1870, Ramsey still enjoyed community support. In addition, he had to apply for a special pardon from President Andrew Johnson because he had held over twenty thousand dollars in property before the war. Johnson approved his pardon, and Ramsey continued a successful business in Beaufort. His oldest son had joined Josiah Pender's regiment in May 1861, though he was discharged for a physical disability two months later. Ramsey had gained permission from Governor Edward Stanly to avoid taking the oath of allegiance as long as possible. The Union provost marshal had accused him of having rebel sympathies, cheering heavy Union casualties at the battles of Fredericksburg and Murfreesboro, and illegally trading salt and moving other goods into Confederate lines. Ramsey's refusal to kowtow to Union authorities enabled him to enjoy postwar success.[60]

But perhaps the most remarkable example of an eastern native whose wartime exploits metamorphosed into a thriving business career is Rufus W. Bell. Bell had led groups of men on clandestine guerrilla raids against Union forces throughout the occupation, and he had once told a New Jersey soldier "that he would rather have his right hand cut off than take the oath of allegiance." In February 1865 he was arrested for aiding southern spy Emeline Pigott. Local whites rewarded his defiance. Once the war ended, Bell, who had never been a merchant, opened a store in December 1865 and gained a level of success that no prominent Unionist ever enjoyed. Within a few years, he amassed over five thousand dollars from the business.[61]

Local whites had welcomed Union soldiers in the spring of 1862. Many of these natives of coastal North Carolina were lukewarm supporters of secession and did not have a strongly developed sense of Confederate nationalism. But three years of military occupation, as well as undesirable economic and social policies imposed by the Federal government, served to drive the majority of residents firmly into the Confederate camp at the very moment that nation ceased to exist.

CONCLUSION

The power of any in-depth study of a community during the Civil War is that it allows for specific lessons to be drawn, grounded in extensive primary research, which can shed light on larger issues of the conflict, such as the fluid nature of loyalty and nationalism and the transformative nature of military occupation. This study of the Carteret-Craven region gives us a greater understanding of how participants in military occupation constructed personal and national identities, and offers a more nuanced way of looking at the war. It demonstrates that loyalties and allegiances are complicated issues that can be influenced by many historical, social, and circumstantial factors. This study also reveals that military occupations are not always resented by the people who are occupied, at least not initially. Whites in Carteret and Craven counties often welcomed the Union troops and the economic advantages they brought with them. Many in the two counties had been lukewarm about secession, and though many had ultimately supported the war, they had a weak attachment to the southern cause and were more concerned with protecting their own property, families, and livelihoods. When Union soldiers first arrived in the spring of 1862, opening the markets back up to commerce and making promises not to disrupt the social status quo, local whites gladly received them.

President Abraham Lincoln and many other Federal authorities had believed the majority of local white citizens would be loyal to the national government. They thought that a show of force and benevolence by the Union army would bring thousands back to the Union fold. Thus, the initial Union policy throughout the South was one of conciliation. Early results seemed positive; indeed, the people of Carteret and Craven counties appeared to be the grateful Unionists Lincoln had envisioned. Residents, seeking to take advantage of new economic opportunities while simultaneously maintaining the social status quo, wedded themselves to the Union. Yet, just a few months after the honeymoon, many apparent Unionists were rejecting their occupiers, primarily due to perceived arbitrary uses of Federal power and serious disagreements over racial policies. But contrary to Lincoln's optimism, the experience of Union occupation ultimately drove local citizens more firmly into the Confederate camp.

While scholars may agree that Union soldiers figuratively took off their kid gloves and displayed "the hard hand of war" in reaction to southern hostility, in eastern North Carolina the hostility of white southerners (including Unionists) was a reaction to what they saw as an oppressive, callous, and racially radical Federal occupation. In the wake of Lincoln's Emancipation Proclamation, white residents realized that what had been a limited war to restore the Union had become a sweeping, society-changing war, much like secessionist fire-eaters had predicted. In Craven and Carteret counties, local whites demonstrated that race was more important than economic interests. The wartime experience of this region informs us why Reconstruction would be so difficult; no matter what economic enticements were offered, southern whites would not be satisfied until they had reestablished racial control.

As the war ended, local whites redefined their community as one based on their view of the Union *before* the war, not the radical new Union the Federal government had thrust upon them during occupation. This meant a Union in which whites were in control of society. As observed by Whitelaw Reid, a northern journalist who traveled through the South in the immediate wake of the war, southern whites were Union men only "if they can have the Union their way — if the Negroes can be kept under, and themselves put foremost." In late 1865 Reid visited with a delegation from Beaufort and listened as the city leaders declared unequivocally that, notwithstanding their successful efforts during wartime occupation, African Americans would "never be able to support themselves in freedom." Reid asserted, "Nothing could overcome this rooted idea, that the negro was worthless, except under the lash."[1]

Former slaves in eastern North Carolina strove during the war to acquire the tools necessary for autonomy. To a large extent they succeeded: enlisting in the army, gaining meaningful employment, and acquiring education. However, it was these very efforts to realize political and economic empowerment, and the support the Union armies gave to these efforts, that increased the hostility of local whites and led to their fierce reaction against the military occupation. Local whites, whether Unionist or secessionist, disapproved of black suffrage and believed that blacks should work as wage laborers rather than as independent proprietors. Freedpeople encountered strong barriers to acquiring land, the foundational requirement for the social autonomy and economic independence they desired. During the war, African Americans had been able to cultivate — often very profitably — the land abandoned by secessionist owners. In many cases, their efforts had tripled or quadrupled the value of the property. Yet when the war ended, Federal authorities generally returned the land to its former owners, even if those owners had been devoted secessionists. After the war, freedpeople needed the dedicated support of the Federal government to solidify the gains they had made, but they received very little. Instead, the government deferred to local whites, who restricted black employment, denied them many voting and basic civil rights, and limited black attempts to win autonomy.

During the Civil War, the Union army, whom freedpeople had welcomed and in whom they had placed so much faith, proved to hinder blacks as much as help them. Blacks had quickly learned that though the Union army sought to free them, few did so for egalitarian motives. Though freedpeople used the Union army as an external agent that could help liberate them from slavery, they also suffered the demeaning racism of their benefactors. While local whites negotiated with their occupiers, African Americans found that they, too, had to negotiate with their supposed liberators. Black men and women found it difficult to achieve a level of independence and equality when neither friend nor foe was inclined to grant them.

The effect of military occupation on northern soldiers and benevolent society members was also revealing. Yankee missionaries and teachers brought to the region their own preconceptions of helpless blacks and a blind confidence in the superiority of a New England system of education. They also introduced very different ideas of how their educational mission should be accomplished. Disagreements led to conflicts among the do-gooders themselves, replete with nasty bickering, reprisals for insults, and much uncivil behavior. Given the often combative nature of the rival northerners' relationships with each other, it is remarkable that the freedpeople were able to acquire the educational skills and degree of autonomy that they did.

For northern soldiers, the original motivations for going to war were tested during their prolonged occupation of an unfamiliar region. The monotony of the occupation itself, the lack of satisfaction in a noncombat role, the enforcement of often distasteful Federal policies, the emerging hostility of local white civilians, prolonged exposure to the petty tyrannies of army life, and the natural and cultural environments of coastal North Carolina all tempered the patriotic convictions of many and transformed the idealistic enlistee into a more cynical veteran. Many experienced sagging morale and even despair during their tedious months of service, but through it all, the majority of Union troops retained a steadfast resolve to see the war through to its conclusion. They knew the stakes for which North and South were fighting, even if they disapproved of the way in which they were being used. However, their extended and intensive interaction with both the agents of the Federal government and a subjected people who challenged that government's legitimacy often altered their perceptions of American society and national policies.

The experience of occupation turned many white residents against the Federal government, and the rapid influx of former Confederates into Carteret and Craven counties after the end of the war ensured that whites maintained a decidedly anti-Unionist perspective. Local whites who had held too steadfastly to their Unionist beliefs, or who had merely pragmatically allied themselves too closely with the Union forces for economic reasons, often found themselves ostracized from the community; many were compelled to abandon their businesses and leave the region. The first few years after the war were tense ones, in which a white leadership base with proto-Confederate sensibilities tried to reinstitute a southern society that looked much like it had in 1860, with the same political, social, and cultural attitudes dominating the community. The whites and blacks who had betrayed these antebellum values found themselves detested and the victims of subtle or overt harassment and violence.

The irony for Carteret and Craven counties is that white residents were more firmly sympathetic with the Confederacy at the war's end than they had ever been during the heady days of secession. Only *conditional Confederates* in 1861, they became *confirmed Confederates* during the very occupation that was supposed to cultivate and encourage loyalty to the Union among the inhabitants. Many whites had flexible loyalties, leaning toward the Union or toward the Confederacy depending on circumstances. At war's end, most of those with flexible loyalties shifted to the Confederate side in response to the radical military occupation and its attempt to reform southern society. This was not the only region in which the presence of the Union army failed to stifle Confederate sentiment. Historian Jacqueline Glass Campbell points out that General William Sherman's 1865 campaign through the Carolinas did not destroy civilian support for the Confederacy as he intended; it actually served as "the first stage in a process of re-dedication to Southern independence" that extended well beyond the war. Similarly, James C. Cobb argues that throughout the South, the ideals of Confederate nationalism became much more powerful once the war was over than they had been during the conflict: "It seems clear that the Confederacy's defeat contributed to the postwar strength of southern patriotism (defined as loyalty to the collective southern white cause)." Noting the irony of southern nationalism, Cobb declares that it took a bitter defeat "to forge anything approaching the sense of unity and common grievance and cause that the white South's leaders had tried to instill" before the war. After all, it was far easier for a man who was angry about Union occupation policies to develop a passionate attachment to an idealized Confederate state that could never really exist and therefore never let him down.[2]

These nationalistic memories remain strong to this day. Paul Branch, an author and park service ranger at Fort Macon State Historic Park in Beaufort, assisted many visitors in their attempts to trace their ancestors' service in the fort's garrison during the war. For several Confederate enthusiasts, Branch wrote, "tracking their ancestor's military service at Fort Macon ended in a manner for which they were completely unprepared." The knowledge that one's great-great-grandfather served in a Yankee North Carolina regiment can be startling and at times emotionally crippling to his descendants. In one case, Branch had to inform an eager southern genealogist that her ancestor who had served in the 1st North Carolina Regiment and was stationed at Fort Macon in 1864 actually wore a Union uniform. The revelation left the woman "completely and utterly devastated." Either ignorant of the Unionism in the region or just assuming that all true southerners would repudiate the Yankees, the woman to whom Branch had to break the bad news was bitterly disconsolate that her ancestor had failed to live up to the mythic ideal of southern resistance. "You mean he was a traitor to the South?" she asked, incredulous. Many contemporary white residents similarly condemned their neighbors who had aided the Union army.[3]

This community case study exposes the degree to which the sentiments of southern Unionists were altered by freedpeople asserting their rights and being supported by Federal authorities. The actions of local whites revealed that white superiority was much more important than economic stability and presaged the contentious Reconstruction years to follow. That those who could most demonstrably prove their Confederate proclivities were the most successful in the immediate postwar years indicates the limited role the Federal government was able to play in constructing a successful Republican interracial coalition. The recalcitrance of white southerners suggested to Federal officials that perhaps the only way the Union could prevent dissent and open revolt was to allow southern whites to dictate racial policy. This was a hard lesson, but one the North eventually learned by 1877, when it cast aside Reconstruction and abandoned African Americans across the South to disfranchisement, lynching, segregation, and Jim Crow.[4]

The experience of Carteret and Craven counties not only sheds more light on the contentious nature of Reconstruction, but also extends beyond the Civil War. As this dual community study suggests, even the noblest intentions of an occupying force (or liberating force, depending on one's point of view) can create hostility and resentment on the ground, especially if the external force does not understand or approve of the dominant local cultural mores. The U.S. government discovered during the Civil War that people under military rule have a peculiar habit of deciding for themselves what they believe is in their own best interests, and they often resent an outside entity that tries to impose significant social and cultural transformations on their society.

NOTES

ABBREVIATIONS

AAS
American Antiquarian Society, Worcester, Mass.

AMA
American Missionary Association Collection, Amistad
Research Center, Tulane University, New Orleans

BHS
Beverly History Society and Museum, Beverly, Mass.

BRVUS
Book Records, Volunteer Union Soldiers Organizations,
RG 94, National Archives, Washington, D.C.

CSR
Compiled Service Records of Volunteer Union Soldiers,
RG 94, National Archives, Washington, D.C.

DU
Rare Book, Manuscript, and Special Collections
Library, Duke University, Durham

ECU
Special Collections, J. Y. Joyner Library,
East Carolina University, Greenville

EU
Special Collections and Archives, Robert W. Woodruff
Library, Emory University, Atlanta

HBS
Baker Library Special Collections, Harvard Business School, Cambridge

LC
Manuscript Division, Library of Congress, Washington, D.C.

MHS
Massachusetts Historical Society, Boston

NA
National Archives, Washington, D.C.

NBDP
New Bern Daily Progress

NBWP
New Bern Weekly Progress

NCC
North Carolina Collection, University of North Carolina, Chapel Hill

NCSA
North Carolina State Archives, Raleigh

OR
U.S. War Department, *The War of the Rebellion: A Compilation of the Official Records of the Union and Confederate Armies. OR* citations take the following form: volume number: page number. All citations are from series 1.

RG 15
Federal Pension Application Files, Records of the Veterans Administration, National Archives, Washington, D.C.

RG 123
Records of the U.S. Court of Claims, National Archives, Washington, D.C.

RG 393
Records of the U.S. Army Continental Commands, National Archives, Washington, D.C.

SCC
Southern Claims Commission, RG 217 (Approved) and RG 233 (Disallowed), National Archives, Washington, D.C.

SHC
Southern Historical Collection, University of North Carolina, Chapel Hill

SHS
Simsbury Historical Society, Simsbury, Conn.

SOR
Janet B. Hewett et al., eds., *Supplement to the Official Records of the Union and Confederate Armies. SOR* citations take the same form as *OR* citations.

INTRODUCTION

1. Sidney Andrews, *The South since the War*, 392.

2. For Union occupation policy, see Grimsley, *Hard Hand of War*. For a more comprehensive look at the effects of military occupation across the South, see Ash, *When the Yankees Came*.

3. For a study of class warfare in eastern North Carolina's Washington County, see Durrill, *War of Another Kind*. For other studies that examine various facets of class warfare, see Ash, *When the Yankees Came*, esp. chap. 6; Sutherland, *Seasons of War*; Maslowski, *Treason Must Be Made Odious*; and Capers, *Occupied City*.

4. Rubin, *Shattered Nation*, 2–3, 50 (quotation), 95; Storey, *Loyalty and Loss*, 6. For varying perspectives on the nature of nationalism, see Gallagher, *Confederate War*, 61–111; Faust, *Creation of Confederate Nationalism*; Carp, "Nations of American Rebels"; and Escott, *After Secession*. For more on the various qualities of Unionism, see Degler, *The Other South*; Current, *Lincoln's Loyalists*; and Inscoe and Kenzer, *Enemies of the Country*.

5. Thomas G. Dyer (*Secret Yankees*) has perceptively written that people have always had multiple loyalties: "Allegiances to family, home, friends, lodges, church, class, state, and region (among others) competed with or complemented national loyalty." In peacetime, loyalties can complement each other, but in wartime "demands arise that national loyalty be paramount and controlling" (p. 4). Dyer also demonstrates that loyalty can be "contingent, circumstantial and subject to a plenitude of definitions shifting over time" (p. 270). I find that in addition to the idea of personal loyalty conflicting with national loyalty, residents of eastern North Carolina had competing national loyalties. For more on the concept of multiple loyalties, see Guetzkow, "Multiple Loyalties," and Fletcher, *Loyalty*.

6. Gordon McKinney ("Layers of Loyalty") found a similar breakdown of allegiances when he examined petitions for amnesty from western North Carolina. Some applicants consistently supported the Union, some consistently supported secession, some shifted away from the Union after secession, and some were neutral. Of the 261 petitioners he surveyed, fewer than 40 percent were consistently Unionist or Confederate. The rest shifted their allegiances, were neutral, or offered no explanation of their loyalty.

7. For more on how the Confederate defeat created a unified southern identity, or a sense of "southern patriotism," see Cobb, *Away Down South*, 34–66. A classic example of fluid loyalties comes from the American Revolution, especially in the southern backcountry, where one's loyalty was often a reflection of how close the British

army was at any given time. See David Hackett Fischer, *Washington's Crossing*, 160–81; Crow and Tise, *Southern Experience*; and Hoffman, Tate, and Albert, *Uncivil War*.

8. In his theoretical analysis of why military occupations succeed or fail, political scientist David Edelstein (*Occupational Hazards*) has argued that "the existence of multiple nationalisms within an occupied territory is likely to make the task of occupation more difficult" (p. 11). Though Edelstein does not consider the Union occupation of the South, or any other intracountry occupation, the theories he derives from military occupations around the world apply equally well to the American Civil War occupation. His book would have been only enhanced by including the Civil War in his analysis.

9. Grimsley, *Hard Hand of War*; Birtle, *U.S. Army Counterinsurgency*, esp. chap. 1.

CHAPTER 1

1. Sharpe, "Completely Coastal Carteret," 4; Bowen, *Adventuring along the Southeast Coast*, 95–96; Watson, *History of New Bern*, 1. See also Sharpe, *New Geography of North Carolina*.

2. "Wild Waterways"; Burke, "History of Portsmouth," 8–9.

3. Crittenden, "Seacoast in North Carolina History," 436, and "Overland Travel," 240–41; William Stuart Morgan, "Commerce of a Southern Port," 83.

4. Watson, *History of New Bern*, 13–54; Paul, "Colonial Beaufort," 144; Cecelski, *Waterman's Song*, 53–60; Sharpe, "Completely Coastal Carteret," 5, 33; Luster, "Help Me to Raise Them," 11–13; U.S. Census, 1860, Carteret County, Population Schedule, Manuscript Census Returns, NA.

5. Dill, "Eighteenth Century New Bern," 47–61; Watson, *History of New Bern*, 37–38, 56–57.

6. William Blackledge to Thomas Jefferson, February 2, 1808, in Keith, *Blount Papers*, 2:101–2.

7. Asbury, *Journal*, 2:272–73; *Population of the United States in 1860*, 358–59.

8. Sharpe, "Completely Coastal Carteret," 4; Bowen, *Adventuring along the Southeast Coast*, 95–96; U.S. Census, 1860, Carteret County, Population Schedule, Manuscript Census Returns, NA; Watson, *History of New Bern*, 250–55; *Agriculture of the United States in 1860*. New Bern and Craven County trailed only Wilmington and New Hanover County in naval stores production in 1860. *Manufactures of the United States in 1860*.

9. *Fifth Census . . . of the United States, 1830*, 90–91; *Sixth Census . . . of the United States, 1840*, 218–19; *Seventh Census of the United States, 1850*, 307–8; *Population of the United States in 1860*, 358–59; Wright, *Political Economy*, 34.

10. Watson, *History of New Bern*, 250.

11. Cecelski, *Waterman's Song*, 141.

12. Ibid., 131, 135–36; Guion Griffis Johnson, *Ante-Bellum North Carolina*, 494. For slave advertisements, see Parker, *Stealing a Little Freedom*. For more on slave escapes, see Schweninger and Franklin, *Runaway Slaves*. For other works that dem-

onstrate the common racial interaction between slaves and whites in low-country regions, see McCurry, *Masters of Small Worlds*; Lockley, *Lines in the Sand*; Olwell, *Masters, Slaves, and Subjects*; Kirsten Fischer, *Suspect Relations*; and Philip D. Morgan, *Slave Counterpoint*.

13. Schweninger and Franklin, *Runaway Slaves*, 154; Watson, *History of New Bern*, 157. For more on the function of southern slave patrols, see Hadden, *Slave Patrols*. The literature on the nature of white unity in the antebellum South is vast. For a recent analysis of the historiographical debates over antebellum white unity, see Browning, "Foundations of Sand."

14. Watson, *History of New Bern*, 207; John Gray Blount to Joseph B. Hinton, December 14, 1830, in Keith, *Blount Papers*, 4:544.

15. Watson, *History of New Bern*, 157, 207–8; W. H. Bryan to E. Pettigrew, September 20, 1840, Pettigrew Papers, NCSA.

16. Crabtree and Patton, *Journal of a Secesh Lady*, November 25, December 12, 1860, 16, 22–23. For differing interpretations of the relationships between slaves and their plantation mistresses, see Fox-Genovese, *Within the Plantation Household*, and Weiner, *Mistresses and Slaves*.

17. Lockley, *Lines in the Sand*; Cecil-Fronsman, *Common Whites*.

18. Watson, *History of New Bern*, 262, 283–89; "Beaufort Long Ago Was Quiet and Good," *Beaufort News*, November 29, 1923, Newspaper Clippings File, NCC (John Edwards); John Rogers Vinson to his mother, February 19, September 21, 1844, Vinson Papers, DU.

19. "Internal Improvements in North Carolina"; Clingman, "North Carolina — Her Wealth, Resources and History," 678; James Manney to David B. Outlaw, March 1, 1850, Manney Papers, SHC; "A Bill to Incorporate the Beaufort and North Carolina Railroad," Sess. 1850–51, S. Doc. 74, and "A Bill to Incorporate the Atlantic and North Carolina Railroad," Sess. 1852–53, H. Doc. 30, in *Proceedings of the Annual Meeting of the Stockholders*, NCC.

20. Walter Gwynn to David S. Reid, October 17, 1854, Sess. 1854–55, H. Doc. 12; John D. Whitford, Esq., to editor of *Beaufort Journal*, December 26, 1857; 2nd reply of *Beaufort Journal* to Whitford, President of A. & N.C.R.R. Co., February 22, 1858 — all in *Proceedings of the Annual Meeting of the Stockholders*, NCC.

21. James Manney to George E. Badger, February 7, 1849, and Manney to Edward Stanly, December 17, 1849, Manney Papers, SHC; Letter to the editor, n.d. (typescript), box 2, Salisbury Collection, NCSA.

22. William Geffrey to David S. Reid, August 30, 1858, Reid Papers, NCSA; William Woods Holden to Miss L. H. Holden, August 6, 1858, in Raper and Mitchell, *Papers of William Woods Holden*, 1:95; "A City by the Sea," by G. F. Stanton, Beaufort Reminiscence, [ca. 1901], box 2, Fales Papers, NCSA; J. Henry to Thomas Henderson, December 16, 1810, in "One Hundred Years Ago Beaufort Had Big Shipbuilding Industry," *Beaufort News*, February 14, 1929, Newspaper Clippings File, NCC.

23. *Greensborough Patriot*, September 17, 1858, in box 3, Salisbury Collection, NCSA; *NBDP*, August 20, 22, 1860.

24. Watson, *History of New Bern*, 183–201, 232; Cheney, *North Carolina Government*, 1328–31; Kruman, *Parties and Politics*, 68–73 (quotation, p. 73). For more on the development of the Whig Party in North Carolina, see Kruman, *Parties and Politics*, 3–28, and Pegg, *Whig Party*. For an analysis of the two parties' stances on internal improvements, see Jeffrey, "Internal Improvements and Political Parties."

25. Cheney, *North Carolina Government*, 1328–31. For more on the development of political parties in the state, see Jeffrey, *State Parties and National Politics*.

26. James Manney to George E. Badger, February 7, 1849, Manney to editors of the *Republic*, [November 1849], and Manney to Zachary Taylor, February 18, 1850, Manney Papers, SHC.

27. Watson, *History of New Bern* (Stanly to New Bern citizens), 233; Sitterson, *Secession Movement* (2nd Stanly quotation, 92).

28. Francis Hawks to John D. Whitford, August 14, 1856, Whitford Collection, NCSA (emphasis in original); Cheney, *North Carolina Government*, 1330–31; Kruman, *Parties and Politics*, 174–78.

29. Howard, "John Brown's Raid," 398–415 (quotations, pp. 402, 410, 415 — emphasis in original).

30. Watson, *History of New Bern*, 240; Nathan H. Street, Peter G. Evans, and John N. Washington to John W. Ellis, in Tolbert, *Papers of . . . Ellis*, 2:345 (quotation); Henry B. Clarke to Ellis, March 20, 1860, Ellis, Governors Papers, NCSA.

31. Nathan H. Street, Peter G. Evans, and John N. Washington to John W. Ellis, in Tolbert, *Papers of . . . Ellis*, 2:346–47.

32. *NBDP*, July 3, 1860.

33. Ibid., August 29, 1860; Cheney, *North Carolina Government*, 1330, 1400; *National Era*, August 26, 1858.

34. *NBDP*, November 9, 1860; Matthias E. Manly to Thomas Ruffin, December 2, 1860, in Hamilton, *Papers of Thomas Ruffin*, 3:104–5 (emphases in original).

35. W. B. Wadsworth to John Ellis, December 12, 1860, Ellis, Governors Papers, NCSA; *NBDP*, December 17, 1860.

36. Crabtree and Patton, *Journal of a Secesh Lady*, October 26, 1860, 11; James Morris to John W. Ellis, February 6, 1861, in Tolbert, *Papers of . . . Ellis*, 2:587; P. W. Biddle to "Rosa," February 19, 1861, Simpson-Biddle Papers, NCSA.

37. *Union Banner* (Beaufort), December 15, 1860, quoted in *NBDP*, December 20, 1860. Carteret County was one of ten counties that held Union meetings after Lincoln's election. For a discussion of the competing secessionist and Unionist meetings, see Sitterson, *Secession Movement*, 191–200. For an excellent study of Upper South conditional Unionists, see Crofts, *Reluctant Confederates*, esp. 144–52 and 330–41.

38. "Voting for Convention," Letter Book, 392–93, Ellis, Governors Papers, NCSA. The final vote for Carteret was 415 yeas and 394 nays, while Craven voted 891 yeas and 362 nays. Overall, the state voted down the convention by a tally of 47,323 to 46,677. Craven sent two delegates, John D. Whitford and George Green, both Southern Rights Democrats, while Carteret sent only one, Charles R. Thomas, chairman of the Union meeting in Beaufort on December 15, 1860. See Cheney, *North Carolina*

Government, 386–87, 399–401; *NBDP*, December 20, 1860, February 28, 1861; and Watson, *History of New Bern*, 246–47. For more on the Unionist debates over secession, see Crofts, *Reluctant Confederates*.

39. John W. Ellis to William H. Gist, October 19, 1860, in Tolbert, *Papers of . . . Ellis*, 2:469–70 (emphasis in original).

CHAPTER 2

1. John W. Ellis Diary, February 13, 1861, in Tolbert, *Papers of . . . Ellis*, 2:478–79. For more on conditional Unionists, see Crofts, *Reluctant Confederates*. The seven states that seceded between December 20, 1860, and February 1, 1861, were (in order) South Carolina, Mississippi, Florida, Alabama, Georgia, Louisiana, and Texas.

2. John W. Ellis to Simon Cameron, April 15, 1861, telegram, in Tolbert, *Papers of . . . Ellis*, 2:612.

3. Harris, *With Charity for All*, 58–59, and *North Carolina and the Coming of the Civil War*, 56; McPherson, *Battle Cry of Freedom*, 276–82; Crofts, *Reluctant Confederates*, 334–52.

4. *NBDP*, April 15, 1861.

5. Ibid., April 16, 17, 1861.

6. S. W. Biddle to Rosa, April 15, 1861, Simpson-Biddle Papers, NCSA; *NBDP*, April 16, 17, 1861.

7. *NBDP*, April 16, 19, 1861; Barrett, *Civil War*, 10–11; Manarin and Jordan, *North Carolina Troops*, 1:14–23.

8. Charles Manly to David L. Swain, April 22, 1861, quoted in Inscoe and McKinney, *Heart of Confederate Appalachia*, 56; *NBDP*, April 16, 1861.

9. J. W. Primrose and E. K. Bryan to John W. Ellis, April 18, 1861, Ellis, Governors Papers, NCSA; Manarin and Jordan, *North Carolina Troops*, 3:462.

10. *NBDP*, April 20, 1861; Manarin and Jordan, *North Carolina Troops*, 3:431–41, 462–79; U.S. Census, 1860, Craven County, Population Schedule, Manuscript Census Returns, NA.

11. Manarin and Jordan, *North Carolina Troops*, 4:171–83, 1:52–61, 138–46; U.S. Census, 1860, Craven County, Population Schedule, Manuscript Census Returns, NA; Henry R. Bryan to "Dear Father," June 25, 1861, John Herritage Bryan Papers, ECU.

12. Manarin and Jordan, *North Carolina Troops*, 2:213–20, 1:406–17, 8:505–12; U.S. Census, 1860, Craven County, Population Schedule, Manuscript Census Returns, NA.

13. *NBDP*, January 2, 25, 1862; Manarin and Jordan, *North Carolina Troops*, 1:465–78, 14:669–77. "Military age" means anyone between the ages of 16 and 39 in the 1860 census, presuming they would be between 17 and 40 in 1861. With few exceptions, no one under 17 or over 40 served in companies from these counties.

14. Powell, *Dictionary of North Carolina Biography*, 5:62–63; Unprocessed material, box 3, Salisbury Collection, NCSA; Bill Stancil, "Laura Pender of Tarboro: Belle of the Blockade Runners," *Rocky Mount Telegram*, March 29, 1970, Newspaper

Clippings File, NCC; North Carolina, vol. 5, p. 176-A, R. G. Dun and Co. Collection, HBS; U.S. Census, 1860, Carteret County, Population and Slave Schedules, Manuscript Census Returns, NA.

15. North Carolina, vol. 5, p. 176-A, R. G. Dun and Co. Collection, HBS; *J. H. Davis v. J. S. Pender*, Fall Term, 1861, Carteret County, Appearance Docket, Superior Court, 1833–69, vol. 2, NCSA; *E. H. Norcum v. J. S. Pender*, November term, 1860, Carteret County Civil Action Papers, NCSA.

16. *NBDP*, April 16, 1861; Manarin and Jordan, *North Carolina Troops*, 1:113–24. Later Pender's company was officially designated as Company G, 10th Regiment of North Carolina State Troops (also referred to as the 1st Regiment, North Carolina Artillery).

17. Manarin and Jordan, *North Carolina Troops*, 1:127; *NBDP*, August 19, December 15, 1860, April 16, 1861; North Carolina, vol. 5, p. 176-A, R. G. Dun and Co. Collection, HBS.

18. Manarin and Jordan, *North Carolina Troops*, 1:124–37; U.S. Census, 1860, Carteret County, Population Schedule, Manuscript Census Returns, NA. For more on the role of violence and combat in the creation and reaffirmation of masculine codes of honor, see Wyatt-Brown, *Southern Honor*; Nisbet and Cohen, *Culture of Honor*; and Spierenburg, *Men and Violence*.

19. *NBDP*, May 23, June 4, 1861; Manarin and Jordan, *North Carolina Troops*, 1:124–37. On September 1, 1861, Pool's unit became Company H, 10th Regiment, North Carolina State Troops (1st Regiment, North Carolina Artillery).

20. Manarin and Jordan, *North Carolina Troops*, 1:124–37.

21. North Carolina, vol. 5, p. 163, R. G. Dun and Co. Collection, HBS; Deposition of Job L. Kinsey, *Calvin Perry v. United States* (case file no. 8958), Deposition of William Rowe, *Arrington Purify, Administrator of Thomas Purify v. United States* (case file no. 7852), and Deposition of Clifford Simpson, *Gabriel Hardison v. United States* (case file no. 8070) — all in RG 123.

22. William A. Blair, *Virginia's Private War*, 141. For an explanation of how national identity interconnects with local identity, see Potter, "The Historian's Use of Nationalism."

23. Benjamin Leecraft to John W. Ellis, June 25, 1861, in Tolbert, *Papers of . . . Ellis*, 2:875–76 (this volume incorrectly cites Leecraft's name as "Seecraft"); Manarin and Jordan, *North Carolina Troops*, 1:269–72, 104–11, 301–11; U.S. Census, 1860, Carteret County, Population Schedule, Manuscript Census Returns, NA. Leecraft's unit would be officially designated as Company G, 36th Regiment of North Carolina Troops (2nd Regiment, North Carolina Artillery). Because the remnants of the unit were reassigned to other companies after the battle of New Bern, Leecraft's company is referred to as 1st Company G (two others would follow as Company G). "Herring's Battery" became Company I of the 36th Regiment, and "Andrew's Battery" became Company F of the 10th Regiment.

24. *NBDP*, June 4, 1861; U.S. Census, 1860, Carteret and Craven Counties, Population Schedules, Manuscript Census Returns, NA. In the 1860 census, there were

1,123 Carteret County white men between the ages of 16 and 39 and 1,522 Craven County white men of military age. To arrive at those figures, I counted the number of enlisted men from each county, using Manarin and Jordan's *North Carolina Troops*, then divided the total into the number of military-age men in each county.

25. Manarin and Jordan, *North Carolina Troops*, 1:52, 60, 104–37, 145, 163, 170, 269–72, 301–11, 468–78, 493, 2:215 (for Carteret County enlistees); 1:52–61, 138–46, 407–17, 465–78, 2:214–20, 3:431–41, 462–79, 4:171–83, 8:505–12, 14:669–77 (for Craven County enlistees); U.S. Census, 1860, Carteret and Craven Counties, Population and Slave Schedules, Manuscript Census Returns, NA. Census records must be used with caution. Though the census can be of great research value, much of what was recorded depended on the methodology of the census takers. It was not unusual for them to misunderstand or fabricate answers, place answers in the wrong place, or misspell key words. They also failed to enumerate every person in every district. As Helen M. Leary and Maurice R. Stirewalt (*North Carolina Research*, 434–37) explain, persons in remote areas often were not counted because they were too few, and persons in urban areas were not counted because they were too many. Some escaped enumeration, while others were listed twice.

26. Crawford, "Confederate Volunteering," 38; Cheney, *North Carolina Government*, 386–87, 399–401; Carteret County Court Minutes, Court of Pleas and Quarters, NCSA. For further examples of community enlistment, see Inscoe and McKinney, *Heart of Confederate Appalachia*, chap. 3; Groce, *Mountain Rebels*, chaps. 3, 4; Sutherland, *Seasons of War*, chap. 2; Brooks, "Social and Cultural Dynamics of Soldiering"; and Logue, "Who Joined the Confederate Army?"

27. Deposition of Sarah F. Trenwith, *Sarah F. Trenwith, Executrix of Clifford F. Simpson, Deceased, v. United States* (case file no. 10014), RG 123. As Reid Mitchell (*Vacant Chair*, 4) has argued, for many Civil War youth, "the very ideas of man, soldier, and citizen were inextricably linked. Remaining a citizen was thought unmanly; going to war a proof of manhood."

28. John W. Ellis to Marshall D. Craton, April 17, 1861, in Tolbert, *Papers of . . . Ellis*, 2:619.

29. Ibid.; Mallison, *Civil War on the Outer Banks*, 24; Barry, "Fort Macon," 168.

30. Barrett, *Civil War*, 11; *NBDP*, May 24, 1861.

31. Walter Gwynn to John W. Ellis, May 27, 1861, in Tolbert, *Papers of . . . Ellis*, 2:794–95.

32. Barrett, *Civil War*, 40–45; Elizabeth Collier Diary, August 30, 1861, in Yearns and Barrett, *Civil War Documentary*, 32.

33. Henry T. Clark to L. P. Walker, August 30, 1861, and Clark to Samuel Cooper, August 30, 1861, *OR* 4:637.

34. H. K. Burgwyn to S. R. Mallory, September 4, 1861, and Henry T. Clark to L. P. Walker, September 7, 1861, *OR* 4:639–40, 643; Turner and Bridgers, *History of Edgecombe County*, 200.

35. Hess, *Lee's Tar Heels*, 7; Archie K. Davis, *Boy Colonel*, 83–84; Rush Hawkins to John Wool, September 19, 1861, *OR* 4:618.

36. Barrett, *Civil War*, 17. For more on mobilization in North Carolina, see Iobst, "North Carolina Mobilizes."

37. Archie K. Davis, *Boy Colonel*, 85–86; Zebulon B. Vance to Henry T. Clark, September 18, 1861, Clark, Governors Papers, NCSA.

38. R. C. Gatlin to Gen. S. Cooper, September 9, 1861, Special Orders No. 166, September 29, 1861, D. H. Hill to Cooper, October 2, 1861, and S. R. Mallory to Secretary of War, October 23, 1861—all in *OR* 4:645, 661, 664, 687.

39. Elizabeth Collier Diary, September 1, 1861, in Yearns and Barrett, *Civil War Documentary*, 32; Manarin and Jordan, *North Carolina Troops*, 2:212–20.

40. J. P. Benjamin to Gen. Gatlin, October 23, 1861, *OR* 4:686; Underwood, *History of the Twenty-sixth Regiment*, 5; Zebulon Vance to his wife, October 13, 17, 1861, in Johnston and Mobley, *Papers of . . . Vance*, 1:118; John Jackson, October 22, 1861, quoted in Hess, *Lee's Tar Heels*, 8.

41. Archie K. Davis, *Boy Colonel*, 91; Morrill, *Civil War in the Carolinas*, 270; William Dixon to Jack Johnson, November 27, 1861, Military Records, Civil War Collection, box 70, folder 75, NCSA; *NBDP*, February 22, 24, 1862.

42. D. H. Hill to Gen. B. Huger, October 1, 1861, and Hill to R. C. Gatlin, October 27, 1861, *OR* 4:664, 694.

43. Testimony of claimant Reuben Fulcher (Carteret County), Disallowed Claims, SCC; Manarin and Jordan, *North Carolina Troops*, 1:270; Testimony of William H. Congleton and Testimony of claimant Joseph B. Whitehurst (Carteret County), Approved Claims, SCC.

44. Testimony of claimant Jesse Fulcher (Carteret County), Disallowed Claims, SCC; Manarin and Jordan, *North Carolina Troops*, 1:117. The Southern Claims Commission, to which Fulcher applied, was established in 1871 so Unionists could apply for compensation for any property that had been confiscated or destroyed by the Union army. Claimants had to prove not only that their property had been damaged or taken by Union troops, but also that they had been loyal to the Union. See Klingberg, *Southern Claims Commission*. An invaluable resource for determining who filed claims with the commission is Mills, *Southern Loyalists*.

45. Deposition of James T. Lewis and of Elijah Ellis, in *Isaac W. Lewis v. United States* (case file no. 4863), and Deposition of George Hardison, in *Gabriel Hardison v. United States* (case file no. 8070)—all in RG 123; Taylor, *Divided Family*, 34. This contrasts with what Margaret Storey ("Civil War Unionists," 89–90) discovered in her study of Alabama Unionists, who, she argues, "took it as a matter of duty that they should reproduce their own political loyalty among their sons, grandsons, and nephews . . . [and] they frequently demanded that the actions of younger male relatives reflect, and sometimes directly extend, their own loyalties to the Union." In eastern North Carolina, many Unionists helplessly watched as their sons rejected, at least initially, their elders' directives.

46. The first to identify the different degrees of dissent—asserting a distinction between passive disaffection and active disloyalty—was Tatum, *Disloyalty in the Confederacy*. For mountain Unionism, see Crawford, *Ashe County's Civil War*,

and Inscoe and McKinney, *Heart of Confederate Appalachia*. For piedmont Unionism, see Auman, "Neighbor against Neighbor," and Auman and Scarboro, "Heroes of America." For coastal plain Unionism, see Thomas, *Divided Allegiances*.

47. McKenzie, "Prudent Silence and Strict Neutrality," 74.

48. Testimony of claimant Alexander Taylor (Craven County), Disallowed Claims, SCC; *NBDP*, July 19, 1861.

49. *NBDP*, May 29, 1861. For further depictions of the methods of community-enforced values, see Wyatt-Brown, *Southern Honor*, 435–38, and pt. III; Ayers, *Vengeance and Justice*.

50. Testimony of claimant Jesse Fulcher (Carteret County), Disallowed Claims, SCC; Deposition of H. B. Hill, *Brief for the Claimant on Loyalty*, December term, 1886, and Deposition of Isaac S. Hill — all in *Nancy C. Hill, Administratrix of the Estate of Isaac S. Hill, Deceased, v. United States* (case file no. 1191), RG 123.

51. Deposition of Zem Garner and of claimant David W. Morton, in *David W. Morton v. United States* (case file no. 6935), RG 123; Judgment of claimant Henry Covert and Testimony of W. H. Pearce (Craven County), Approved Claims, SCC. Morton's nephew, Joseph A. Bell, joined Stephen Decatur Pool's company in May 1861. Captured at Fort Macon, he returned to his unit after being exchanged. He was then taken prisoner at Washington, N.C., on September 6, 1862, and never returned to his unit. Manarin and Jordan, *North Carolina Troops*, 1:127. Morton experienced some relief when the Union army captured New Bern. When the first Union troops came marching down the railroad toward Beaufort, Morton was the first to greet them. He took them into his house and fed the soldiers and their officers. As one witness recalled, "The captain came up and called us all 'brothers,' Mr. Morton brothered him back again." Depositions of J. T. Dennis and Lewis McCain, in *David W. Morton v. United States* (case file no. 6935), RG 123.

52. Testimony of claimant Thomas Hall (Carteret County), Approved Claims, SCC.

53. Cecelski, *Waterman's Song*, xvi, 141–91.

54. Testimony of David Parker, in Caesar Manson's claim (Carteret County), Disallowed Claims, SCC; Manarin and Jordan, *North Carolina Troops*, 1:127.

55. Manarin and Jordan, *North Carolina Troops*, 1:114; Unprocessed material, box 3, Salisbury Collection, NCSA; Maurice Davis, "History of the Hammock House" (unpublished typescript), NCC; *NBDP*, December 20, 1860. After his dismissal, Pender turned to a career as a blockade-runner; in 1864 he returned to Union-occupied Beaufort, where he died of yellow fever. Browning and Smith, *Letters*, 237–38.

56. Hess, *Lee's Tar Heels*, 7–9; Barrett, *Civil War*, 95–98, 113.

57. Barrett, *Civil War*, 96; Zeb Vance to Allen Davidson, March 4, 1862, in Johnston and Mobley, *Papers of . . . Vance*, 1:119.

58. Dehlia Mabrey Diary, February 19, 1862, Crisp Papers, ECU; J. T. Shaffner to Christian Thomas Pfohl, January 17, February 4, 1862, Pfohl Papers, SHC; John Quincy Adams to Nathan Adams, January 29, 1862, Adams and Partin Family Papers, NCSA.

59. Clarissa Phelps Hanks Diary, January 26, 1862, Hanks Papers, ECU; Archie K. Davis, *Boy Colonel*, 91, 99–100.

60. Archie K. Davis, *Boy Colonel*, 100, 105.

CHAPTER 3

1. *NBDP*, January 23, February 22, March 7, 8, 1862.

2. *NBDP*, May 28, 1861, January 23, 1862 (emphasis in original); Mary Norcott Bryan, "Recollections of Old-Time Dixie," in Thornton, "New Bern, North Carolina, 1862–1865" (unpublished typescript), 5, NCC.

3. Mary Norcott Bryan, "Recollections of Old-Time Dixie"; White Diary, March 17, 1862, AAS.

4. Alonzo Cushman to Miss Caroline D. Cushman, March 21, 1862, Cushman Letters, AAS; L. G. Hunt to "My dear sister," April 10, 1862, box 1, folder C, Grimes-Bryan Papers, ECU. For a fuller account of the battle, see Sauers, *Burnside Expedition*, and Barrett, *Civil War*, esp. chap 2.

5. W. A. Curtis, "A Journal of Reminiscences of the War," *Our Living and Our Dead*, 2, no. 3 (May 1875), 288, quoted in Thornton, "New Bern, North Carolina, 1862–1865" (unpublished typescript), 11, NCC; Spear, "Army Life" (unpublished typescript), 54, MHS; Oliver Cromwell Case to his sister, March 16, 1862 (typescript), Case Letters, SHS; Denny, *Wearing the Blue*, 104.

6. Hayden Diary, March 15, 1862, LC; Daniel Read Larned to his sister, March 18, 1862, Larned Papers, LC; Spear, "Army Life" (unpublished typescript), 60, MHS. For more on depredations, see F. B. Spruz to "Friend," [March 1862], Humiston Family Collection, USAMHI; Hayden Diary, March 15, 1862, LC; Draper, *Recollections*, 67.

7. Allen, *Forty-six Months*, 97; James M. Drennan to his wife, March 15, 1862, Drennan Papers, WHM; William Alexander to "My own dear wife," March 25, 1862, Alexander Letters, SHC; Putnam, *Story of Company A*, 114.

8. Denny, *Wearing the Blue*, 104; Daniel Read Larned to "Uncle," March 20, 1862, Larned Papers, LC; J. Madison Drake, *Ninth New Jersey*, 66–67; George H. Baxter to Jim, April 6, 1862, Baxter Letters, MHS; Charles S. Wilder to Rev. Alonzo Hill, June 1, 1862, box 1, folder 7a, Civil War Collection, AAS.

9. Oliver Case to his sister, June 3, 1862, Case Letters, SHS; John G. Parke to Ambrose Burnside, March 23, 24, 26, 1862, *OR*, 9:276–80. See also Wyeth, *Leaves from a Diary*, 15.

10. Rumley Diary, undated entry and March 17, 1862, in Browning, *Southern Mind*, 29–30; *The Look Out*, January 7, 1910; Davis and Hamilton, *Heritage of Carteret County*, 5; John G. Parke to Ambrose Burnside, March 23, 1862, *OR* 9:277. There is a truncated version of Rumley's diary in *The Look Out*.

11. Rumley Diary, March 25, 1862, in Browning, *Southern Mind*, 31; John G. Parke to Ambrose Burnside, March 24, 26, 1862, 9:278–80; Allen, *Forty-six Months*, 101. Allen says that his company took Beaufort on March 21, but Parke's official report,

a contemporary source, states that he ordered Allen to Beaufort on the night of March 25; hence I have favored Parke's report over Allen's postwar recollection.

12. Mallison, *Civil War on the Outer Banks*, 103; Spear, "Army Life" (unpublished typescript), 66, MHS, April 28, 1862; Daniel Read Larned to Henry Howe, March 26, 1862, Larned Papers, LC.

13. Moses J. White to Theophilus H. Holmes, May 4, 1862, *OR* 9:293; Oliver Case to his sister, April 6, 1862, Case Letters, SHS.

14. Manarin and Jordan, *North Carolina Troops*, 1:105, 110, 115–37; U.S. Census, 1860, Carteret County, Population Schedule, Manuscript Census Returns, NA.

15. John G. Parke to Lewis Richmond, May 9, 1862, and Ambrose Burnside to Edwin Stanton, April 29, 1862, *OR* 9:284, 274; Rumley Diary, April 25, 1862, in Browning, *Southern Mind*, 34–35; James Monroe Hollowell Journal, April 25, 1862, in *SOR* 1(1):604. For more on the fort's bombardment and surrender, see Branch, *Siege of Fort Macon*.

16. "Terms of Capitulation," *OR* 9:276; Oliver Case to his sister, April 28, 1862, Case Letters, SHS.

17. Historian Mark Grimsley (*Hard Hand of War*, 3) has asserted: "The central assumption underlying [conciliation] was a faith that most white Southerners were lukewarm about secession, and if handled with forbearance, would withdraw their allegiance from the Confederacy once Union armies entered their midst."

18. George McClellan to Don Carlos Buell, November 7, 1861, quoted in Grimsley, *Hard Hand of War*, 35; Ambrose Burnside, "Proclamation to the People of North Carolina," February 16, 1862, *OR* 9:363–64. For further discussion of the strategy of conciliation and its ultimate failure, see Grimsley, *Hard Hand of War*, 23–92; Ash, *When the Yankees Came*, 1–38; and Harsh, "Lincoln's Tarnished Brass," 124–41.

19. Daniel Read Larned to Mrs. Ambrose E. Burnside, March 30, 1862, and Larned to "Sis," April 22, 1862, Larned Papers, LC. For examples of discontent with Burnside's parole terms, see Charles M. Duren to his mother and father, April 27, 1862, Duren Papers, EU; Oliver Case to his sister, April 28, 1862, Case Letters, SHS; Priest, *From New Bern to Fredericksburg*, 26.

20. For Lincoln's vision and plan of wartime Reconstruction in the South and specifically North Carolina, see Harris, *With Charity for All*, esp. pp. 58–72.

21. Ash, *When the Yankees Came*, 76; Daniel Read Larned to Henry Howe, March 26, 1862, Larned Papers, LC; *Philadelphia Inquirer*, March 31, 1862, quoted in Mamré Marsh Wilson, *A Researcher's Journal*, 39; Burlingame, *Fifth Regiment of Rhode Island Heavy Artillery*, 59; John A. Hedrick to Benjamin S. Hedrick, June 20, 1862, in Browning and Smith, *Letters*, 7; Joseph Barlow to Ellen Barlow, April 29, 1862, Barlow Papers, USAMHI.

22. William A. Musson to "Friend Mary," June 8, 1862, Brown and Musson Papers, Norwich Civil War Round Table, USAMHI; Allen, *Forty-six Months*, 116–17.

23. All quotations are from Beringer et al., *Why the South Lost the Civil War*, 70.

24. Ibid.; Testimony of claimant Alexander Taylor (Craven County), Disallowed

Claims, SCC. See also Roark, *Masters without Slaves*, 2–7; Crofts, *Reluctant Confeder-ates*, esp. chaps. 4, 5.

25. Testimony of claimant Elijah W. Ellis and Testimony of Ellsworth Hawks (Cra-ven County), Disallowed Claims, SCC.

26. Testimony of Elijah W. Ellis, in Solomon Witherington's Claim (Craven County), Disallowed Claims, SCC. Witherington's name is also spelled "Worthing-ton."

27. Rumley Diary, April [n.d.], 1862, in Browning, *Southern Mind*, 33; John A. Hedrick to Benjamin S. Hedrick, June 20, 1862, October 25, 1863, in Browning and Smith, *Letters*, 7–8, 163–64. The Atlantic Hotel became Hammond General Hospital from April 1862 until it was closed on January 14, 1865. See Cleveland Diary, Janu-ary 14, 1865, SHC.

28. North Carolina, vol. 5, pp. 173, 176-A, R. G. Dun and Co. Collection, HBS.

29. John A. Hedrick to Benjamin S. Hedrick, June 20, 1862, October 25, 1863, in Browning and Smith, *Letters*, 7–8, 163–64; North Carolina, vol. 5, pp. 173, 176-A, R. G. Dun and Co. Collection, HBS; Mann, *Forty-fifth Regiment*, 202. After the Ocean House burned down in October 1863, Taylor found other ways to serve Union authorities.

30. North Carolina, vol. 5, p. 176-E, and vol. 7, p. 289, R. G. Dun and Co. Col-lection, HBS; U.S. Census, 1860, Craven County, Population Schedule, Manuscript Census Returns, NA.

31. E. A. Harkness to Southard Hoffman, March 5, 1863, box 2, pt. I, Letters Re-ceived, Department of North Carolina, RG 393; John A. Hedrick to Benjamin S. Hedrick, June 20, 1862, August 2, 1863, in Browning and Smith, *Letters*, 7, 141.

32. J. Jourdan to B. B. Foster, October 25, 1863, B. A. Ensley to Jourdan, Janu-ary 28, 1864, pt. II, Letters Sent, October 1863–March 1864, District and Subdistrict of Beaufort, Entry 940, RG 393.

33. Circular Issued from Headquarters Provost Marshal, Beaufort, July 20, 1862, Martine Papers, SHC; Rumley Diary, June 7, 1862, in Browning, *Southern Mind*, 38.

34. John A. Hedrick to Benjamin S. Hedrick, June 20, 1862, in Browning and Smith, *Letters*, 7–8.

35. North Carolina, vol. 5, p. 176-L, R. G. Dun and Co. Collection, HBS; U.S. Census, 1850, 1860, Carteret County, Population and Slave Schedules, Manuscript Census Returns, NA; William B. Fowle Jr. to Southard Hoffman, January 14, 1863, box 2, pt. I, Department of North Carolina, RG 393; Manarin and Jordan, *North Carolina Troops*, 1:128.

36. John A. Hedrick to Benjamin S. Hedrick, September 7, 1862, in Browning and Smith, *Letters*, 33; *NBWP*, September 20, 1862.

37. Manarin and Jordan, *North Carolina Troops*, 1:128–29, 134, 434; Cleveland Diary, February 16, 1865, January 12, 1865, SHC; John A. Hedrick to Benjamin S. Hedrick, June 22, July 10, 1862, in Browning and Smith, *Letters*, 7–8, 13.

38. Benjamin Leecraft to C. C. Lee, March 14, 1862, *SOR* 1(1):598–99; Manarin and Jordan, *North Carolina Troops*, 1:269–72. Leecraft never returned to Beaufort,

even after the war. The numbers do not exactly match up, because a handful of the men from Leecraft's company later reported for duty.

39. When I refer to those who "abandoned" their regiments, I refer not only to deserters, but also to those who did not return to their regiments after capture and exchange, those troops listed as "absent without leave" from some point to the end of the war, and those who have no further records after 1862. Those who died, officers who resigned for health reasons, or men who were legitimately discharged for disability or other reasons are not considered to have "abandoned" their regiments.

40. J. Madison Drake, *Ninth New Jersey*, 79; Testimony of claimant James B. Roberts (Carteret County), Approved Claims, SCC; Deposition of Isaac S. Hill, in *Nancy C. Hill, Administratrix of the Estate of Isaac S. Hill, Deceased, v. United States* (case file no. 1191), RG 123. Roberts's brother, David W. Roberts, served in Pool's company, while another brother, Richard, served in 1st Company I, 36th North Carolina Regiment. See Manarin and Jordan, *North Carolina Troops*, 1:134, 311.

41. Browning, "'Little-souled Mercenaries?.'" Many prospective enlistees were rejected because they were over age forty-five. See A. W. Woodhull to Maj. Southard Hoffman, September 9, 1862, box 1, pt. I, Letters Received, Department of North Carolina, RG 393. There is no clear origin of the appellation "buffaloes." For more information on the 1st and 2nd North Carolina Union regiments and the etymology of "buffaloes," see Browning, "'Little-souled Mercenaries,'" 337–42.

42. General Affidavit, December 10, 1901, Easton Arnold pension file, RG 15.

43. Deposition of William Fillingum, October 19, 1900, Fillingum pension file, and Deposition of John Lincoln, August 15, 1900, Lincoln pension file, both in RG 15; Manarin and Jordan, *North Carolina Troops*, 1:412, 8:507; John Lincoln service file, First North Carolina Infantry, CSR.

44. Henry Sawyer to "Commissioner of Pensions," June 13, 1895, and General Affidavit, June 27, 1890, Henry Sawyer pension file, RG 15; Manarin and Jordan, *North Carolina Troops*, 1:414; Henry Sawyer service file, First North Carolina Infantry, CSR.

45. J. Madison Drake, *Ninth New Jersey*, 71. As Stephen V. Ash ("Poor Whites in the Occupied South") notes, throughout the occupied regions of the South the Union armies employed three tactics in dealing with poor whites to cultivate their perceived latent Unionist sympathies: give them provisions, smite aristocrats while treating poor whites benevolently, and change their situation through education.

46. Rumley Diary, October [n.d.], 1862, in Browning, *Southern Mind*, 45; Charles Henry Tubbs to his wife, February 4–11, 1863, Tubbs Letters, NCSA. For a deeper exploration of the motivations of men enlisting in these two regiments, see Browning, "'Little-souled Mercenaries?.'"

47. I computed average wealth by cross-referencing the company rosters with the census population schedules. For average household wealth, I added the total value of personal property and the value of real estate from the 1860 census for the households in which each enlistee lived and then divided that sum by the total number of enlistees for whom records could be found. The enlistee did not have to personally own the

wealth in the household. The sample was undeniably small, but still large enough to give a clear impression of the disparity in wealth.

48. J. M. McChesney to Maj. R. S. Davis, April 6, 1864, Regimental Letter and Endorsement Book, First North Carolina Infantry, BRVUS; Deposition of Britton Ambrose, July 17, 1889, Joseph Fulcher pension file, RG 15; Wilbur F. Stevens to Col. E. E. Potter, October 21, 1862, Stevens file, First North Carolina Infantry, CSR.

49. Priest, *From New Bern to Fredericksburg,* 13; I. N. Roberts to Ebenezer Hunt, May 24, 1862, Hunt Papers, MHS; Daniel Read Larned to Henry Howe, March 20, 1862, Larned Papers, LC. For more on how women formed a strong resistance to Federal occupation in many areas of the South, see the essays in Whites and Long, *Occupied Women.*

50. Perhaps the most famous examples come from Gen. Benjamin Butler's occupation of New Orleans in 1862, when women crossed the street rather than acknowledge Union soldiers and refused to share their churches or public transportation with the troops; some even dumped the contents of their chamber pots on the heads of passing officers. As George Rable ("'Missing in Action'") has suggested in a persuasive article, women took such aggressive actions not only to demonstrate their own defiance, but also to shame southern men who seemed too ready to abandon their masculine duties. "For women who accepted traditional definitions of masculine honor," Rable wrote, "their menfolk had thoroughly disgraced themselves, first by surrendering the city and then by fitting their necks to the despot's yoke" (p. 139). See also Rable, *Civil War.*

51. I. N. Roberts to Ebenezer Hunt, May 24, July 19, 1862, Hunt Papers, MHS; William Amerman to "Cousin Aletta," June 30, 1862, Amerman Papers, Norwich Civil War Round Table, USAMHI.

52. Mitchell, *Vacant Chair,* 100. Men were not granted such leniency. When Haney Smith cursed a guard, he was thrown in jail immediately. Mrs. Haney Smith to Gen. John G. Foster, September 3, 1862, box 1, pt. 1, Letters Received, Department of North Carolina, RG 393.

53. Frederick Osborne to "Dear mother," June 25, July 25, 1862, in Osborne, *Private Osborne,* 85, 92.

54. Valentine, *Story of Co. F,* 61; James Edward Glazier to "Dear Parents," August 1, 1862, Glazier Papers, Huntington Library, San Marino, Calif.; *New York Times,* August 2, 1862; Ladd Diary, July 26, 1862, Ladd Papers, Civil War Miscellany Collection, USAMHI; Stephen Driver to George Driver, July 26, 1862, Driver Papers, Hooker Collection, ECU; Herbert Eugene Valentine Diary, July 26, 1862, Valentine Collection, NCSA.

55. Caroline Howard to "Cousin Harvey," August 21, 1862, Beckwith Papers, SHC; Dr. Hall Curtis to General Foster, [September 9, 1862], box 1, pt. I, Letters Received, Department of North Carolina, RG 393.

56. Edwin M. Stanton to Ambrose Burnside, May 20, 1862, OR 9:391; Powell, *Dictionary of North Carolina Biography,* 5:423; Caroline Howard to "Cousin Harvey," August 21, 1862, Beckwith Papers, SHC.

57. Daniel Read Larned to Mrs. Ambrose E. Burnside, May 27, 1862, Larned Papers, LC; Gerteis, *From Contraband to Freedman*, 30; Special Order No. 65, March 30, 1862, pt. I, General Records, Correspondence, General and Special Orders, Departments of North Carolina and Virginia, 1861–65, RG 393; Brown, *Edward Stanly*, 207; Charles Duren to "mother and father," May 2, 1862, Duren Papers, EU.

58. Rumley Diary, June 7, 1862, in Browning, *Southern Mind*, 37; Ambrose Burnside to Edwin Stanton, May 28, 30, 1862, *OR* 9:393–94, 396; Daniel Read Larned to Mrs. Ambrose E. Burnside, May 28, 1862, Larned Papers, LC. For more about closing the school, see Maxine D. Jones, "'A Glorious Work,'" 29–30.

59. Burnside, "Proclamation to the People of North Carolina," February 16, 1862, *OR* 9:363–64; *NBDP*, March 26, 1862. See also Harris, *With Charity for All*, 62.

60. Edward Stanly to Edwin Stanton, June 12, 1862, *OR* 9:400–401; R. R. Clarke to Dr. J. G. Metcalf, June 5, 1862, box 3, folder 5, Civil War Collection, AAS; Daniel Read Larned to Mrs. Ambrose E. Burnside, May 28, 1862, Larned Papers, LC. For more on the Bray incident, see Brown, *Edward Stanly*, 208–14.

61. Edward Stanly to Edwin Stanton, June 12, 1862, *OR* 9:400–401.

CHAPTER 4

1. William B. Fowle Jr. to Maj. Southard Hoffman, January 14, 1863, box 2, pt. I, Letters Received, Department of North Carolina, RG 393; John A. Hedrick to Benjamin S. Hedrick, January 11, 16, 1863, in Browning and Smith, *Letters*, 80–83 (weather conditions). Joel Henry Davis and Henry Rieger were prosperous merchants in Beaufort. North Carolina, vol. 5, pp. 175, 176-L, R. G. Dun and Co. Collection, HBS.

2. William B. Fowle Jr. to Maj. Southard Hoffman, January 14, 1863, box 2, pt. I, Letters Received, Department of North Carolina, RG 393. William B. Fowle Jr. was captain of Company C, 43rd Massachusetts Militia Volunteers. His unit mustered in on September 22, 1862, and mustered out on July 30, 1863. See *SOR* 29(2):378–80.

3. For more on the use of violent physical demonstrations against the body to send political messages, see Nudelman, *John Brown's Body*.

4. Ash, *When the Yankees Came*, chap. 4; Rose, *Rehearsal for Reconstruction*. For works that grant blacks more agency in their emancipation experience, see Berlin, *Slaves No More*; Harding, *There Is a River*; Hahn, *Nation under Our Feet*; and Litwack, *Been in the Storm So Long*.

5. H. S. Beals to Rev. S. S. Jocelyn, August 18, 1863, doc. 99706, roll 150, AMA (emphasis added); *American Missionary* 7 (October 1863): 231.

6. Rumley Diary, January 1, 1863, in Browning, *Southern Mind*, 54. Though slaves developed their own methods of dealing with harsh economic and political subordination, they were unable to operate completely free from white control. Southern slaves, in contrast to bondsmen in other slave societies (notably the West Indies), lived in constant contact with their white masters. In fact, in Carteret and Craven counties, the vast majority of slaves lived in households containing five or fewer slaves.

They could not simply establish a new life apart from whites. For more on the development and strength of slave communities, see Blassingame, *Slave Community*; Rawick, *From Sundown to Sunup*; Escott, *Slavery Remembered*; and Joyner, *Down by the Riverside*. For more on black and white interaction, see Genovese, *Roll, Jordan, Roll*. For a good synthesis of scholarly works on slavery, see Kolchin, *American Slavery*.

7. Daniel Read Larned to his sister, March 18, 1862, Larned Papers, LC; White Diary, March 13, 1862, AAS; Col. Heckman to Gov. Olden, March 15, 1862, in J. Madison Drake, *Ninth New Jersey*, 65–66; "Extracts from Letters," April 9, 1862, William L. Norton Papers, Connecticut Historical Society, Hartford; Denny, *Wearing the Blue*, 104.

8. Ambrose Burnside to Edwin Stanton, March 21, 1862, vol. 9, Union Battle Reports, ser. 729, War Records Office, quoted in Berlin et al., *Freedom . . . Series I*, 80–81; James Drennan to his wife, March 15, 1862, Drennan Papers, WHM; Draper, *Recollections*, 67.

9. Rumley Diary, June 7, 1862, in Browning, *Southern Mind*, 38; I. N. Roberts to Ebenezer Hunt, May 24, 1862, Hunt Papers, MHS.

10. Dehlia Mabrey Diary, March 27, 1862, Crisp Papers, ECU.

11. Daniel Read Larned to Henry Howe, March 28, 1862, Larned Papers, LC; Colyer, *Report of the Services Rendered*, 33.

12. R. R. Clarke to Dr. J. G. Metcalf, April 26, 1862, box 3, folder 5, Civil War Collection, AAS; Cecelski, *Waterman's Song*, 205; Emmerton, *Twenty-third Regiment*, 95.

13. William Lind to his brother, August 13, 1862, Lind Papers, USAMHI; Joseph Barlow to Ellen Barlow, November 19, 1862, Barlow Papers, USAMHI; Osborne, *Private Osborne*, 78 (James Emmerton).

14. Rawick, *American Slave*, 14:373, 81.

15. Thornton, "New Bern, North Carolina, 1862–1865" (unpublished typescript), p. 5, NCC (Colyer); R. R. Clarke to Dr. J. G. Metcalf, April 26, 1862, box 3, folder 5, Civil War Collection, AAS; Testimony of Capt. C. B. Wilder, May 9, 1863, in Berlin et al., *Freedom . . . Series I*, 89.

16. James, *Annual Report*, 43–44; Emily Gill to Rev. Jocelyn, January 11, 1864, doc. 99734, roll 150, AMA; Rawick, *American Slave*, 14:452.

17. U.S. Census, 1860, Carteret and Craven Counties, Population and Slave Schedules, Manuscript Census Returns, NA; "Order of Exercises at the Installation of Rev. Horace James," AAS; James, *Annual Report*, 3, 6; Cecelski, *Waterman's Song*, xvi, 141–51.

18. See Chapter 3 for the full account.

19. Though the Emancipation Proclamation exempted several occupied sections of the Confederacy from its authority (notably parts of Virginia and Louisiana and the entire state of Tennessee), North Carolina in its entirety came under the power of the Proclamation. See "Emancipation Proclamation," in Michael P. Johnson, *Abraham Lincoln*, 218–19. For more on the effect of the Proclamation in North Carolina, see Harris, *With Charity for All*, esp. chap. 3.

20. George H. Weston to "Dear Sir," February 15, 1863, New Bern Occupation Papers, SHC; Oliver W. Peabody to Mary Peabody, November 20, 1862, Peabody Papers, MHS; Rev. E. Cummings to George Whipple, January [n.d.], 1864, doc. 99765, roll 150, AMA; Benjamin H. Day Journal, January 11, 1863, Civil War Collection, BHS; James, *Annual Report*, 44.

21. Derby, *Bearing Arms*, 216; H. S. Beals to the editor, August 18, 1863, *American Missionary* 7 (October 1863): 231.

22. Rumley Diary, January 1, 1863, in Browning, *Southern Mind*, 55; George Greene to George Whipple, February 5, 1864, doc. 99767, AMA.

23. Ash, *When the Yankees Came*, 162; Daniel Read Larned to Henry Howe, March 20, 1862, Larned Papers, LC; Carolina Howard to Cousin Harvey, August 21, 1862, Beckwith Papers, SHC.

24. General Order No. 25, April 8, 1862, Entry 3239, vol. 33, pt. I, General Records, Correspondence, General and Special Orders, Departments of North Carolina and Virginia, 1861–65, RG 393; J. M. Drennan Diaries, August 2, 1862, SHC; Frederick Osborne to his mother, May 30, 1862, in Osborne, *Private Osborne*, 77; Cleveland Diary, March 20, 1865, SHC; James, *Annual Report*, 4.

25. Horace James to "My dear friends at the O. S. Sabbath School," June 21, 1862, James Correspondence, AAS; Corporal [Zenas T. Haines], *Letters from the Forty-fourth Regiment . . .* (Boston, 1863), 90, quoted in Ash, *When the Yankees Came*, 171–72.

26. James, *Annual Report*, 4. For more on black employment, see Gerteis, *From Contraband to Freedman*; Holt, *Making Freedom Pay*; and Saville, *Work of Reconstruction*.

27. R. R. Clarke to Dr. J. G. Metcalf, April 26, 1862, box 3, folder 5, Civil War Collection, AAS; Claim of Mary Washington (No. 166090), Douglass Papers, Horner Collection, ECU; Charles Glover to "My dear mother and father," April 1, 1862, Glover Papers, ECU; Testimony of claimant Willis M. Lewis (Craven County), Approved Claims, SCC; Deposition of Jacob Grimes, in *Gabriel Hardison v. United States* (case file no. 8070), RG 123.

28. Colyer, *Report of the Services Rendered*, 9–10; Mobley, *James City*, 8.

29. Rumley Diary, April [n.d.], 1862, in Browning, *Southern Mind*, 33 (emphasis in original); Spear, "Army Life" (unpublished typescript), 61, MHS; Barden, *Letters to the Home Circle*, 39.

30. Edward Bartlett to Martha, November 1, 1862, Bartlett Papers, MHS; Day Journal, December 1, 1862, BHS; Horatio Newhall to George, November 17, 1862, Newhall Papers, Civil War Miscellany Collection, USAMHI.

31. James, *Annual Report*, 10; Testimony of Eliza Garner, Testimony of Richard Rice, and Testimony of claimant John Pender (Carteret County), Disallowed Claims, SCC.

32. Testimony of claimant Caesar Manson (Carteret County), Disallowed Claims, SCC; Mann, *Forty-fifth Regiment*, 202; James, *Annual Report*, 19; Testimony of claimant Andrew Ward (Carteret County), Approved Claims, SCC.

33. Mobley, *James City*, 22–24; Cecelski, *Waterman's Song*, 187.

34. Cecelski, *Waterman's Song*, 181–89 (1st quotation, p. 181; 2nd quotation, p. 188).

35. Testimony of John Pender and Testimony of David Parker, Caesar Manson's Claim (Carteret County), Disallowed Claims, SCC; James, *Annual Report*, 12.

36. James, *Annual Report*, 11–12. For further analysis of how North Carolina freedpeople used employment after the war, see Holt, *Making Freedom Pay*.

37. Rumley Diary, August [n.d.], 1862, March 25, 1863, in Browning, *Southern Mind*, 42, 62.

38. Rumley Diary, June 1, 1863, January 1, 1864, in Browning, *Southern Mind*, 71, 118. For more on black enlistment, see Smith, *Black Soldiers in Blue*; Glatthaar, *Forged in Battle*; Berlin et al., *Freedom . . . Series II*; Cornish, *Sable Arm*; Keith P. Wilson, *Campfires of Freedom*; Jenkins, *Climbing Up to Glory*, chap. 2; and Richard M. Reid, *Freedom for Themselves*.

39. "Notes from North Carolina," *American Missionary* 7 (March 1863): 58; H. S. Beals to Rev. S. S. Jocelyn, August 18, 1863, doc. 99706, AMA; Claim of Mary Washington (No. 166090), Douglass Papers, Horner Collection, ECU. For more on how black men saw military service as proving their manhood, see Shaffer, *After the Glory*.

40. Singleton, *Recollections*, 188; William Augustus Willoughby to wife, January 22, 1863, Willoughby Papers, AAS; Richard M. Reid, *Freedom for Themselves*, 29. In July 1862, the Second Confiscation Act and the Militia Act gave President Lincoln the right to recruit black soldiers. Lincoln endorsed arming black troops in the Emancipation Proclamation. In February 1863 the Federal government began recruiting black troops, and on May 22, 1863, the War Department created the Bureau of Colored Troops to oversee and regulate black enlistment. See Keith P. Wilson, *Campfires of Freedom*, 1–2, and Urwin, "United States Colored Troops," 4:2002–3.

41. Mann, *Forty-fifth Regiment*, 301–2 (quotations); Cecelski, *Waterman's Song*, 181; Edward A. Wild to Edward W. Kinsley, November 30, 1863, Kinsley Papers, DU; Richard M. Reid, *Freedom for Themselves*, 30–31.

42. James Owens to Gen. [Henry] Wessells, February 20, 1863, box 2, pt. I, Letters Received, Department of North Carolina, RG 393; Jeremiah Stetson to "Dear ones at home," April 21, 1863, Stetson Papers, SHC; Spear, "Army Life" (unpublished typescript), 156, MHS; Richard M. Reid, *Freedom for Themselves*, 13–14, 28–33.

43. Mann, *Forty-fifth Regiment*, 324; Honey, "War within the Confederacy," 75–76.

44. Richard M. Reid, *Freedom for Themselves*, 46–50.

45. Henry Clapp to Willie, April 10, 1863, in Barden, *Letters to the Home Circle*, 176; Edward J. Bartlett to Martha, February 26, 1863, Bartlett Papers, MHS.

46. Cornelius, *"When I Can Read My Title Clear,"* 3; Slave Narrative of Hannah Crasson and Slave Narrative of Patsy Michner, in Hurmence, *My Folks Don't Want Me to Talk about Slavery*, 18, 77.

47. Horace James to "My Dear Friends," May 25, 1863, James Correspondence,

AAS; Singleton, *Recollections*, 41; "The Experience of Reverend Thomas H. Jones," in William L. Andrews, *North Carolina Slave Narratives*, 220–21 (emphases in original).

48. Henry A. Clapp to his mother, March 14, 1863, in Barden, *Letters to the Home Circle*, 150. W. E. B. DuBois suggested that about 5 percent of slaves learned to read, while historian Eugene D. Genovese believed the percentage may have been somewhat higher. See Genovese, *Roll, Jordan, Roll*, 563.

49. Maxine D. Jones, "'A Glorious Work,'" 29–30 (AMA correspondent); Horace James to "My dear friends at the O. S. Sabbath School," June 21, 1862, James Correspondence, AAS.

50. *The Liberator*, June 20, July 11, 1862.

51. Maxine D. Jones, "'A Glorious Work,'" 45–51; Valentine, *Story of Co. F*, 65; Miss Emily Gill to Rev. S. S. Jocelyn, January 11, 1864, doc. 99734, roll 150, AMA.

52. Valentine, *Story of Co. F*, 65; Maxine D. Jones, "'A Glorious Work,'" 47; Horace James to Old South Sabbath School, May 25, 1863, James Correspondence, AAS. For more on James's prewar educational activities, see J. B. Miles to Horace James, January 7, 1861, James to George Chandler, July 14, 1860, and Robert Allyn to James, January 21, 1856, James Correspondence, AAS.

53. Henry Wellington to Abby, April 15, 1863, Wellington Papers, MHS; Horace James to Old South Sabbath School, May 25, 1863, James Correspondence, AAS; Carrie Getchell to George Whipple, February 29, 1864, doc. 99777, roll 150, AMA.

54. Emmerton, *Twenty-third Regiment*, 97; Mary Peabody to Livy, February 23, 1863, Peabody Papers, MHS; Maxine D. Jones, "'A Glorious Work,'" 41–42 (William Briggs); Cleveland Diary, November 16, 1864, SHC; Rev. G. N. Greene to the editor, October 23, 1863, *American Missionary* 7 (December 1863): 280.

CHAPTER 5

1. Susan A. Hosmer to "Honored Father," September 11, 1863, doc. 99713, roll 150, AMA; Anderson, *The Education of Blacks*, 5. Hosmer was one of the four teachers who taught on the opening of the first two missionary schools in New Bern on July 23, 1863. See James, *Annual Report*, 39.

2. "Appeal for the Freedmen," *American Missionary* 7 (January 1863): 13. Heeding the advice of my friend and freedpeople's education scholar, Ronald E. Butchart, I try to avoid lumping all teachers and missionaries together. While many missionaries were teachers, not all teachers were missionaries, and some (often serving under the auspices of the New England Freedmen's Aid Society and National Freedmen's Relief Association) objected to the narrow sectarianism of true missionaries like those with the AMA. Hence, I try to separate the northerners who came South as missionaries and those who came as teachers, recognizing that there was much overlap as well as distinctions between the two groups.

3. Susan A. Hosmer to "Honored Father," September 11, 1863, doc. 99713, roll 150, AMA.

4. George W. Jenkins to Sarah, June 29, 1864, doc. 99895, roll 150, AMA.

5. For more on the small number of abolitionist white teachers, see Butchart, "Perspectives on Gender, Race."

6. Silber, "A Compound of Wonderful Potency."

7. "Appeal for the Freedmen," *American Missionary* 7 (January 1863): 13. See also Butchart, "Remapping Racial Boundaries." For more on black education initiatives in other regions, see Span, "'I Must Learn Now or Not at All.'"

8. *The Liberator*, June 20, 1862; Richard Bryant Drake, "American Missionary Association," 1–7; Beard, *Crusade of Brotherhood*, 23–32; Joe M. Richardson, *Christian Reconstruction*, 20.

9. Wolfe, "Women Who Dared," 31; Joe M. Richardson, *Christian Reconstruction*, 166 (George Whipple); Mary S. Williams to E. P. Smith, July 20, 1868, doc. 92052, Williams to Smith, August 25, 1868, doc. 92150, roll 150, AMA. For more on the teachers, see Butchart, "Perspectives on Gender, Race"; Small, "Yankee Schoolmarm"; Swint, *Northern Teacher in the South*; and Andrea Heather Williams, *Self-Taught*.

10. James, *Annual Report*, 20 (quotations); Reilly, "Reconstruction through Regeneration," 73–74.

11. James, *Annual Report*, 39; Fen, "Notes on the Education of Negroes," 25.

12. H. S. Beals to Rev. S. S. Jocelyn, August 18, 1863, doc. 99706, roll 150, AMA; Joe M. Richardson, *Christian Reconstruction*, 164, 168; Susan A. Hosmer to "Honored Father," September 11, 1863, doc. 99713, roll 150, AMA.

13. [Rev.] George Greene to Rev. S. S. Jocelyn, October 23, 1863, doc. 99732, roll 150, AMA; Alexander, *North Carolina Faces the Freedmen*, 157.

14. Fen, "Notes on the Education of Negroes," 26n11.

15. W. T. Briggs to George Whipple, March 3, 1865, doc. 99970, Sarah M. Pearson, Monthly Report, February 1864, doc. 99778, and Horace James to [George Whipple], August 24, 1863, doc. 99710, roll 150, AMA; Maxine D. Jones, "'A Glorious Work,'" 48–51.

16. Emily Gill to Rev. S. S. Jocelyn, February 24, 1864, doc. 99775, and Gill to Jocelyn, March 2, 1864, doc. 99784, roll 150, AMA; *American Missionary*, 8 (May 1864): 128–29.

17. Farnham and King, "'March of the Destroyer'"; Benjamin, *Great Epidemic in New Berne*; Horace James to George Whipple, March 16, 1864, doc. 99792, and E. J. Harness to Whipple, March 15, 1864, doc. 99790, roll 150, AMA.

18. Carrie Getchell to George Whipple, February 15, 1864, doc. 99773, roll 150, AMA; B. F. Maxwell to Horace James, March 17, 1864, James Correspondence, AAS.

19. Miss A. L. Etheridge to Rev. S. S. Jocelyn, November 30, 1863, doc. 99721, roll 150, AMA.

20. Joe M. Richardson, *Christian Reconstruction*, 171 (Lymans); Horace James to George Whipple, August 15, 1864, doc. 99877, roll 150, AMA; Horace James to the editor, *The Congregationalist*, February 7, 1862.

21. Nellie Stearns to "Lizzie," November 5, 1865, Stearns Papers, DU.

22. William Briggs to George Whipple, December 3, 1864, doc. 99910, and

Carrie M. Getchell to Whipple, January 18, 1864, doc. 99744, roll 150, AMA; Joe M. Richardson, *Christian Reconstruction*, 28.

23. Horace James to "Dear Bro," January 16, 1864, doc. 99742 (emphasis in original), William Hamilton to "Bro. Jocelyn," January 25, 1864, doc. 99756, and William Briggs to George Whipple, April 24, 1865, doc. 100005 (emphasis in original), roll 150, AMA; Eli Whittlesey to George Whipple, August 2, 1865, Letters Sent, Vol. 1, July 4, 1865–July 13, 1867, roll 1, Records of the Assistant Commissioner for the State of North Carolina, Bureau of Refugees, Freedmen, and Abandoned Lands, 1865–70, Record Group 105, National Archives, Washington, D.C.

24. Rev. William Hamilton to "My Dear Rev. Jocelyn," January 19, 1864, doc. 99732, and Hamilton to "Bro. Jocelyn," January 25, 1864, doc. 99756, roll 150, AMA.

25. Rev. William Hamilton to "My Dear Rev. Jocelyn," January 19, 1864, doc. 99732, roll 150, AMA.

26. Cecelski, *Waterman's Song*, 170–71; Horace James to Rev. George Whipple, September 15, 1863, doc. 99717, roll 150, AMA (emphases in original); Reilly, "Reconstruction through Regeneration," 69.

27. Horace James to "Dear Bro" January 4, 1864, doc. 99731 (emphasis in original), James to "Dear Bro," January 16, 1864, doc. 99742, and James to "Dear Bro," January 20, 1864, doc. 99746, roll 150, AMA.

28. Horace James to "Dear Bro," January 16, 1864, doc. 99742 (emphasis in original), and James to George Whipple, September 15, 1863, doc. 99717, roll 150, AMA; Richard Bryant Drake, "American Missionary Association," 13; Reilly, "Reconstruction through Regeneration," 63–65 (relief statistics, p. 64). It is difficult to ascertain how many freedmen's aid societies developed during and after the war. One scholar identifies eighty-one societies, while Richard Drake ("American Missionary Association," 14) believes there were probably even more than that.

29. G. N. Greene to "Bro. Jocelyn," October 10, 1863, doc. 99719 (emphasis in original), and William Briggs to George Whipple, January 6, 1865, doc. 99934 (emphasis in original), roll 150, AMA.

30. Susan A. Hosmer to "Honored Father," September 11, 1863, doc. 99713, roll 150, AMA; Horace James to "My Dear Friends of the O. S. Sabbath School," June 21, 1862, James Correspondence, AAS; Cecelski, *Waterman's Song*, 167–69. Cecelski (p. 167) notes that former slaves in the region held on to traditional African religious practices — particularly Ba-Kongo and Yoruba — as well. These were syncretic religions that merged African communal religious practices with Christian teachings. Some soldiers were disturbed by the spiritual rituals that often accompanied baptisms and funerals.

31. Horace James to "Reverend and Dear Sir" [Rev. S. S. Jocelyn], June 10, 1863, doc. 99702, roll 150, AMA.

32. Timothy Lyman to George Whipple, August 30, 1864, doc. 99881 (emphases in original), and Lyman to Whipple, February 27, 1865, doc. 99958 (emphases in original), roll 150, AMA. For more on northern missionaries' views of freedpeople's religion, see Jacqueline Jones, *Soldiers of Light and Love*, and Click, *Time Full of Trial*.

33. Hubbard, *Campaign of the Forty-fifth Regiment*, 82; H. S. Beals to the editor, August 1863, *American Missionary* 7 (October 1863): 230; Timothy Lyman to George Whipple, February 27, 1865, doc. 99958, roll 150, AMA.

34. Henry Wellington to Abby, April 7, 1863, Wellington Papers, MHS; Timothy Lyman to George Whipple, February 27, 1865, doc. 99958, roll 150, AMA (emphasis in original).

35. Horace James to the editor, *The Congregationalist*, June 8, 1866. For similar sentiments, see Joe M. Richardson, *Christian Reconstruction*, 22, and Wolfe, "Women Who Dared," 12. James's attitudes (and the same quotation) can also be found in Reilly, "Reconstruction through Regeneration," 159.

36. Miss Burnap to the editor, January 18, 1864, *American Missionary* 8 (March 1864): 65; Miss E. James to the editor, [December 1863], *American Missionary* 8 (February 1864): 39.

37. Chaplain Talbot to the editor, *American Missionary* (January 1865): 6.

CHAPTER 6

1. William Augustus Walker to his sister, July 11, 14, 1862, in Silber and Sievers, *Yankee Correspondence*, 61–62.

2. Daniel Read Larned to Henry Howe, March 20, 1862, Larned to Mrs. Ambrose E. Burnside, March 23, 1862, and Larned to his sister, March 30, 1862, Larned Papers, LC; John A. Hedrick to Benjamin S. Hedrick, June 6, 1862, in Browning and Smith, *Letters*, 2.

3. For the power of the sense of duty as a motivator of northern soldiers, see McPherson, *For Cause and Comrades*. My interpretation (and McPherson's) differs from that of Gerald Linderman (*Embattled Courage*), who argues that Union soldiers became disillusioned with the war and desired to get out before seeing the cause through to ultimate victory. Linderman focuses on how combat affected motivation, whereas this work explores how the monotony of occupation affected motivation.

4. White Diary, August [n.d.], November 17, 1861, AAS; U.S. Census, 1860, Worcester County, Mass., Population Schedule, Manuscript Census Returns, NA.

5. Samuel Storrow to his father, October 12, 1863, Storrow Civil War Letters, MHS, and Storrow Civil War Journals, MS 192, Woodson Research Center, Fondren Library, Rice University, Houston, Tex.

6. Charles Duren to "my dear father," July 1, 1861, Duren Papers, EU (emphasis in original); Benjamin H. Day Journal, November 25, 186, BHS; Mann, *Forty-fifth Regiment*, 183.

7. Abraham Lincoln to Ambrose E. Burnside, December 26, 1861, in Michael P. Johnson, *Abraham Lincoln*, 149.

8. For more on Burnside's expedition, see Sauers, *Burnside Expedition*. For more on Beaufort's wartime role as a blockading port, see Dan Blair, "'One Good Port.'"

9. Chase, "Service with Battery F," 6.

10. Charles E. Briggs to "Lizzie," November 22, 1862, Briggs Letters, MHS; Henry

Clapp to Helen, April 28, 1863, in Barden, *Letters to the Home Circle*, 195. Porte Crayon, the pseudonym of David Hunter Strother, wrote many travel accounts for national magazines such as *Harper's Weekly*.

11. Edward Bartlett to Ripley, December 27, 1862, Bartlett Papers, MHS; Emerson, *A Report on the Trees and Shrubs*; Massachusetts, Adjutant General's Office, *Massachusetts Soldiers*, 4:291; Mann, *Forty-fifth Regiment*, 316.

12. Dexter B. Ladd Diary, April 12, 1862, Ladd Papers, Civil War Miscellany Collection, USAMHI; Oliver Case to his sister, May 8, 1862, Case Letters, SHS; Farnham and King, "'March of the Destroyer,'" 449, 471. For more soldiers' complaints about the natural adversaries they encountered, see William Lind to Thomas Lind, May 20, 1862, William W. Lind Papers, USAMHI; Daniel Read Larned to his sister, June 2, 1862, box 1, Larned Papers, LC; Wyeth, *Leaves from a Diary*, May 2, 1863, 52; Edward J. Bartlett to Martha, March 9, 1863, Bartlett Papers, MHS; and William Augustus Willoughby to his wife, October 29, 1862, Willoughby Papers, AAS.

13. John E. Bassett Diary, July 8, 1862, MHS; Isaac Newton Parker to Caroline Parker, June 26, 1864, in Hauptman, *A Seneca Indian*, 82; George Jewett to "Deck," July 8, 1862, Jewett Papers, LC. For more on how nineteenth-century Americans viewed climate as integrally related to health, see Bolton-Valencius, *The Health of the Country*.

14. White Diary, March 18, 1862, AAS; Daniel Read Larned to Mrs. Ambrose E. Burnside, March 23, 1862, and Larned to his sister, March 24, 1862, Larned Papers, LC.

15. Alfred Otis Chamberlin to his sister, October 7, 1862, Chamberlin Papers, DU; George Jewett to "Deck," June 1, 1862, Jewett Papers, LC; Henry Clapp to his mother, November 14, 1862, in Barden, *Letters to the Home Circle*, 22.

16. Ladd Diary, June 4, 7, 1863, Ladd Papers, Civil War Miscellany Collection, USAMHI; Edward J. Bartlett to Martha, March 25, 1863, Bartlett Papers, MHS; U.S. Census, 1860, Craven County, Population Schedule, Manuscript Census Returns, NA; Manarin and Jordan, *North Carolina Troops*, 3:436.

17. Edward J. Bartlett to Ripley, May 6, 1863, Bartlett Papers, MHS; 1860 U.S. Census, Craven County, Population and Slave Schedules, Manuscript Census Returns, NA; Barden, *Letters to the Home Circle*, 203; D. A. Maynard to "Dear Brother," February 22, 1864, Military Records, Civil War Collection, box 85, folder 14, NCSA. For more on marriages, see J. Madison Drake, *Ninth New Jersey*, 75; Mamré Marsh Wilson, *A Researcher's Journal*, 22–23; and Deposition of Clifford Simpson and of Sarah Trenwith, *Sarah F. Trenwith, Executrix of Clifford F. Simpson, Deceased, v. United States* (case file no. 10014), RG 123. The 1860 census reported that Israel Disosway owned eleven slaves and that Jane, age fifteen, was his oldest daughter.

18. William Augustus Walker to his sister, July 11, 14, 1862, in Silber and Sievers, *Yankee Correspondence*, 62; Alfred Holcomb to Emma, May 31–June 1, 1863, Alfred Holcomb to his father, July 12, 1863, in Lind, *Long Road for Home*, 130, 134; William G. Leonard to John G. Foster, April 26, 1863, box 2, pt. I, Letters Received, Department of North Carolina, RG 393. For more on Union perceptions,

see Daniel Read Larned to Henry Howe, March 20, 1862, box 1, Larned Papers, LC; Spear, "Army Life" (unpublished typescript), 62, MHS; Horatio Newhall to George, December 1, 1862, Newhall Papers, Civil War Miscellany Collection, USAMHI. For more on racial attitudes of northern soldiers, see Cecere, "Carrying the Home Front to War."

19. Edward Bartlett to "Lizzie," February 17, 1863, Bartlett Papers, MHS; Dexter B. Ladd Diary, December 18, 1862, Ladd Papers, Civil War Miscellany Collection, USAMHI.

20. Nathan G. Newton to his mother, November 22, 1862, Newton Letters, EU; Inner lining of Ladd Diary, Ladd Papers, Civil War Miscellany Collection, USAMHI. See also "Carl" to "My Dear Parents," April 6, 1863, folder 44, Federal Soldiers Letters, SHC. Other soldiers made sport of trying to steal the wares that blacks tried to peddle to Union troops. See Lyman Alfred Chamberlin to Miss Maria Willard, August 11, 1862 (typescript), Hammond General Hospital Box, Carteret County Historical Society, Morehead City, N.C.

21. White images of blacks were, in David Cecere's words ("Carrying the Home Front to War," 297), initially "marked by two dimensional understandings of African Americans: blacks were subhuman, simple-minded, amusing pets, often the butt of jokes." For more on the development of racial thought, see Jordan, *White Man's Burden*, and Fredrickson, *Black Image*, esp. chaps. 1, 2. For more on Free Soil political thought, see Foner, *Free Soil*, esp. chap. 2.

22. Alfred Holcomb to Emma, August 4, 1863, in Lind, *Long Road for Home*, 139; Oliver Case to his sister, May 24, 1862, Case Letters, SMS.

23. Rumley Diary, May [n.d.], 1862, in Browning, *Southern Mind*, 37; Edwin Fish to Lucy Fish, September 25, 1862, Fish Letters, EU; Isaac N. Roberts to Dr. Ebenezer Hunt, December 5, 1862, Hunt Papers, MHS.

24. Alfred Holcomb to Milton, August 29, 1862, Holcomb Papers, Civil War Miscellany Collection, USAMHI; Hale Wesson to his father, September 26, 1863, Wesson Papers, EU.

25. Rumley Diary, May 30, July 3, 1863, in Browning, *Southern Mind*, 70, 79; Mary Peabody to [unknown], March 1, 1863, Peabody Papers, MHS.

26. Charles Codman Reminiscence, 1897 vol., pp. 240–42, Codman Papers, MHS. For another example, see James Cartwright to his mother, February 25, 1863, Cartwright Family Papers, *Civil War Times Illustrated* Collection, USAMHI.

27. Spear, "Army Life" (unpublished typescript), 173, MHS; William F. Keeler to Anna Keeler, June 30, 1863, in McPherson, *For Cause and Comrades*, 127. Union soldier Charles Tournier also was impressed by the local blacks who became soldiers: "They look strong and healthy [and] thoroughly enjoy wearing the uniforms and handling the guns." Tournier Diary, May 19, 1865, New Bern Historical Society Papers, ECU.

28. Historian Chandra Manning (*What This Cruel War Was Over*) has argued that many Union soldiers developed a strong commitment to abolition as they ventured

into the South and observed the effects of slavery. Joseph T. Glatthaar (*March to the Sea*) found similar changes in attitude among soldiers when they were exposed to African Americans or the institution of slavery.

29. J. Madison Drake, *Ninth New Jersey*, 75; Mary Peabody to Livy, February 23, 1863, Peabody Papers, MHS. For more on guerrillas elsewhere, see Grimsley, *Hard Hand of War*, 111–19; Fellman, *Citizen Sherman*, 137–48; Frazier, "'Out of Stinking Distance'"; and Mackey, *Uncivil War*.

30. George Frederick Jourdan to his wife, May 3, 1863, box 1, folder 9, Civil War Collection, AAS; Jeremiah Stetson to his wife, July 4, 1863, Stetson Papers, SHC; William Jackson to George Root, December 4, 1864, Root Papers, DU; James Gifford to parents, April 3, 1864, Gifford Papers, SHC.

31. Hale Wesson to his father, September 2, 1862, Wesson Papers, EU; Capt. Cole to Southard Hoffman, November 15, 1862, box 1, Letters Received, Department of North Carolina, RG 393. For another example, see Kirwan, *Memorial History*, 125.

32. Spear, "Army Life" (unpublished typescript), 126–27, MHS; Thorpe, *History of the Fifteenth Connecticut*, 181; Burlingame, *Fifth Regiment of Rhode Island Heavy Artillery*, 56.

33. Frederick Osborne to his mother, July 25, 1862, in Osborne, *Private Osborne*, 92–93; Hale Wesson to his father, August 15, 1862, Wesson Papers, EU; Mann, *Forty-fifth Regiment*, 219; Rowland M. Hall letter, n.d., Julia Ward Stickley Papers, NCSA, in Fort Macon Archival Box, vol. 42, Carteret County Historical Society, Morehead City.

34. John Timmerman to Mary, August 4, 1862, Timmerman Papers, USAMHI; Isaac Newton Parker to Martha Hoyt Parker, April 1, 1864, in Hauptman, *A Seneca Indian*, 97.

35. Collins, "War Crime or Justice? ." For more on the use of corpses to send political messages, see Nudelman, *John Brown's Body*, and Myers, *Executing Daniel Bright*. Indeed, such clandestine acts of violence only heightened the desire for retribution among the occupiers. Historian Michael Fellman (*Citizen Sherman*) asserts, "Guerrillas broke all the conventions of honorable war and led the occupying forces into a deepening cycle of attack and counterattack, revenge and retaliation, in a war that blurred all distinctions between the civilian and the military, thus deepening war and brutalizing the combatants" (p. 140). Though not as omnipresent as guerrilla warfare was in other occupied parts of the Confederacy, this "deepening" of war did occur in the Carteret-Craven region as well.

36. Mrs. Haney Smith to John G. Foster, September 3, 1862, Owen Sempler to Foster, September 25, 1862, box 1, pt. I, Letters Received, Department of North Carolina, RG 393; James Williams to Brig. Gen. Heckman, August 8, 1863, recorded in Herbert Valentine Diary, Valentine Papers, SHC. See also Janda, "Shutting the Gates of Mercy."

37. William Lind to Thomas Lind, July 28, 1862, August 1, 1862, Lind Papers, USAMHI; Alfred Holcomb to Milton Holcomb, August 22, 1862, Holcomb Papers,

Civil War Miscellany Collection, USAMHI; John S. Bartlett to "My Dear Affectionate Sister," June 4, [1862], box 1, Civil War Papers, Connecticut Historical Society, Hartford.

38. Oliver Peabody to Mary Peabody, January 3, 1863, Peabody Papers, MHS; George H. Weston to "Dear Sir," February 15, 1863, New Bern Occupation Papers, SHC. For another example, see Henry Wellington to "Sister Abby," March [15], 1863, Wellington Papers, MHS.

39. McPherson, *Battle Cry of Freedom*, 500; Edward Bartlett to Martha, November 1, 1862, Bartlett Papers, MHS; Ladd Diary, October 27, 1862, Ladd Papers, Civil War Miscellany Collection, USAMHI; Joseph Barlow to Ellen Barlow, August 25, 1863, Barlow Papers, USAMHI. Massachusetts was charged with raising 19,090 men for nine months of service through voluntary enlistment or a draft. Barden, *Letters to the Home Circle*, xxi.

40. Joseph Barlow to Ellen Barlow, July 5, 1862, Barlow Papers, USAMHI; Edward Bartlett to Martha, April 23, May 12, 1863, Bartlett Papers, MHS; Alfred Holcomb to Milton Holcomb, June 21, 1862, Holcomb Papers, Civil War Miscellany Collection, USAMHI.

41. John A. Hedrick to Benjamin S. Hedrick, August 6, 1863, in Browning and Smith, *Letters*, 142; Ladd Diary, November 27, 1862, Ladd Papers, Civil War Miscellany Collection, USAMHI; Record of the Regimental Court Martial, June 15, 1862, Regimental Order Book, 27th Massachusetts Infantry, BRVUS; Walcott, *Twenty-first Regiment, Massachusetts Volunteers*, 88.

42. Samuel C. Hunt to "dearest," December 23, 1862, quoted in L. G. Williams, *A Place for Theodore*, 73; Stephen Driver to George Driver, July 26, 1862, Driver Papers, Hooker Collection, ECU; Denny, *Wearing the Blue*, 116.

43. Alfred Holcomb to Milton Holcomb, June 21, 1862, Holcomb Papers, Civil War Miscellany Collection, USAMHI; William Augustus Willoughby to his wife, January 11, 1863, Willoughby Papers, AAS; J. M. McChesney to Maj. R. S. Davis, October 8, 1864, vol. 3, Regimental Descriptive Books, 1st North Carolina Infantry Regiment, BRVUS. For more on the antagonism between enlisted men and their officers in a democratic army, see Mitchell, *Vacant Chair*, 39–54.

44. For more on low morale, see McPherson, *Battle Cry of Freedom*, esp. chap. 20, and Roland, *An American Iliad*, esp. chap 6.

45. William Lind to Thomas Lind, September 12, 1862, in Lind, *Long Road for Home*, 105; Isaac N. Roberts to Dr. Ebenezer Hunt, September 12, 1862, Hunt Papers, MHS; Jacob Roberts to "Hon. B. F. Carter," October 5, 1862, Roberts Correspondence, Hinch Collection, USAMHI.

46. David Lucius Craft to his sister, November 19, 1862, Craft Papers, DU; Isaac N. Roberts to Dr. Ebenezer Hunt, November 10, 1862, Hunt Papers, MHS; Edward Bartlett to Martha, December 26, 1862, Bartlett Papers, MHS; Joseph Barlow to Ellen Barlow, December 26, 1862, Barlow Papers, USAMHI.

47. David P. Reynolds Diary, January 1, 1863, Reynolds Papers, DU; Eben Thomas Hale to his mother, June 9, 1863, Hale Papers, SHC.

48. As military psychologists Reuven Gal and Frederick Manning ("Morale and Its Components," 389) postulate, "Perhaps it should not be surprising that in an all-volunteer force there is a stronger relationship between the soldier's morale and the extent to which he perceives his service as meaningful. The volunteer, after all, made a conscious decision that military service was a worthwhile endeavor. His feelings of whether this service makes a contribution to his country" are "reflected in his level of morale."

49. Nathaniel Warner ("Morale of Troops on Occupation Duty," 749) has argued that morale is "the net satisfaction derived from acceptable progress toward goals or from the attaining of goals." Sociologist William E. Hocking ("Nature of Morale," 303) has concluded that morale "is a measure of one's disposition to give one's self to the objective in hand." Most scholars agree that one's level of morale is directly influenced by "a sense of fruitful participation in [one's] work" (Baynes, *Morale*, 108). As Reuven Gal ("Unit Morale," 561), writing about another conflict, has noted, when "the course of war carried you far away from your country's borders and from your own home, when the justification of such a war becomes questionable — then the issue of the perceived legitimacy of that war by the soldier becomes a crucial factor concerning his morale and combat readiness."

50. Joseph Barlow to Ellen Barlow, May 22, 1863, Barlow Papers, USAMHI; William Jackson to George A. Root, October 28, 1864, Root Papers, DU. For similar reports on morale among American enlisted men in other wars, see Seidule, "Morale in the American Expeditionary Forces"; Moskos, *The American Enlisted Man*; Kellett, *Combat Motivation*; and Wong et al., *Why They Fight*.

51. Baynes, *Morale*, 237, quoted in McPherson, *For Cause and Comrades*, 155.

52. Several recent scholarly works debate the sustaining nature of soldiers' motivations. This study of eastern North Carolina agrees with James McPherson (*For Cause and Comrades*) that despite the unpleasant nature of their work, soldiers maintained a strong motivation to fulfill their duty. McPherson referred to soldiers on both sides and in all theaters of war, not just those involved in military occupation. For a differing viewpoint — that soldiers lost their motivation to continue the fight — see Linderman, *Embattled Courage*. For different variations on these themes, see Robertson, *Soldiers Blue and Gray*, and Hess, *Union Soldier in Battle*.

53. Charles Quick to "Sister Mary," March 26, 1863, July 30, 1862, Quick Correspondence, SHC.

54. Josiah Wood to Reanna, December 22, 1862, May 12, 31, 1863, Wood Papers, DU; Henry Clapp to Willie, May 12, 1863, in Barden, *Letters to the Home Circle*, 204.

55. Herbert Cooley to "Dear Father," April 8, July 26, 1863, Cooley Papers, SHC.

56. John Richter Jones to Joseph A. Clay, May 18, 1863 [printed in unidentified newspaper clipping], in Jones Papers, SHC.

57. Nelson Chapin to "My dear wife," March 6, 1864, Chapin Papers, *Civil War Times Illustrated* Collection, USAMHI; Mary Peabody to [unknown], March 1, 1863, Peabody Papers, MHS.

58. Joseph Barlow to Ellen, June 30, October 23, 1862, Barlow Papers, USAMHI; Charles Duren to his father, September 21, 1861, Duren Papers, EU (emphasis in original); Spear, "Army Life" (unpublished typescript), 110, MHS. For more on soldiers' recognition of slavery as the primary reason for the war, see Manning, *What This Cruel War Was Over*.

59. Day Journal, January 10, 1863, BHS; Spear, "Army Life" (unpublished typescript), 132, MHS; Nelson Chapin to "My dear wife," January 6, 1863, Chapin Papers, *Civil War Times Illustrated* Collection, USAMHI.

CHAPTER 7

1. Allen, *Forty-six Months*, 104, 106, 116–17, 119.

2. Edward J. Bartlett to "Dear Martha," January 30, 1863, Bartlett Papers, MHS; Charles Henry Tubbs to "My dear wife," March 1, 1863, Tubbs Letters, NCSA; John A. Hedrick to Benjamin S. Hedrick, August 9, 1863, in Browning and Smith, *Letters*, 144; James E. Glazier to "Dear Parents," February 2, 1863, Glazier Papers, Huntington Library, San Marino, Calif.

3. For Lincoln's vision and plan of wartime Reconstruction in the South and specifically in North Carolina, see Harris, *With Charity for All*, esp. 58–72. In one of the best treatments of Union military policy in occupied areas, Mark Grimsley (*Hard Hand of War*, 3, 47–119) argues that conciliation died with the Union defeats outside of Richmond in 1862. Federal authorities then moved toward a "pragmatic" policy, one between conciliation and hard war.

4. Allen, *Forty-six Months*, 116; Kirwan, *Memorial History*, 251–52; *NBDP*, April 23, 1862. For an in-depth look at how the prospects of trade influenced local allegiances in other parts of eastern North Carolina, see Meekins, *Elizabeth City*.

5. John A. Hedrick to Benjamin S. Hedrick, August 6, October 3, 21, 1863, in Browning and Smith, *Letters*, 143, 159, 163. In Natchez, Miss., some Union officers benefited from corrupt trading practices, and in the Sea Islands of South Carolina, they also profited from the confiscation of nonwar-related valuables. In Memphis, Tenn., a Union official cursed the private cotton brokers who followed General Grant's army into Mississippi, claiming that a "mania for sudden fortunes made in cotton has to an alarming extent corrupted and demoralized the army. Every colonel, captain, or quartermaster is in secret partnership with some operator in cotton; every soldier dreams of adding a bale of cotton to his monthly pay." Smithers, "Profit and Corruption"; Duncan, *Blue-eyed Child*, 331–70; Doyle, *Faulkner's County*, 235.

6. William B. Fowle Jr. to Edward Stanly, December 27, 1862, box 1, pt. I, Letters Received, Department of North Carolina, RG 393.

7. John J. Bowen to Southard Hoffman, November 3, 1862, box 1, John A. Hedrick to Henry Wessells, April 22, 1863, box 2, pt. I, Department of North Carolina, RG 393; Cleveland Diary, December 17, 1864, SHC.

8. *New York Times*, August 2, 1862; William B. Fowle Jr. to Southard Hoffman, January 14, 1863, box 2, pt. I, Department of North Carolina, RG 393 (Stanly); Un-

processed material, box 2, Salisbury Collection, NCSA; North Carolina, vol. 5, pp. 176-B, 163, 167, 170, R. G. Dun and Co. Collection, HBS.

9. William B. Fowle Jr. to Southard Hoffman, January 14, 1863, and Luke Lyman to Hoffman, February 4, 1863, box 2, pt. I, Department of North Carolina, RG 393.

10. Mary Peabody to Livy, March 11, 1863, Peabody Papers, MHS; Mann, *Forty-fifth Regiment*, 219; Brown, *Edward Stanly*, 238–41.

11. John A. Hedrick to Benjamin S. Hedrick, January 10, April 9, May 3, 1863, in Browning and Smith, *Letters*, 80, 106, 114; *New York Times*, April 7, 1863 (Lincoln's proclamation).

12. Testimony of [unknown], Testimony of Edmund D. Jones, and Testimony of Elijah Ellis, Solomon Witherington's Claim (Craven County), Disallowed Claims, SCC.

13. J. Madison Drake, *Ninth New Jersey*, 140–41; U.S. Census, 1860, Carteret County, Population Schedule, Manuscript Census Returns, NA; Orders that forbade trade can be found in General Order No. 25, March 14, 1863, Lt. Col. Luke Lyman, Regimental Order Book, 27th Massachusetts Infantry, BRVUS.

14. John A. Hedrick to Benjamin S. Hedrick, September 27, 1863, in Browning and Smith, *Letters*, 157; J. W. Atwill to William J. Riggs, May 15, 1865, pt. II, Letters Sent, December 1864–October 1865, District of New Bern, Entry 1660, Polynomous Succession of Commands, RG 393.

15. Edward Stanly to John G. Foster, March 28, 1863, box 2, and November 13, 1862, box 1, pt. I, Letters Received, Department of North Carolina, RG 393.

16. Harris, "*In the Country of the Enemy*," 95, 102.

17. Ibid., 94; Zebulon B. Vance to James Seddon, December 21, 1863, in Johnston and Mobley, *Papers of . . . Vance*, 2:344–45.

18. Edward Stanly to John G. Foster, March 28, 1863, box 2, pt. I, Letters Received, Department of North Carolina, RG 393; Kirwan, *Memorial History*, 131–32.

19. William Augustus Willoughby to his wife, January 22, 1863, in Silber and Sievers, *Yankee Correspondence*, 97; Agnes Paton Foy Memoir (typescript), p. 12, ECU.

20. Mann, *Forty-fifth Regiment*, 407–8; Ladd Diary, Undated Entry [May 1, 1862], Ladd Papers, Civil War Miscellany Collection, USAMHI.

21. Leonidas Polk to his wife, March 17, 1863 (typescript), Denmark Collection, NCSA. For a view on the relatively limited nature of the destructive expeditions, see Neely, "Was the Civil War a Total War?" and *The Civil War and the Limits of Destruction*.

22. James Glazier to Annie G. Monroe, October 26, 1862, Glazier Papers, Huntington Library, San Marino, Calif.; Alfred Otis Chamberlain to "Dear father and mother," October 25, 1862, Chamberlin Papers, DU. See also Massey, "Confederate Refugees."

23. George Kimball to his wife, April 20, 1863, Kimball Papers, USAMHI; John A. Hedrick to Benjamin S. Hedrick, June 24, 1863, in Browning and Smith, *Letters*, 132; Hill, *Bethel to Sharpsburg*, 238 (Stanly). For a parallel example, see Gerteis, "'A Friend of the Enemy.'"

24. Spear, "Army Life" (unpublished typescript), 124–25, MHS.

25. Ibid., 106, 152; Isaac N. Roberts to Dr. Ebenezer Hunt, July 19, 1862, Hunt Papers, MHS.

26. Calvin Jarrett, "The Spy Was a Lady," *Greensboro Daily News*, September 29, 1963, in Newspaper Clippings File, NCC; [Emeline Pigott] Diary, February 7 (1st quotation—emphasis in original), 8, 1865, Royal Papers, SHC; Cleveland Diary, February 9, 10, 17 (2nd quotation), 1865, SHC; *Old North State*, February 11, 18, 1865; "Sketch of Miss Emeline Pigott," Pigott Collection, NCSA.

27. Benjamin Roberson to Edward Stanly, July 29, 1862, and Roberson to Southard Hoffman, November 1, 1862, box 1, pt. I, Letters Received, Department of North Carolina, RG 393; Claim of Benjamin Roberson (Carteret County), Disallowed Claims, SCC. For more on the Southern Claims Commission, see Klingberg, *Southern Claims Commission*.

28. Testimony of Nelson E. Hamilton, Reuben Fulcher's claim, Testimony of claimant Daniel Bell, Testimony of claimant Daniel B. Dickinson, Testimony of claimant William H. Dickinson, Testimony of claimant David W. Bell, Testimony of claimant David S. Quinn Sr., and Testimony of claimant Jesse Fulcher—all in Disallowed Claims (Carteret County), SCC.

29. Judgment of William H. Dickinson (Carteret County), Disallowed Claims, SCC.

30. Judgment of David S. Quinn Sr. (Carteret County), Disallowed Claims, SCC.

31. John A. Hedrick to Benjamin S. Hedrick, April 9, 1863, in Browning and Smith, *Letters*, 106; Col. J. Jourdan to J. J. Peck, November 25, 1863, and Jourdan, General Order No. 26, n.d. [December 1863], both in pt. II, Letters Sent, October 1863–March 1864, District and Subdistrict of Beaufort, RG 393. For an examination of standard procedures under U.S. Army occupation policy, see Birtle, *U.S. Army Counterinsurgency*.

32. John A. Hedrick to Benjamin S. Hedrick, November 29, 1863, March 13, 1864, in Browning and Smith, *Letters*, 170, 191; Rumley Diary, November 21, 1863, October [n.d.], 1862, in Browning, *Southern Mind*, 97, 44.

33. Capt. C. A. Lynn to Edward Stanly, March 13, 1863, box 2, pt. I, Letters Received, Department of North Carolina, RG 393; C. C. Graves to "Union Paymaster at Fort Monroe, VA," March 11, 1864, First North Carolina Infantry Regimental Descriptive Books, vol. 3, BRVUS; C. H. Foster to J. B. Frye, January 5, 1864, Second North Carolina Infantry Regimental Letter, Endorsement and Order Book, BRVUS.

34. H. W. Barrow to Christian Thomas Pfohl, February 17, 1864, Pfohl Papers, SHC. For more on the capture and execution, see Rumley Diary, March 2, 1864, in Browning, *Southern Mind*, 127; Honey, "War within the Confederacy," 76–77; Collins, "War Crime or Justice?"; and Hawkins, *Assassination of Loyal Citizens*. For the effect of the massacre on the victims' families, see Gordon, "'In Time of War.'"

35. C. H. Foster to B. B. Foster, March 13, 1864, Second North Carolina Infantry Regimental Letter, Endorsement and Order Book, BRVUS; Innis N. Palmer to Edwin M. Stanton, May 15, 1864, *OR* 26(2):809.

36. J. M. McChesney to Maj. R. S. Davis, April 6, 1864, First North Carolina Infantry, Regimental Descriptive Books, vol. 3, BRVUS; Innis N. Palmer to E. B. French, November 9, 1864, pt. II, Letters Sent, December 1864–October 1865, District of New Bern, Entry 1660, Polynomous Succession of Commands, RG 393.

37. Rumley Diary, April 24, 1864, in Browning, *Southern Mind*, 132; George W. Jones to Walter S. Poor, April 15, 1864, George W. Jones Service File, Second North Carolina Infantry, CSR.

38. Harris, "*In the Country of the Enemy*," 80–81 (Zenas Haines). For scholars' views of emancipation as a war measure, see Ash, *When the Yankees Came*, 153; Gerteis, *From Contraband to Freedman*, 32; and Woodward, "Equality: The Deferred Commitment."

39. Guion Griffis Johnson, *Ante-Bellum North Carolina*, 602 (James West Bryan); Powell, *Dictionary of North Carolina Biography*, 1:255; Edward Stanly to Edwin Stanton, June 12, 1862, *OR* 9:400–401.

40. Watson, *History of New Bern*, 385; Delaney, "Charles Henry Foster and the Unionists"; John A. Hedrick to Benjamin S. Hedrick, December 16, 21, 25, 1862, in Browning and Smith, *Letters*, 64–69.

41. John A. Hedrick to Benjamin S. Hedrick, January 10, 1863, in Browning and Smith, *Letters*, 79–80; Stanly, *Military Governor among Abolitionists*, 46–47; Harris, *With Charity for All*, 70; Brown, *Edward Stanly*, 256.

42. Rumley Diary, May [n.d.], 1862, January 1, 1863, in Browning, *Southern Mind*, 37, 52; Thornton, "New Bern, North Carolina, 1862–1865" (unpublished typescript), 30, NCC; John A. Hedrick to Benjamin S. Hedrick, July 29, 1862, in Browning and Smith, *Letters*, 19.

43. Charles Henry Foster to John G. Foster, November 19, 1862, box 1, and William B. Fowle Jr., to Southard Hoffman, January 16, 1863, box 2, pt. I, Letters Received, Department of North Carolina, RG 393.

44. Rumley Diary, May 30, June 1, March 25, 1863, in Browning, *Southern Mind*, 71, 59; John A. Hedrick to Benjamin S. Hedrick, July 26, June 19, May 3, 1863, in Browning and Smith, *Letters*, 140, 130, 115; Charles Duren to his mother and father, June 16, 1862, Duren Papers, EU.

45. James, *Annual Report*, 44, 9, 20. Jesse William Page identified in Barden, *Letters to the Home Circle*, 105.

46. Henry Clapp to his mother, November 14, 1862, in Barden, *Letters to the Home Circle*, 22; Edward Bartlett to "Dear Martha," November 15, 1862, January 30, 1863, Bartlett Papers, MHS. For more on the experience of poor whites during Union occupation, see Ash, "Poor Whites in the Occupied South."

47. Cleveland Diary, November 28, 1864, SHC; Fen, "Notes on the Education of Negroes," 26n11; Joseph Barlow to Ellen Barlow, June 18, 1865, Barlow Papers, USAMHI.

48. Thomas J. Carey Diary, April 11, 1865, SHC; Elizabeth Oakes Smith to Mr. & Mrs. Spence, June 30, 1874, Oaksmith Papers, SHC.

49. Solon A. Carter to Col. John H. Holman, June 22, 1865, pt. II, Letters Sent,

December 1864–October 1865, District of New Bern, Entry 1660, Polynomous Succession of Commands, RG 393.

50. Dehlia Mabrey Diary, May 12, 1865, Crisp Papers, ECU.

51. Elijah S. Smith to Benjamin F. Butler, February 15, 1869, in Padgett, "Reconstruction Letters from North Carolina," 71; Oscar Eastmond to Lt. Col. J. A. Campbell, June 10, 1865, 1st North Carolina Infantry, Regimental and Endorsement Book, BRVUS; Denny, *Wearing the Blue*, 227.

52. Craven County is more difficult to use because most of its merchants fled the region upon the Union army's approach, and few records exist to prove which merchants returned during occupation and which did not.

53. E. A. Harkness to Southard Hoffman, March 5, 1863, box 2, pt. I, Letters Received; B. A. Ensley to J. Jourdan, January 28, 1864, pt. II, Letters Sent, October 1863–March 1864, District and Subdistrict of Beaufort, Entry 940, Department of North Carolina, RG 393; North Carolina, vol. 5, p. 176-E, R. G. Dun and Co. Collection, HBS.

54. North Carolina, vol. 5, pp. 176-A, 185, R. G. Dun and Co. Collection, HBS.

55. Deposition of John B. Wolf, in *John B. Wolf v. United States* (case file no. 12389), RG 123; North Carolina, vol. 5, p. 165, R. G. Dun and Co. Collection, HBS; U.S. Census, 1860, Carteret County, Population Schedule, Manuscript Census Returns, NA.

56. Manarin and Jordan, *North Carolina Troops*, 1:116, 128, 4:174; North Carolina, vol. 5, pp. 176-R, 176-Q, R. G. Dun and Co. Collection, HBS.

57. John A. Hedrick to Benjamin S. Hedrick, September 8, 1862, in Browning and Smith, *Letters*, 34; *NBWP*, September 20, 1862; North Carolina, vol. 5, pp. 176-L, 176-D, R. G. Dun and Co. Collection, HBS; Deposition of Lewis McCain, Deposition of J. T. Dennis, and Deposition of Josiah L. Bell — all in *David W. Morton v. United States* (case file no. 6935), RG 123. Joel Henry Davis Sr. died in 1868, but his son, Joel Henry Jr., who had left the Confederate service and taken the oath of allegiance in April 1862, continued to operate the business with Henry Rieger. The stigma of Unionism clung to them both after the war.

58. Journal of James Monroe Hollowell, April 25, 1862, *SOR* 1:602–4; Tom Stevenson to Hannah, October 9, 1862, Walcott Family Papers II, MHS; Daniel R. Goodloe to B. S. Hedrick, April 24, 1867, Hedrick Papers, DU.

59. Manarin and Jordan, *North Carolina Troops*, 1:115; North Carolina, vol. 5, p. 176-Z, R. G. Dun and Co. Collection, HBS.

60. North Carolina, vol. 5, p. 176-Z 2, R. G. Dun and Co. Collection, HBS; William B. Fowle Jr. to Southard Hoffman, January 16, 1863, pt. I, Letters Received, box 2, Department of North Carolina, RG 393; Manarin and Jordan, *North Carolina Troops*, 1:134; U.S. Census, 1860, 1870, Carteret County, Population Schedules, Manuscript Census Returns, NA.

61. Cleveland Diary, February 9, 1865, SHC; "Statement of Amanda Gaskill, thos. Rudderforth & B. F. Bloodgood in relation to Force on Adams Creek," October 21,

1862, box 1, pt. I, Letters Received, Department of North Carolina, RG 393; North Carolina, vol. 5, pp. 164, 176-T, R. G. Dun and Co. Collection, HBS.

CONCLUSION

1. Alexander, *North Carolina Faces the Freedmen*, 34 (1st quotation); Reid, *After the War*, 33–34.

2. Campbell, *When Sherman Marched North*, 69; Cobb, *Away Down South*, 59–60. For another interpretation of how a region's Confederate identity became much stronger after the war, see Marshall, "'A Strange Conclusion to a Triumphant War.'" While not entirely analogous, for Kentucky never seceded, Marshall argues that pro-Confederate sentiment became strongest in Kentucky after Lee's surrender at Appomattox.

3. Branch, "Fort Macon as a Shelter for Buffaloes," ⟨http://www.clis.com/friends/bufffaloes.htm⟩ (December 8, 2005).

4. The best comprehensive work on Reconstruction and its failures remains Foner, *Reconstruction*. For a work that conveys how whites used racial violence to accomplish their conservative political ends during Reconstruction, see Rable, *But There Was No Peace*. For works that discuss how sectional reconciliation and postwar politics shifted the focus away from African American civil rights, see Heather Cox Richardson, *Death of Reconstruction*; Blight, *Race and Reunion*; and Silber, *The Romance of Reunion*.

BIBLIOGRAPHY

PRIMARY SOURCES

Manuscripts
Atlanta, Georgia
    Special Collections and Archives, Robert W. Woodruff Library,
        Emory University
        Charles M. Duren Papers
        Edwin R. Fish Letters (microfilm)
        Nathan G. Newton Papers
        Hale Wesson Papers
Beverly, Massachusetts
    Beverly Historical Society and Museum
        Benjamin H. Day Journal, Civil War Collection
Boston, Massachusetts
    Massachusetts Historical Society
        Edward J. Bartlett Papers
        John E. Bassett Diary (microfilm)
        George H. Baxter Letters (microfilm)
        Charles E. Briggs Letters
        Charles Codman Papers
        Ebenezer Hunt Papers
        Oliver W. Peabody Papers
        Samuel Storrow Civil War Letters (microfilm)
        Walcott Family Papers II
        Henry F. Wellington Papers (typescript) (microfilm)
Cambridge, Massachusetts
    Baker Library, Harvard University
        R. G. Dun and Company Collection
Carlisle, Pennsylvania
    U.S. Army Military History Institute
        Joseph Barlow Papers
        Civil War Miscellany Collection
            Alfred Holcomb Papers

Humiston Family Collection

Dexter B. Ladd Papers

Horatio Newhall Papers

Civil War Times Illustrated Collection

Cartwright Family Papers

Nelson Chapin Papers

Lowry Hinch Collection

Jacob Roberts Correspondence

George W. Kimball Papers

William W. Lind Papers

Norwich Civil War Round Table

William P. Amerman Papers

James O. Brown and William A. Musson Papers

John D. Timmerman Papers

Chapel Hill, North Carolina

North Carolina Collection, Louis Round Wilson Library, University of North Carolina

Newspaper Clippings File

Proceedings of the Annual Meeting of the Stockholders of the Atlantic and North Carolina Railroad

Southern Historical Collection, Louis Round Wilson Library, University of North Carolina

William Alexander Letters

Edmund Ruffin Beckwith Papers

Thomas J. Carey Diary

Edmund J. Cleveland Diary

Herbert A. Cooley Papers

J. M. Drennan Diaries

Federal Soldiers Letters

James E. Gifford Papers

John Richter Jones Papers

James Manney Papers

Alfred H. Martine Papers

New Bern Occupation Papers

Appleton Oaksmith Papers

Christian Thomas Pfohl Papers (microfilm)

Charles B. Quick Correspondence

Benjamin Franklin Royal Papers

Jeremiah Stetson Papers

Herbert Eugene Valentine Papers

Durham, North Carolina

Rare Book, Manuscript and Special Collections Library, Duke University

Alfred Otis Chamberlin Papers

David Lucius Craft Papers
Benjamin Sherwood Hedrick Papers
Edward W. Kinsley Papers
David P. Reynolds Papers
George A. Root Papers
Nellie F. Stearns Papers
John Rogers Vinson Papers
Josiah Wood Papers
Greenville, North Carolina
Special Collections, J. Y. Joyner Library, East Carolina University
John Herritage Bryan Papers
Lucy Cherry Crisp Papers
Agnes Paton Foy Memoir
Charles F. Glover Papers
Grimes-Bryan Papers
Clarissa Phelps Hanks Papers
William Howard Hooker Collection
George H. S. Driver Papers
William L. Horner Collection
Frederick C. Douglass Papers
New Bern Historical Society Papers
Charles Tournier Diary
Hartford, Connecticut
Connecticut Historical Society
Civil War Papers
William L. Norton Papers
Houston, Texas
Woodson Research Center, Fondren Library, Rice University
Samuel Storrow Civil War Journals, 1863–65
Morehead City, North Carolina
Carteret County Historical Society
Fort Macon Archival Box, vol. 42
Hammond General Hospital Box
New Orleans, Louisiana
Amistad Research Center, Tulane University
American Missionary Association Collection
Raleigh, North Carolina
North Carolina State Archives, North Carolina Division of Archives and History
Adams and Partin Family Papers
Carteret County, Minutes of the Superior Court, 1851–61
Carteret County Civil Action Papers, 1858–64
Carteret County Court Minutes, Court of Pleas and Quarters, 1858–68
Civil War Collection, Military Records

Henry T. Clark, Governors Papers

L. Polk Denmark Collection

John W. Ellis, Governors Papers

Alida F. Fales Papers

Pettigrew Papers

Levi Woodbury Pigott Collection

David Settle Reid Papers

F. C. Salisbury Collection

Simpson-Biddle Papers

Charles Henry Tubbs Letters

Herbert Eugene Valentine Collection, reel 1, Miscellaneous Military Records
(microfilm)

John D. Whitford Collection

San Marino, California

Henry E. Huntington Library

James Edward Glazier Papers

Simsbury, Connecticut

Simsbury Historical Society

Oliver Case Letters, Civil War Collection

Washington, D.C.

Manuscripts Division, Library of Congress

Levi Hayden Diary

George O. Jewett Papers

Daniel Read Larned Papers

National Archives

Compiled Service Records of Volunteer Union Soldiers, Record Group 94

Federal Pension Application Files, Records of the Veterans Administration,
Record Group 15

Manuscript Census Returns, Eighth Census of the United States, 1860,
Population and Slave Schedules, National Archives Microfilm Series
M-653

Records of the Accounting Officers of the Department of the Treasury, Settled
Case Files for Claims Approved by the Southern Claims Commission,
1871–80, Record Group 217

Records of the Adjutant General's Office, Book Records of Volunteer Union
Soldiers Organizations, Record Group 94

Records of the Assistant Commissioner for the State of North Carolina,
Bureau of Refugees, Freedmen, and Abandoned Lands, 1865–70, Record
Group 105 (microfilm, M843)

Records of the Southern Claims Commission, 1871–80, Disallowed Claims,
Record Group 233

Records of the U.S. Army Continental Commands, Department of North
Carolina, Record Group 393

Records of the U.S. Court of Claims, Record Group 123
Worcester, Massachusetts
   American Antiquarian Society
      Civil War Collection
      Alonzo Cushman Letters, Octavo Volume
      Horace James Correspondence
      Henry White Diary
      William Augustus Willoughby Papers (typescript)
   Worcester Historical Museum
      James M. Drennan Papers

Unpublished Typescripts

Cleveland, Edmund J. "The Late Campaigns in North Carolina as Seen through the Eyes of a New Jersey soldier." Southern Historical Collection, University of North Carolina at Chapel Hill.

Davis, Maurice. "History of the Hammock House and Related Trivia." North Carolina Collection, University of North Carolina at Chapel Hill.

Spear, John M. "Army Life in the Twenty-fourth Regiment, Massachusetts Volunteer Infantry, Dec. 1861 to Dec. 1864, 1892." Massachusetts Historical Society, Boston.

Thornton, Mary Lindsey. "New Bern, North Carolina, 1862–1865: A Southern Town under Federal Occupation." North Carolina Collection, University of North Carolina at Chapel Hill.

Newspapers

American Missionary
Beaufort News
The Congregationalist (Boston)
Greensboro Daily News
The Liberator (Boston)
The Look Out (Beaufort)

National Era (Washington, D.C.)
New Bern Daily Progress
New Bern Weekly Progress
New York Times
Old North State (Beaufort)
Rocky Mount Telegram

Published Primary Documents

Agriculture of the United States in 1860: Compiled from the Original Returns of the Eighth Census, under the Direction of the Secretary of the Interior, by Joseph C. G. Kennedy, Superintendent of Census. Washington, D.C.: Government Printing Office, 1864.

Allen, George. *Forty-six Months with the Fourth R.I. Volunteers in the War of 1861 to 1865: Comprising a History of the Marches, Battles, and Camp Life, Compiled from Journals Kept While on Duty in the Field and Camp, by Corp. Geo. H. Allen, of Company B.* Providence, R.I.: J. A. and R. A. Reid, Printers, 1887.

Andrews, William L., ed. *North Carolina Slave Narratives: The Lives of Moses Roper, Lunsford Lane, Moses Grandy and Thomas H. Jones.* Chapel Hill: University of North Carolina Press, 2003.

Andrews, Sidney. *The South since the War; as Shown by Fourteen Weeks of Travel and Observation in Georgia and the Carolinas*. 1866. Reprint, Boston: Houghton-Mifflin, 1971.

Asbury, Francis. *The Journal of the Rev. Francis Asbury, Bishop of the Methodist Episcopal Church from August 7, 1771 to December 7, 1815*. 3 vols. New York: N. Bangs and T. Mason, 1821.

Barden, John R., ed. *Letters to the Home Circle: The North Carolina Service of Pvt. Henry A. Clapp, Company F, Forty-fourth Massachusetts Volunteer Militia, 1862–1863*. Raleigh: Division of Archives and History, North Carolina Department of Cultural Resources, 1998.

Benjamin, W. S. *Great Epidemic in New Berne and Vicinity, September and October, 1864*. New Berne, N.C.: George Mills Joy, 1865.

Berlin, Ira, Barbara J. Fields, Thavolia Glymph, Joseph P. Reidy, and Leslie S. Rowland, eds. *Freedom: A Documentary History of Emancipation: Series I, The Destruction of Slavery*. Cambridge: Cambridge University Press, 1985.

———. *Freedom: A Documentary History of Emancipation, 1861–1867: Series II, The Black Military Experience*. Cambridge: Cambridge University Press, 1982.

Browning, Judkin. *The Southern Mind under Union Rule: The Diary of James Rumley, Beaufort, North Carolina, 1862–1865*. Gainesville: University Press of Florida, 2009.

Browning, Judkin, and Michael Thomas Smith, eds. *Letters from a North Carolina Unionist: The Civil War Letters of John A. Hedrick, 1862–1865*. Raleigh: North Carolina Division of Archives and History, 2001.

Burlingame, John K. *History of the Fifth Regiment of Rhode Island Heavy Artillery*. Providence: Snow and Farnham, 1892.

Butler, Lindley S., ed. *The Papers of David Settle Reid, Vol. 1, 1829–1852*. Raleigh: North Carolina Historical Publications, 1993.

Chase, Philip S. "Service with Battery F, First Rhode Island Light Artillery in North Carolina." *Soldiers and Sailors Historical Society of Rhode Island, Personal Narratives, 3rd Series, No. 7*. Providence: Snow and Farnham, 1884.

Cheney, John L., Jr., ed. *North Carolina Government, 1585–1979: A Narrative and Statistical History*. Raleigh: North Carolina Department of the Secretary of State, 1981.

Clingman, T. L. "North Carolina — Her Wealth, Resources and History." *DeBow's Review* 25 (December 1858): 664–79.

Colyer, Vincent. *Report of the Services Rendered by the Freed People to the United States Army, in North Carolina, in the Spring of 1862, after the Battle of Newbern*. New York: V. Colyer, 1864.

Crabtree, Beth G., and James W. Patton, eds. *Journal of a Secesh Lady: The Diary of Catherine Ann Devereux Edmondston, 1860–1866*. Raleigh: Division of Archives and History, 1979.

Denny, J. Waldo. *Wearing the Blue in the Twenty-fifth Massachusetts Volunteer Infantry, with Burnside's Coast Division, 18th Army Corps, and Army of the James*. Worcester, Mass.: Putnam and Davis, Publishers, 1879.

Derby, W. P. *Bearing Arms in the Twenty-seventh Regiment of Massachusetts Volunteers Infantry during the Civil War, 1861–1865*. Boston: Wright and Potter, 1883.

Drake, J. Madison. *The History of the Ninth New Jersey Veteran Vols.: A Record of Its Service from Sept. 13th, 1861, to July 12th, 1865*. Elizabeth, N.J.: Journal Printing House, 1889.

Draper, William Franklin. *Recollections of a Varied Career*. Boston: Little, Brown, 1908.

Duncan, Russell, ed. *Blue-eyed Child of Fortune: The Civil War Letters of Colonel Robert Gould Shaw*. Athens: University of Georgia Press, 1992.

Emerson, George B. *A Report on the Trees and Shrubs Growing Naturally in the Forests of Massachusetts*. 1846. 3rd ed. Boston: Little, Brown, 1878.

Emmerton, James A. *A Record of the Twenty-third Regiment, Massachusetts Volunteer Infantry in the War of the Rebellion, 1861–1865*. Boston: William Ware, 1886.

Fifth Census or Enumeration of the Inhabitants of the United States, 1830. Washington, D.C.: Duff Green, 1832; reprint, New York: Norman Ross Publishing, 1990.

Hamilton, J. G. de Roulhac, ed. *The Papers of Thomas Ruffin, Volume III*. Raleigh: Edwards and Broughton Printing Co., 1920.

Harris, William. C., ed. *"In the Country of the Enemy": The Civil War Reports of a Massachusetts Corporal*. Gainesville: University Press of Florida, 1999.

Hauptman, Laurence M., ed. *A Seneca Indian in the Union Army: The Civil War Letters of Sergeant Isaac Newton Parker, 1861–1865*. Shippensburg, Pa.: Burd Street Press, 1995.

Hawkins, Rush Christopher. *Account of the Assassination of Loyal Citizens of North Carolina, for Having Served in the Union Army, Which Took Place at Kingston in the Months of February and March, 1864*. New York: J. H. Folan, 1897.

Hewett, Janet B., et al., eds. *Supplement to the Official Records of the Union and Confederate Armies*. 100 vols. Wilmington, N.C.: Broadfoot, 1994–99.

Hubbard, Charles Eustis. *The Campaign of the Forty-fifth Regiment, Massachusetts Volunteer Militia: "The Cadet Regiment."* Boston: J. S. Adams, 1882.

Hurmence, Belinda, ed. *My Folks Don't Want Me to Talk about Slavery: Twenty-one Oral Histories of Former North Carolina Slaves*. Winston-Salem: Blair, 1984.

James, Horace. *Annual Report of the Superintendent of Negro Affairs in North Carolina, 1864; With an Appendix Containing the History and Management of Freedmen in This Department up to June 1st 1865*. Boston: W. F. Brown, 1865.

Johnson, Michael P., ed. *Abraham Lincoln, Slavery, and the Civil War: Selected Writings and Speeches*. Boston: Bedford, St. Martin's Press, 2001.

Johnston, Frontis W., and Joe A. Mobley, eds. *The Papers of Zebulon Baird Vance*. 2 vols. Raleigh: North Carolina Division of Archives and History, 1963–.

Keith, Alice Barnwell, ed. *John Gray Blount Papers*. 4 vols. Raleigh: State Department of Archives and History, 1952–1982.

Kirwan, Thomas. *Memorial History of the Seventeenth Regiment, Massachusetts Volunteer Infantry (Old and New Organizations) in the Civil War from 1861–1865*. Edited and completed by Henry Splaine. Salem, Mass.: Salem Press Co., 1911.

Lind, Henry C., ed. *The Long Road for Home: The Civil War Experiences of Four Farmboy Soldiers of the Twenty-seventh Massachusetts Regiment of Volunteer Infantry as Told by Their Personal Correspondence, 1861–1864*. Rutherford, N.J.: Fairleigh Dickinson University Press, 1992.

Manarin, Louis H., and Weymouth T. Jordan Jr., comps. *North Carolina Troops, 1861–1865: A Roster*. 15 vols. Raleigh: Division of Archives and History, Department of Cultural Resources, 1966–.

Mann, Albert W. *History of the Forty-fifth Regiment, Massachusetts Volunteer Militia*. Boston: W. Spooner, 1908.

Manufactures of the United States in 1860. Washington, D.C.: Government Printing Office, 1865; reprint, New York: Norman Ross Publishing, 1990.

Massachusetts, Adjutant General's Office. *Massachusetts Soldiers, Sailors, and Marines in the Civil War*. 8 vols. Norwood, Mass.: Norwood Press, 1931–35.

"Order of Exercises at the Installation of Rev. Horace James as Pastor of the Old South Church, Worcester, Thursday, February 3d, 1853" (broadside). Worcester, Mass.: C. B. Webb, Printer, Aegis Office, 1853.

Osborne, Frederick. *Private Osborne, Massachusetts 23rd Volunteers: Burnside Expedition, Roanoke Island, Second Front against Richmond*. Edited by Frank B. Marcotte. Jefferson, N.C.: McFarland, 1999.

Padgett, James A., ed. "Reconstruction Letters from North Carolina, Part 10: Letters to Benjamin Franklin Butler." *North Carolina Historical Review* 20 (April 1943): 46–71.

Parker, Freddie L., ed. *Stealing a Little Freedom: Advertisements for Slave Runaways in North Carolina, 1791–1840*. New York: Garland Publishing, 1994.

Population of the United States in 1860: Compiled from the Original Returns of the Eighth Census, under the Direction of the Secretary of the Interior, by Joseph C. G. Kennedy. Washington, D.C.: Government Printing Office, 1864; reprint, New York: Norman Ross Publishing, 1990.

Priest, John Michael, ed. *From New Bern to Fredericksburg: Captain James Wren's Diary, B Company, 48th Pennsylvania Volunteers, February 20, 1862–December 17, 1862*. Shippensburg, Pa.: White Mane Publishing Co., 1990.

Putnam, Samuel H. *The Story of Company A, Twenty-fifth Regiment, Massachusetts, Volumes on the War of the Rebellion*. Worcester: Putnam, Davis and Co., 1886.

Raper, Horace W., and Thornton W. Mitchell, eds. *The Papers of William Woods Holden, 1841–1868*. 2 vols. Raleigh: Division of Archives and History, Department of Cultural Resources, 2001.

Rawick, George P. *The American Slave: A Composite Autobiography; Volume 14, North Carolina Narratives, Part I*. Westport, Conn.: Greenwood Publishing Co., 1977.

Reid, Whitelaw. *After the War: A Tour of the Southern States, 1865–1866*. Edited by C. Vann Woodward. New York: Harper and Row, 1965.

Seventh Census of the United States, 1850. Washington, D.C.: Robert Armstrong, 1853; reprint, New York: Norman Ross Publishing, 1990.

Silber, Nina, and Mary Beth Sievers, eds. *Yankee Correspondence: Civil War Letters between New England Soldiers and the Home Front*. Charlottesville: University of Virginia Press, 1996.

Singleton, William Henry. *Recollections of My Slavery Days*. Edited and annotated by Katherine Mellen Charron and David S. Cecelski. Raleigh: Division of Archives and History, North Carolina Department of Cultural Resources, 1999.

Sixth Census or Enumeration of the Inhabitants of the United States, as Corrected at the Department of State, in 1840. Washington, D.C.: Blair and Rives, 1841; reprint, New York: Norman Ross Publishing, 1990.

Stanly, Edward A. *Military Governor among Abolitionists: A Letter from Edward Stanly to Charles Sumner*. New York: N.p., 1865.

Thorpe, Sheldon B. *The History of the Fifteenth Connecticut Volunteers in the War for the Defense of the Union, 1861–1865*. New Haven, Conn.: Price, Lee and Adkins Co., 1893.

Tolbert, Noble J., ed. *The Papers of John W. Ellis, Vol. 2*. Raleigh: State Department of Archives and History, 1964.

Underwood, George C. *History of the Twenty-sixth Regiment of the North Carolina Troops in the Great War, 1861–1865*. Goldsboro. N.C.: Nash Brothers, Book and Job Printers, n.d.; reprint, Wendell, N.C.: Broadfoot's Bookmark, 1978.

U.S. War Department. *The War of the Rebellion: A Compilation of the Official Records of the Union and Confederate Armies*. 128 vols. Washington, D.C.: Government Printing Office, 1880–1901.

Valentine, Herbert E. *Story of Co. F., 23d Massachusetts Volunteers in the War for the Union, 1861–1865*. Boston: W. B. Clarke, 1896.

Walcott, Charles F. *History of the Twenty-first Regiment, Massachusetts Volunteers, in the War for the Preservation of the Union, 1861–1865*. Boston: Houghton, Mifflin, and Co., 1882.

Wyeth, John J. *Leaves from a Diary, Written While Serving in Co. A, 44 Massachusetts from September, 1862 to June, 1863*. Boston: L. F. Lawrence, 1878.

Yearns, W. Buck, and John G. Barrett, eds. *North Carolina Civil War Documentary*. Chapel Hill: University of North Carolina Press, 1980.

SECONDARY SOURCES

Books

Alexander, Roberta Sue. *North Carolina Faces the Freedmen: Race Relations during Presidential Reconstruction, 1865–67*. Durham: Duke University Press, 1985.

Anderson, James D. *The Education of Blacks in the South, 1860–1935*. Chapel Hill: University of North Carolina Press, 1988.

Ash, Stephen V. *When the Yankees Came: Conflict and Chaos in the Occupied South, 1861–1865*. Chapel Hill: University of North Carolina Press, 1995.

Ayers, Edward L. *Vengeance and Justice: Crime and Punishment in the 19th-Century American South*. New York: Oxford University Press, 1984.

Barrett, John G. *Civil War in North Carolina*. Chapel Hill: University of North Carolina Press, 1963.

Baynes, John. *Morale: A Study of Men and Courage*. New York: Frederick A. Praeger, 1967.

Beard, Augustus Field. *A Crusade of Brotherhood: A History of the American Missionary Association*. New York: AMS Press, 1972.

Beringer, Richard E., Herman Hattaway, Archer Jones, and William N. Still Jr. *Why the South Lost the Civil War*. Athens: University of Georgia Press, 1986.

Berlin, Ira. *Slaves No More: Three Essays on Emancipation and the Civil War*. Cambridge: Cambridge University Press, 1992.

Birtle, Andrew J. *U.S. Army Counterinsurgency and Contingency Operations Doctrine, 1860–1941*. Washington, D.C.: U.S. Army Center for Military History, 1998.

Blair, William A. *Virginia's Private War: Feeding Body and Soul in the Confederacy, 1861–1865*. New York: Oxford University Press, 1998.

Blassingame, John W. *The Slave Community: Plantation Life in the Antebellum South*. Rev. ed. New York: Oxford University Press, 1979.

Blight, David W. *Race and Reunion: The Civil War in American Memory*. Cambridge: Belknap Press of Harvard University Press, 2001.

Bolton-Valencius, Conevery. *The Health of the Country: How American Settlers Understood Themselves and Their Land*. New York: Basic Books, 2003.

Bowen, John. *Adventuring along the Southeast Coast: The Sierra Club Guide to the Low Country, Beaches, and Barrier Islands of North Carolina, South Carolina, and Georgia*. San Francisco: Sierra Club Books, 1993.

Branch, Paul, Jr. *Siege of Fort Macon*. Morehead City, N.C.: Herald Printing Co., 1982.

Brown, Norman D. *Edward Stanly: Whiggery's Tarheel "Conqueror."* University, Ala.: University of Alabama Press, 1974.

Butchart, Ronald E. *Northern Schools, Southern Blacks, and Reconstruction: Freedmen's Education, 1862–1875*. Westport, Conn.: Greenwood Press, 1980.

Campbell, Jacqueline Glass. *When Sherman Marched North from the Sea: Resistance on the Confederate Home Front*. Chapel Hill: University of North Carolina Press, 2003.

Capers, Gerald M. *Occupied City: New Orleans under the Federals, 1862–1865*. Lexington: University of Kentucky Press, 1965.

Cashin, Joan E., ed. *The War Was You and Me: Civilians in the American Civil War*. Princeton, N.J.: Princeton University Press, 2002.

Cecelski, David S. *The Waterman's Song: Slavery and Freedom in Maritime North Carolina*. Chapel Hill: University of North Carolina Press, 2001.

Cecil-Fronsman, Bill. *Common Whites: Class and Culture in Antebellum North Carolina*. Lexington: University Press of Kentucky, 1992.

Click, Patricia C. *Time Full of Trial: The Roanoke Island Freedmen's Colony, 1862–1867*. Chapel Hill: University of North Carolina Press, 2001.

Clinton, Catherine, and Nina Silber, eds. *Divided Houses: Gender and the Civil War*. New York: Oxford University Press, 1992.

Cobb, James C. *Away Down South: A History of Southern Identity*. New York: Oxford University Press, 2005.

Cornelius, Janet Duitsman. *"When I Can Read My Title Clear": Literacy, Slavery and Religion in the Antebellum South*. Columbia: University of South Carolina Press, 1991.

Cornish, Dudley T. *The Sable Arm: Negro Troops in the Union Army, 1861–1865*. New York: W. W. Norton, 1966.

Crawford, Martin. *Ashe County's Civil War: Community and Society in the Appalachian South*. Charlottesville: University of Virginia Press, 2001.

Crofts, Daniel. *Reluctant Confederates: Upper South Unionists in the Secession Crisis*. Chapel Hill: University of North Carolina Press, 1989.

Crow, Jeffrey J., and Larry E. Tise, eds. *The Southern Experience in the American Revolution*. Chapel Hill: University of North Carolina Press, 1978.

Current, Richard Nelson. *Lincoln's Loyalists: Union Soldiers from the Confederacy*. Boston: Northeastern University Press, 1992.

Davis, Archie K. *Boy Colonel of the Confederacy: The Life and Times of Henry King Burgwyn, Jr*. Chapel Hill: University of North Carolina Press, 1985.

Davis, Pat Dula, and Kathleen Hill Hamilton. *The Heritage of Carteret County, North Carolina, Vol. 1, to 1982*. Beaufort: Carteret Historical Research Association, 1982.

Degler, Carl N. *The Other South: Southern Dissenters in the Nineteenth Century*. New York: Harper and Row, 1974.

Doyle, Don. *Faulkner's County: The Historical Roots of Yoknapatawpha*. Chapel Hill: University of North Carolina Press, 2001.

Durrill, Wayne K. *War of Another Kind: A Southern Community in the Great Rebellion*. New York: Oxford University Press, 1990.

Dyer, Thomas G. *Secret Yankees: The Union Circle in Confederate Atlanta*. Baltimore: Johns Hopkins University Press, 1999.

Edelstein, David M. *Occupational Hazards: Success and Failure in Military Occupation*. Ithaca, N.Y.: Cornell University Press, 2008.

Escott, Paul D. *After Secession: Jefferson Davis and the Failure of Confederate Nationalism*. Baton Rouge: Louisiana State University Press, 1978.

———. *Slavery Remembered: A Record of Twentieth-Century Slave Narratives*. Chapel Hill: University of North Carolina Press, 1979.

Faust, Drew Gilpin. *The Creation of Confederate Nationalism: Ideology and Identity in the Confederate South*. Baton Rouge: Louisiana State University Press, 1988.

Fellman, Michael. *Citizen Sherman: A Life of William Tecumseh Sherman*. New York: Random House, 1995.

Fischer, David Hackett. *Washington's Crossing*. New York: Oxford University Press, 2004.

Fischer, Kirsten. *Suspect Relations: Sex, Race, and Resistance in Colonial North Carolina*. Ithaca, N.Y.: Cornell University Press, 2002.

Fletcher, George P. *Loyalty: An Essay on the Morality of Relationships.* New York: Oxford University Press, 1993.

Foner, Eric. *Free Soil, Free Labor, Free Men: The Ideology of the Republican Party before the Civil War.* New York: Oxford University Press, 1970.

———. *Reconstruction: America's Unfinished Revolution, 1863–1877.* New York: Harper and Row, 1988.

Fox-Genovese, Elizabeth. *Within the Plantation Household: Black and White Women of the Old South.* Chapel Hill: University of North Carolina Press, 1988.

Fredrickson, George M. *The Black Image in the White Mind: The Debate on Afro-American Character and Destiny, 1817–1914.* New York: Harper and Row., 1971.

Gallagher, Gary W. *The Confederate War.* Cambridge: Harvard University Press, 1997.

Genovese, Eugene D. *Roll, Jordan, Roll: The World the Slaves Made.* New York: Pantheon Books, 1972.

Gerteis, Louis S. *From Contraband to Freedman: Federal Policy toward Southern Blacks, 1861–1865.* Westport, Conn.: Greenwood Press, 1973.

Glatthaar, Joseph T. *Forged in Battle: The Civil War Alliance of Black Soldiers and White Officers.* New York: Macmillan, 1990.

———. *The March to the Sea and Beyond: Sherman's Troops in the Savannah and Carolinas Campaign.* Baton Rouge: Louisiana State University Press, 1985.

Grimsley, Mark. *The Hard Hand of War: Union Military Policy toward Southern Civilians, 1861–1865.* Cambridge: Cambridge University Press, 1995.

Groce, W. Todd. *Mountain Rebels: East Tennessee Confederates and the Civil War, 1860–1870.* Knoxville: University of Tennessee Press, 1999.

Hadden, Sally E. *Slave Patrols: Law and Violence in Virginia and the Carolinas.* Cambridge: Harvard University Press, 2001.

Hahn, Steven. *A Nation under Our Feet: Black Political Struggles in the Rural South, from Slavery to the Great Migration.* Cambridge, Massachusetts: Belknap Press of Harvard University Press, 2003.

Harding, Vincent. *There Is a River: The Black Struggle for Freedom in America.* New York: Harcourt Brace Jovanovich, 1981.

Harris, William C. *North Carolina and the Coming of the Civil War.* Raleigh: North Carolina Department of Cultural Resources, 1988.

———. *With Charity for All: Lincoln and the Restoration of the Union.* Lexington: University Press of Kentucky, 1997.

Heidler, David S., and Jeanne T. Heidler, eds. *Encyclopedia of the American Civil War: A Political, Social, and Military History.* 5 vols. Santa Barbara, Calif.: ABC-CLIO Press, 2000.

Hess, Earl J. *Lee's Tar Heels: The Pettigrew-Kirkland-MacRae Brigade.* Chapel Hill: University of North Carolina Press, 2002.

———. *The Union Soldier in Battle: Enduring the Ordeal of Combat.* Lawrence: University of Kansas Press, 1997.

Hill, Daniel Harvey. *History of North Carolina in the War between the States: Bethel to Sharpsburg.* Raleigh: Edwards and Broughton Printing Co., 1926.

Hoffman, Ronald, Thad W. Tate, and Peter J. Albert, eds. *An Uncivil War: The Southern Backcountry during the American Revolution*. Charlottesville: University of Virginia Press, 1985.

Holt, Sharon Ann. *Making Freedom Pay: North Carolina Freedpeople Working for Themselves, 1865–1900*. Athens: University of Georgia Press, 2000.

Inscoe, John C., and Robert C. Kenzer, eds. *Enemies of the Country: New Perspectives on Unionists in the Civil War South*. Athens: University of Georgia Press, 2001.

Inscoe, John C., and Gordon B. McKinney. *The Heart of Confederate Appalachia: Western North Carolina in the Civil War*. Chapel Hill: University of North Carolina Press, 1997.

Jeffrey, Thomas E. *State Parties and National Politics: North Carolina, 1815–1861*. Athens: University of Georgia Press, 1989.

Jenkins, Wilbert L. *Climbing Up to Glory: A Short History of African Americans during the Civil War and Reconstruction*. Wilmington, Del.: SR Books, 2002.

Johnson, Guion Griffis. *Ante-Bellum North Carolina: A Social History*. Chapel Hill: University of North Carolina Press, 1937.

Jones, Jacqueline. *Soldiers of Light and Love: Northern Teachers and Georgia Blacks, 1865–1873*. Athens: University of Georgia Press, 1980.

Jordan, Winthrop D. *The White Man's Burden: Historical Origins of Racism in the United States*. New York: Oxford University Press, 1974.

Joyner, Charles W. *Down by the Riverside: A South Carolina Slave Community*. Urbana: University of Illinois Press, 1984.

Kellett, Anthony. *Combat Motivation: The Behavior of Soldiers in Battle*. Boston: Kluwer-Nijhoff Pub., 1982.

Klingberg, Frank W. *The Southern Claims Commission*. Berkeley: University of California Press, 1955.

Kolchin, Peter. *American Slavery, 1619–1877*. Rev. ed. New York: Hill and Wang, 2003.

Kruman, Marc W. *Parties and Politics in North Carolina, 1836–1865*. Baton Rouge: Louisiana State University Press, 1983.

Leary, Helen M., and Maurice R. Stirewalt, eds. *North Carolina Research: Genealogy and Local History*. Raleigh: North Carolina Genealogical Society, 1980.

Linderman, Gerald F. *Embattled Courage: The Experience of Combat in the American Civil War*. New York: Free Press, 1987.

Litwack, Leon F. *Been in the Storm So Long: The Aftermath of Slavery*. New York: Knopf, 1979.

Lockley, Timothy. *Lines in the Sand: Race and Class in Lowcountry Georgia, 1750–1860*. Athens: University of Georgia Press, 2001.

Mackey, Robert. *The Uncivil War: Irregular Warfare in the Upper South, 1861–1865*. Norman: University of Oklahoma Press, 2004.

Mallison, Fred M. *The Civil War on the Outer Banks: A History of the Late Rebellion along the Coast of North Carolina from Carteret to Currituck*. Jefferson, N.C.: McFarland, 1998.

Manning, Chandra. *What This Cruel War Was Over: Soldiers, Slavery, and the Civil War*. New York: Knopf, 2007.

Maslowski, Peter. *Treason Must Be Made Odious: Military Occupation and Wartime Reconstruction in Nashville, Tennessee*. Millwood, N.Y.: KTO Press, 1978.

McCurry, Stephanie. *Masters of Small Worlds: Yeoman Households, Gender Relations, and the Political Culture of the Antebellum South Carolina Lowcountry*. New York: Oxford University Press, 1995.

McPherson, James M. *Battle Cry of Freedom: The Civil War Era*. New York: Oxford University Press, 1988.

————. *For Cause and Comrades: Why Men Fought in the Civil War*. New York: Oxford University Press, 1997.

Meekins, Alex Christopher. *Elizabeth City, North Carolina, and the Civil War: A History of Battle and Occupation*. Charleston, S.C.: History Press, 2007.

Mills, Gary B. *Southern Loyalists in the Civil War: The Southern Claims Commission, a Composite Directory of Case Files Created by the U.S. Commissioner of Claims, 1871–1880*. Baltimore: Genealogical Publishing Co., 1994.

Mitchell, Reid. *The Vacant Chair: The Northern Soldier Leaves Home*. New York: Oxford University Press, 1993.

Mobley, Joe A. *James City: A Black Community in North Carolina, 1863–1900*. Raleigh: North Carolina Division of Archives and History, 1981.

Morgan, Philip D. *Slave Counterpoint: Black Culture in the Eighteenth-Century Chesapeake and Lowcountry*. Chapel Hill: University of North Carolina, 1998.

Morrill, Dan L. *The Civil War in the Carolinas*. Charleston, S.C.: Nautical and Aviation Publishing Co. of America, 2002.

Moskos, Charles C. *The American Enlisted Man: The Rank and File in Today's Military*. New York: Russell Sage Foundation, 1970.

Myers, Barton E. *Executing Daniel Bright: Race, Loyalty, and Guerrilla Violence in a Coastal Carolina Community, 1861–1865*. Baton Rouge: Louisiana State University Press, 2009.

Neely, Mark E. *The Civil War and the Limits of Destruction*. Cambridge: Harvard University Press, 2007.

Nisbet, Richard E., and Dov Cohen. *Culture of Honor: The Psychology of Violence in the South*. Boulder, Colo.: Westview Press, 1996.

Nudelman, Franny. *John Brown's Body: Slavery, Violence, and the Culture of War*. Chapel Hill: University of North Carolina Press, 2004.

Olwell, Robert. *Masters, Slaves, and Subjects: The Culture of Power in South Carolina's Lowcountry, 1740–1790*. Ithaca, N.Y.: Cornell University Press, 1998.

Parker, Freddie L. *Running for Freedom: Slave Runaways in North Carolina, 1775–1840*. New York: Garland Publishing, 1993.

Pegg, Herbert D. *The Whig Party in North Carolina*. Chapel Hill: Colonial Press, 1968.

Powell, William S., ed. *Dictionary of North Carolina Biography*. 6 vols. Chapel Hill: University of North Carolina Press, 1979–96.

Rable, George C. *But There Was No Peace: The Role of Violence in the Politics of Reconstruction*. Athens: University of Georgia Press, 1984.

——. *Civil Wars: Women and the Crisis of Southern Nationalism*. Urbana: University of Illinois Press, 1989.

Rawick, George P. *From Sundown to Sunup: The Making of the Black Community*. Westport, Conn.: Greenwood Publishing Co., 1972.

Reid, Richard M. *Freedom for Themselves: North Carolina's Black Soldiers in the Civil War Era*. Chapel Hill: University of North Carolina Press, 2008.

Richardson, Heather Cox. *The Death of Reconstruction: Race, Labor, and Politics in the Post–Civil War North, 1865–1901*. Cambridge: Harvard University Press, 2001.

Richardson, Joe M. *Christian Reconstruction: The American Missionary Association and Southern Blacks, 1861–1890*. Athens: University of Georgia Press, 1986.

Roark, James L. *Masters without Slaves: Southern Planters in the Civil War and Reconstruction*. New York: W. W. Norton, 1977.

Robertson, James I. *Soldiers Blue and Gray*. Columbia: University of South Carolina Press, 1988.

Roland, Charles P. *An American Iliad: The Story of the Civil War*. 2nd ed. New York: McGraw-Hill, 2002.

Rose, Willie Lee. *Rehearsal for Reconstruction: The Port Royal Experiment*. Indianapolis: Bobbs-Merrill, 1964.

Rubin, Anne Sarah. *A Shattered Nation: The Rise and Fall of the Confederacy, 1861–1868*. Chapel Hill: University of North Carolina Press, 2005.

Sauers, Richard A. *The Burnside Expedition in North Carolina: A Succession of Honorable Victories*. Dayton, Ohio: Morningside House, 1996.

Saville, Julie. *The Work of Reconstruction: From Slave to Wage Laborer in South Carolina, 1860–1870*. Cambridge: Cambridge University Press, 1996.

Schweninger, Loren, and John Hope Franklin. *Runaway Slaves: Rebels on the Plantation*. New York: Oxford University Press, 1999.

Shaffer, Donald R. *After the Glory: The Struggles of Black Civil War Veterans*. Lawrence: University Press of Kansas, 2004.

Sharpe, Bill. *A New Geography of North Carolina*. Raleigh: Sharpe Publishing Co., 1954.

Silber, Nina. *The Romance of Reunion: Northerners and the South, 1865–1900*. Chapel Hill: University of North Carolina Press, 1993.

Sitterson, J. Carlyle. *The Secession Movement in North Carolina*. Chapel Hill: University of North Carolina Press, 1939.

Smith, John David, ed. *Black Soldiers in Blue: African American Troops in the Civil War Era*. Chapel Hill: University of North Carolina Press, 2002.

Spierenburg, Pieter, ed. *Men and Violence: Gender, Honor, and Rituals in Modern Europe and America*. Columbus: Ohio State University Press, 1998.

Storey, Margaret M. *Loyalty and Loss: Alabama's Unionists in the Civil War and Reconstruction*. Baton Rouge: Louisiana State University Press, 2004.

Sutherland, Daniel E., ed. *Guerrillas, Unionists, and Violence on the Confederate Home Front*. Fayetteville: University of Arkansas Press, 1999.

———. *Seasons of War: The Ordeal of a Confederate Community, 1861–1865*. New York: Free Press, 1995.

Swint, Henry Lee. *The Northern Teacher in the South, 1862–1870*. New York: Octagon Books, 1967.

Tatum, Georgia Lee. *Disloyalty in the Confederacy*. Chapel Hill: University of North Carolina Press, 1934.

Taylor, Amy Murrell. *The Divided Family in Civil War America*. Chapel Hill: University of North Carolina Press, 2005.

Thomas, Gerald. *Divided Allegiances: Bertie County in the Civil War*. Raleigh: North Carolina Historical Publications, 1996.

Turner, J. Kelly, and John L. Bridgers. *History of Edgecombe County, North Carolina*. Raleigh: Edwards and Broughton Printing Co., 1920.

Watson, Alan D. *A History of New Bern and Craven County*. New Bern: Tryon Palace Commission, 1987.

Weiner, Marli. *Mistresses and Slaves: Plantation Women in South Carolina, 1830–1880*. Urbana: University of Illinois Press, 1998.

Whites, LeeAnn, and Alecia P. Long, eds. *Occupied Women: Gender, Military Occupation, and the American Civil War*. Baton Rouge: Louisiana State University Press, 2009.

Williams, Andrea Heather. *Self-Taught: African American Education in Slavery and Freedom*. Chapel Hill: University of North Carolina Press, 2005.

Williams, L. G. *A Place for Theodore: The Murder of Dr. Theodore Parkman, Boston, Massachusetts & Whitehall, North Carolina: A True Story*. Greenville, N.C.: Holly Two Leaves Press, 1997.

Wilson, Keith P. *Campfires of Freedom: The Camp Life of Black Soldiers during the Civil War*. Kent, Ohio: Kent State University Press, 2002.

Wilson, Mamré Marsh. *A Researcher's Journal: Beaufort, NC & the Civil War*. Beaufort: M. M. Wilson, 1999.

Wong, Leonard, et al. *Why They Fight: Combat Motivation in the Iraq War*. Carlisle, Pa.: Strategic Studies Institute, Army War College, 2003.

Wright, Gavin. *The Political Economy of the Cotton South: Households, Markets, and Wealth in the Nineteenth Century*. New York: W. W. Norton, 1978.

Wyatt-Brown, Bertram. *Southern Honor: Ethics and Behavior in the Old South*. New York: Oxford University Press, 1982.

Articles

Ash, Stephen V. "Poor Whites in the Occupied South, 1861–1865." *Journal of Southern History* 57 (February 1991): 39–62.

Auman, William T. "Neighbor against Neighbor: The Inner Civil War in the Randolph County Area of Confederate North Carolina." *North Carolina Historical Review* 61 (January 1984): 59–92.

Auman, William T., and David D. Scarboro. "The Heroes of America in Civil War North Carolina." *North Carolina Historical Review* 66 (January 1989): 61–86; 67 (April 1989): 179–210.

Barry, Richard S. "Fort Macon: Its History." *North Carolina Historical Review* 27 (April 1950): 163–77.

Blair, Dan. "'One Good Port': Beaufort Harbor, North Carolina, 1863–1864." *North Carolina Historical Review* 79 (July 2002): 301–26.

Branch, Paul. "Fort Macon as a Shelter for Buffaloes." *Ramparts* (Spring 1997), ⟨http://www.clis.com/friends/bufffaloes.htm⟩.

Brooks, Charles E. "The Social and Cultural Dynamics of Soldiering in Hood's Texas Brigade." *Journal of Southern History* 67 (August 2001): 535–72.

Browning, Judkin. "Foundations of Sand: Evaluating the Historical Assessments of Antebellum Southern White Unity." *Gulf South Historical Review* 19 (Spring 2004): 6–38.

———. "'Little-souled Mercenaries?' The Buffaloes of Eastern North Carolina during the Civil War." *North Carolina Historical Review* 77 (July 2000): 337–63.

———. "Removing the Mask of Nationality: Unionism, Racism, and Federal Military Occupation in North Carolina, 1862–1865." *Journal of Southern History* 71 (August 2005): 589–620.

Butchart, Ronald E. "Perspectives on Gender, Race, Calling, and Commitment in Nineteenth-Century America: A Collective Biography of the Teachers of the Freedpeople, 1862–1875." *Vitae Scholastica* 13 (Spring 1994): 15–32.

———. "Remapping Racial Boundaries: Teachers as Border Police and Boundary Transgressors in Post-Emancipation Black Education, USA, 1861–1876." *Paedagogica Historica: International Journal of the History of Education* 43 (February 2007): 61–78.

Carp, Benjamin L. "Nations of American Rebels: Understanding Nationalism in Revolutionary North America and the Civil War South." *Civil War History* 48 (March 2002): 5–33.

Cecere, David A. "Carrying the Home Front to War: Soldiers, Race, and New England Culture during the Civil War." In *Union Soldiers and the Northern Home Front: Wartime Experiences and Postwar Adjustments*, edited by Paul A. Cimbala and Randall M. Miller, 293–323. New York: Fordham University Press, 2002.

Collins, Donald E. "War Crime or Justice? General George Pickett and the Mass Execution of Deserters in Civil War Kinston, North Carolina." In *The Art of Command in the Civil War*, edited by Steven E. Woodworth, 50–83. Lincoln: University of Nebraska Press, 1998.

Crawford, Martin. "Confederate Volunteering and Enlistment in Ashe County, North Carolina, 1861–1862." *Civil War History* 37 (March 1991): 29–50.

Crittenden, Charles Christopher. "Overland Travel and Transportation in North Carolina, 1763–1789." *North Carolina Historical Review* 8 (July 1931): 239–57.

———. "The Seacoast in North Carolina History, 1763–1789." *North Carolina Historical Review* 7 (October 1930): 433–42.

Delaney, Norman C. "Charles Henry Foster and the Unionists of Eastern North Carolina." *North Carolina Historical Review* 37 (July 1960): 348–66.

Dill, Alonzo Thomas. "Eighteenth Century New Bern: A History of the Town and Craven County, 1700–1800: Political and Commercial Rise of New Bern." *North Carolina Historical Review* 23 (January 1946): 47–78.

Farnham, Thomas J., and Francis P. King. "'The March of the Destroyer': The New Bern Yellow Fever Epidemic of 1864." *North Carolina Historical Review* 73 (October 1996): 435–83.

Fen, Sing-Nan. "Notes on the Education of Negroes in North Carolina during the Civil War." *Journal of Negro Education* 36 (Winter 1967): 24–31.

Frazier, Donald Shaw. "'Out of Stinking Distance.'" In *Guerrillas, Unionists, and Violence on the Confederate Home Front*, edited by Daniel E. Sutherland, 151–70. Fayetteville: University of Arkansas Press, 1999.

Gal, Reuven. "Unit Morale: From a Theoretical Puzzle to an Empirical Illustration — An Israeli Example." *Journal of Applied Social Psychology* 16 (June 1986): 549–64.

Gal, Reuven, and Frederick J. Manning. "Morale and Its Components: A Cross-National Comparison." *Journal of Applied Social Psychology* 17 (April 1987): 369–91.

Gerteis, Louis S. "'A Friend of the Enemy': Federal Efforts to Suppress Disloyalty in St. Louis during the Civil War." *Missouri Historical Review* 96 (April 2002): 165–87.

Gordon, Lesley J. "'In Time of War': Unionists Hanged in Kinston, North Carolina, February 1864." In *Guerrillas, Unionists, and Violence on the Confederate Home Front*, edited by Daniel E. Sutherland, 45–58. Fayetteville: University of Arkansas Press, 1999.

Guetzkow, Harold. "Multiple Loyalties: Theoretical Approach to a Problem in International Organization." Princeton, N.J.: Center for Research on World Political Institutions, 1955.

Harsh, Joseph L. "Lincoln's Tarnished Brass: Conservative Strategies and the Attempt to Fight the Early Civil War as a Limited War." In *The Confederate High Command & Related Topics: Themes in Honor of T. Harry Williams*, edited by Roman J. Heleniak and Lawrence L. Hewitt, 121–41. Shippensburg, Pa.: White Mane Publishing, 1988.

Hocking, William Ernest. "The Nature of Morale." *American Journal of Sociology* 47 (November 1941): 302–20.

Honey, Michael K. "War within the Confederacy: White Unionists of North Carolina." *Prologue* 18 (Summer 1986): 74–93.

Howard, Victor B. "John Brown's Raid at Harpers Ferry and the Sectional Crisis in North Carolina." *North Carolina Historical Review* 55 (October 1978): 396–420.

"Internal Improvements in North Carolina." *North American Review* 12 (January 1821): 16–38.

Janda, Lance. "Shutting the Gates of Mercy: The American Origins of Total War, 1860–1880." *Journal of Military History* 59 (January 1995): 7–26.

Jeffrey, Thomas E. "Internal Improvements and Political Parties in Antebellum North Carolina." *North Carolina Historical Review* 55 (April 1978): 11–56.

Logue, Larry M. "Who Joined the Confederate Army? Soldiers, Civilians, and Communities in Mississippi." *Journal of Social History* 26 (Fall 1993): 611–23.

Massey, Mary E. "Confederate Refugees in North Carolina." *North Carolina Historical Review* 40 (April 1963): 158–82.

McKenzie, Robert Tracy. "Prudent Silence and Strict Neutrality: The Parameters of Unionism in Parson Brownlow's Knoxville, 1860–1863." In *Enemies of the Country: New Perspectives on Unionists in the Civil War South*, edited by John C. Inscoe and Robert C. Kenzer, 73–96. Athens: University of Georgia Press, 2001.

McKinney, Gordon B. "Layers of Loyalty: Confederate Nationalism and Amnesty Letters from Western North Carolina." *Civil War History* 51 (March 2005): 5–22.

Morgan, William Stuart, III. "The Commerce of a Southern Port, New Bern, North Carolina, 1783–1789." *American Neptune* 49 (Spring 1989): 77–90.

Neely, Mark E., Jr. "Was the Civil War a Total War?" *Civil War History* 37 (March 1991): 5–28.

Paul, Charles Livingston. "Colonial Beaufort." *North Carolina Historical Review* 42 (April 1965): 139–52.

Potter, David M. "The Historian's Use of Nationalism and Vice Versa." In *The South and the Sectional Conflict*, edited by David M. Potter, 34–83. Baton Rouge: Louisiana State University Press, 1968.

Rable, George C. "'Missing in Action': Women of the Confederacy." In *Divided Houses: Gender and the Civil War*, edited by Catherine Clinton and Nina Silber, 134–46. New York: Oxford University Press, 1992.

Sharpe, Bill. "Completely Coastal Carteret." *The State* 21 (June 27, 1953): 3–5, 33–38.

Silber, Nina. "A Compound of Wonderful Potency." In *The War Was You and Me: Civilians in the American Civil War*, edited by Joan E. Cashin, 35–59. Princeton, N.J.: Princeton University Press, 2002.

Small, Sandra E. "The Yankee Schoolmarm in Freedmen's Schools: An Analysis of Attitudes." *Journal of Southern History* 45 (August 1979): 381–402.

Smithers, Leslie. "Profit and Corruption in Civil War Natchez: A Case History of Union Occupation Government." *Journal of Mississippi History* 64 (Winter 2002): 17–32.

Span, Christopher M. "'I Must Learn Now or Not at All': Social and Cultural Capital in the Education Initiatives of Formerly Enslaved African Americans in Mississippi, 1862–1869." *Journal of African American History* 87, no. 2 (2002): 196–222.

Storey, Margaret M. "Civil War Unionists and the Political Culture of Loyalty in Alabama." *Journal of Southern History* 69 (February 2003): 71–106.

Urwin, Gregory J. W. "United States Colored Troops." In *Encyclopedia of the American Civil War: A Political, Social, and Military History*, edited by David S. Heidler and Jeanne T. Heidler. 5 vols. Santa Barbara, Calif.: ABC-CLIO Press, 2000.

Warner, Nathaniel. "The Morale of Troops on Occupation Duty." *American Journal of Psychiatry* 102 (May 1946): 749–57.

"Wild Waterways: North Carolina Rivers." *ExplorNet's Trailblazer Magazine* (Spring 2000), ⟨http://www.trailblazermagazine.com/February00/html/features_2.htm⟩.

Woodward, C. Vann. "Equality: The Deferred Commitment." In *The Burden of Southern History*. Edited by C. Vann Woodward. 3rd ed. Baton Rouge: Louisiana State University Press, 1993.

Dissertations and Theses

Burke, Kenneth E., Jr. "The History of Portsmouth, North Carolina, from Its Founding in 1753 to Its Evacuation in the Face of Federal forces in 1861." M.A. thesis, University of Richmond, 1958.

Drake, Richard Bryant. "The American Missionary Association and the Southern Negro, 1861–1880." Ph.D. dissertation, Emory University, 1957.

Iobst, Richard. "North Carolina Mobilizes: Nine Crucial Months, December 1860–August 1861." Ph.D. dissertation, University of North Carolina at Chapel Hill, 1968.

Jones, Maxine D. "'A Glorious Work': The American Missionary Association and Black North Carolinians, 1863–1880." Ph.D. dissertation, Florida State University, 1982.

Luster, John Michael. "Help Me to Raise Them: The Menhaden Chanteymen of Beaufort, North Carolina." Ph.D. dissertation, University of Pennsylvania, 1994.

Marshall, Anne E. "'A Strange Conclusion to a Triumphant War': Memory, Identity and the Creation of a Confederate Kentucky." Ph.D. dissertation, University of Georgia, 2004.

Meekins, Alex Christopher. "Caught between Scylla and Charybdis: The Civil War in Northeastern North Carolina." M.A. thesis, North Carolina State University, 2001.

Reilly, Stephen Edward. "Reconstruction through Regeneration: Horace James' Work with the Blacks for Social Reform in North Carolina, 1862–1867." Ph.D. dissertation, Duke University, 1983.

Seidule, James Tyrus. "Morale in the American Expeditionary Forces during World War I." Ph.D. dissertation, Ohio State University, 1997.

Wolfe, Allis. "Women Who Dared: Northern Teachers of the Southern Freedmen, 1862–1872." Ph.D. dissertation, City University of New York, 1982.

Barbour, Mary, 87

Barlow, Joseph, 64, 86, 139, 143, 144, 146, 147, 171

Bartlett, Edward J., 100, 139, 143, 171

Baynes, John, 144

Beals, H. S., 82, 83, 109

Beaufort, N.C.: African American church threatened in, 171; African American conflicts with whites in, 90; African American enlistments in, 96, 169; African Americans living in, 168; African American population in, 88; as African American religious center, 117; African Americans work for Union forces in, 93; AMA schools in, 108; AMA teachers in, 103, 108; antebellum population of, 12; beating of African Americans in, 81; business returns to, 64; captured by Union forces, 56, 59–60; celebration of firing on Fort Sumter in, 30; complaints by Union soldiers of African Americans in, 123; Confederate enlistments in, 32, 36; Confederate reinforcements arrive in, 42–43; defensive preparations of, 45; depredations in, 84; development of, 9; early description of, 16; female spy arrested in, 159–60; guerrilla attacks against, 135; harbor of, 11, 17; hostility toward African Americans in, 169; illegal liquor sales in, 151; inefficiency of teachers in, 112; map of, 10; naval stores industry in, 151; postwar, 172–76, 178; prepares for Union attack, 41; prostitutes in, 142; railroad controversy in, 17; reaction to Union troops' arrival in, 149; as refuge for blockading ships, 126; residents abandon Confederate army, 70; resistance by female population of, 75; as resort area, 18, 19; during Revolution, 12; school burned in, 171; settlement of, 11; slaves escape to, 88; threatened with bombardment, 60, 62; trade on waterways near, 154; trade prohibitions in, 153; trade welcomed in, 150; travel difficulties from, 11;

Union forces fear attack in, 89; Unionist merchants ostracized in, 173–75; Unionists in, 48, 50, 63, 64; Union meetings in, 23–24, 33, 50, 70; Union organizations in, 72; Union soldiers demoralized in, 144; Union soldiers seize property in, 66–68; visited by northern journalist after war, 1; white attitudes toward Union army in, 172; yellow fever in, 111

Beaufort County, N.C., 173

Beaufort Harbor Guards, 33

Beauregard Rifles, 30, 31

Beecher, Henry Ward, 107

Bell, Daniel, 161

Bell, David W., 162

Bell, John, 22

Bell, Joseph A., 193 (n. 51)

Bell, Rufus W., 159, 176

Benevolent societies: conflicts between, 116–17; number of, 205 (n. 28); preconceptions of African Americans by members of, 119–20; rejected by poor whites, 171; varieties of, 117

Blair, William A., 35

Bloodgood, Joseph, 61

Bogue Banks (North Carolina), 9, 60

Bogue Island (North Carolina), 93, 154

Boston, Mass., 16, 68, 107, 116, 117, 125

Boston Society, 117

Branch, Lawrence O'Bryan, 43, 44, 45, 49, 50, 51, 56

Branch, Paul, 181

Bray, Nicholas, 79, 88

Breckinridge, John C., 22

Bridgers, John L., 41

Briggs, William, 113, 114, 117

Brown, John, 21, 96

Brownlow, William "Parson," 47

Bryan, Edward K., 30

Bryan, Henry R., 31

Bryan, James West, 166

Bryan, Mary Norcott, 55, 56

Buchanan, James, 20, 22

Buffaloes, 72, 163, 164, 165, 173, 197 (n. 41)

Core Creek (North Carolina), 162

Covert, Henry, 48, 49

Crasson, Hannah, 100

Craton, Marshall D., 39

Craven County, N.C.: African American enlistments in, 99; commerce in, 12, 16; Confederate soldiers return to, 175; demographics of soldiers from, 37, 74; enlistments into Confederate army in, 30–32; enlistments into Union army in, 72–74; evictions from, 158; in no-man's-land, 63–64; politics in, 3, 9, 19–20; prepares for abolitionist attack, 21; railroad controversy in, 16–17; residents aid Union army, 71; rumors of slave rebellions in, 14, 15; slavery in, 12–16; soldiers abandon Confederate army, 71; support for secession in, 23, 24; Unionist attitudes in, 20, 22, 46–48, 64–66; votes in 1860 election, 22

Croatoan Line, 51

Croome, Caroline E., 108

Danvers, Mass., 142

Davenport, H. K., 133

Davis, Anson, 174

Davis, James, 69, 70

Davis, Jefferson, 153

Davis, Joel Henry: accepts secession, 68; beats African American woman, 81, 82, 90; becomes prominent Unionist, 70; death of, 216 (n. 57); as merchant, 199 (n. 1); postwar fate of, 174; supports Confederacy, 69; takes oath of allegiance, 70

Davis, Joel Henry, Jr., 69, 70, 216 (n. 57)

Davis, Sutton, 85

Davis Island (North Carolina), 85

Day, Benjamin, 125, 147

Day, John W., 70

Derby, William, 89

Deserters, 175; in Beaufort, 163; from Carteret County, 70; coerced into Union army, 163; executed, 137; flee to New Bern, 138; from Fort Macon, 61

Dickinson, Daniel, 162

Dickinson, William H., 162

Disosway, Israel, 130, 207 (n. 17)

Disosway, Jane, 130, 207 (n. 17)

Douglas, Stephen A., 21, 22

Drake, Richard, 205 (n. 28)

Draper, William, 84

Driver, Stephen, 141

DuBois, W. E. B., 203 (n. 48)

Duncan, Thomas, 152

Duren, Charles, 125, 147, 169

Dyer, Thomas G., 185 (n. 5)

Eastmond, Oscar, 173

Edelstein, David, 186 (n. 8)

Edenton, N.C., 11

Edgecombe County, N.C., 41, 51, 85

Edmondston, Catherine Ann Devereux, 15, 23

Education: African American attempts to acquire, 100–104; difficulties associated with, 102; poor white desires for, 109–10; white opposition to, 110

Education Commission of Boston, 117

Edwards, John, 16

Ellis, Elijah W., 65, 66, 154

Ellis, John W., 21, 22, 24, 36, 37; death of, 39, 42; fears coercion of southern states, 27; organized state's defenses, 39–40

Elm City Rifles (also Elm City Cadets), 46; composition of, 38; formed, 21, 29; joins Confederate service, 31

Emancipation Proclamation: African American understanding of, 88–89; denounced by Stanly, 167; emboldens African Americans, 81; endorses enlistment of African American troops, 202 (n. 40); issued by Lincoln, 80, 178; North Carolina not exempted from, 88, 200 (n. 19); Union soldier support for, 147

Emmerton, James, 85, 86

Hammond General Hospital (Beaufort), 196 (n. 27)

Hardison, Cassandra, 130

Hardison, Council, 46

Hardison, Elijah, 130

Hardison, Eliza, 130

Hardison, Gabriel, 46

Harker's Island (North Carolina), 11

Harris, George W., 87

Hartford Convention, 146

Harvard College, 125, 139

Hatteras, 40, 72, 112

Hawkins, Rush, 42

Hedrick, John A.: arrives in Beaufort, 64; befriends James Rumley, 68; comments on evictions from Beaufort, 158; comments on self-interest of local traders, 154; describes suicide of Union officer, 140; desires removal of African Americans, 169; discusses coercion of Confederate deserters, 163; discusses freedom of African Americans, 168; dislikes trade restrictions, 153; doubts loyalty in region, 149; hires local man as assistant, 70; opposes Charles Henry Foster, 167; racist attitudes of, 123; seizes illegal liquor, 151; takes residence in Ocean House, 67

Herring's Artillery, 36, 43

Hill, Daniel Harvey, 43, 44, 45, 49, 50, 157

Hill, Isaac, 48, 72

Hocking, William E., 211 (n. 49)

Holcomb, Alfred, 131, 132, 133, 138, 139, 141

Holden, William Woods, 18

Hosmer, Susan A., 105, 106, 109, 117, 203 (n. 1)

Howard, Caroline, 77

Howe, Miss, 113

Hubbard, Charles, 119

Huggins, Alex, 88

Hughes, Edward, 90

Hunt, Ebenezer, 142, 143

Hunt, Samuel C., 141

Hurtt, Daniel W., 31

Hyde County, N.C., 173

Jackson, William H., 144

James, Horace: African American settlement named after, 93; attempts to acquire quality teachers for region, 102, 108, 116; censured, 114; complains of incompetent teachers, 114, 116; complaints against AMA authorities to, 112; conducts census of African Americans in eastern North Carolina, 88; describes African American employment, 93, 95–96; describes dangers facing African Americans, 91; describes intelligence of African American children, 103; dispenses donations to freedpeople, 117; hears African American complaints, 100, 116; opposes African American teachers, 116; pictured, 115; praises teachers, 111; prefers New England methods, 120; recognizes legal freedom of slaves, 89; reports on need for ministers, 118; reports on skilled African Americans in New Bern, 92; views African Americans more favorably than local whites, 169–70; wants "purified" Union, 90

James, Mrs. Horace, 114

James City, N.C., 93

Jenkins, George W., 106

Jewett, George, 128, 129

Jim Crow, 182

Johnson, Andrew, 175

Jones, John Richter, 146

Jones County, N.C., 47, 87

Jourdan, James, 163

Kinnegay, William, 14

Kinsey, Job L., 35

Kinsley, Edward W., 97, 98

Kinston, N.C., 17, 71, 91; executions at, 164, 165, 166; Union expedition to, 86, 155

Kirwan, Thomas, 156

Kruman, Marc W., 19

Ladd, Dexter B., 128, 129, 131, 140

Lane, James S., 31, 43

Macon, 61; departs Beaufort with company, 34–35; described by Union soldiers, 128–29; as editor of *Union Banner*, 22, 33; military company of, 49, 50; organizes Confederate military company, 33–34; postwar fate of, 175; returns with company, 41

Poor whites, 5, 14, 16; and education, 109, 110; enlist in Union army, 73–74; reject benevolent societies, 171; Union authorities disapprove of, 169–71; Union soldiers describe, 128, 129

Porte Crayon, 126, 207 (n. 10)

Portsmouth, N.C., 10, 76, 136, 158, 159

Quick, Charles B., 144

Quinn, David S., 162

Rable, George, 198 (n. 50)

Raleigh, N.C., 15, 27, 41, 43, 87

Raleigh, Sir Walter, 9

Ramsey, Isaac, 152, 175, 176

Reconstruction, 178, 181, 182

Reid, Whitelaw, 178

Reynolds, David P., 143

Rhode Island units: 4th Regiment Infantry, 60, 149

Rieger, Henry, 69, 70, 174, 199 (n. 1), 216 (n. 57); beats African American woman, 81, 82, 90

Roanoke Island (North Carolina), 32, 50, 114, 120, 126

Roberson, Benjamin L., 160

Roberts, David W., 197 (n. 40)

Roberts, Isaac N., 132

Roberts, James B., 71

Roberts, Richard, 197 (n. 40)

Rodman, N.Y., 128

Rowe, William, 35

Rubin, Anne Sarah, 3, 4

Ruffin, Thomas, 22

Rumley, James: anger at African American enlistment, 96, 169; believes slaves are content, 83; complains of African American indifference to whites, 89; complains of legal rights for African Americans, 168; complains of Union employment of African Americans, 92; denounces black confiscation of white property, 84; discusses Union recruitment tactics, 73; disdains occupation, 80; granted trade pass by Stanly, 152; keeps outrage private, 68; meets with John G. Parke, 60; pictured, 170; postwar fate of, 175; talks with Stanly, 77

Rutherford County, N.C., 85

Santo Domingo, 14, 96

Sawyer, Henry, 73

Scott, George W., 61

Scott, Winfield, 47

Sea Islands (South Carolina), 212 (n. 5)

Secession convention: of North Carolina, 23, 24; of Virginia, 65

Segregation, 182

Sempler, Owen, 138

Seward, William Henry, 124

Sherman, William, 125, 180

Silber, Nina, 107

Simpson, Clifford, 35

Singleton, William Henry, 97, 100

Slaves: attempts to acquire education during slavery, 101–6, 203 (n. 48); dig fortifications, 44; duties in Carteret County, 13; duties in Craven County, 13; employed by Burnside, 77; escape, 14, 85–90; exposure to outside influences, 13; fears of rebellion of, 14; rejoice at Union arrival, 83, 84; WPA interviews of, 100. *See also* African Americans

Smith, Elijah S., 172

Smith, Elizabeth Oakes, 172

Smith, Haney, 138, 198 (n. 52)

Smyrna, N.C., 85

Snowdon, Lizzie, 142

Southbridge, Mass., 128

Southern Claims Commission, 160, 162, 172, 192 (n. 44)

chase alcohol, 151; marriage of, 130; morale of, 137–44; motivations for enlisting, 124–25; oppose reenlisting, 143; oppose slavery, 146–47; and physical attacks on whites, 155; plunder New Bern, 57–58; pride in pillaging prowess of, 157; racist attitudes of, 123, 130–32, 169; reactions to southern women, 129–30; response to black religion, 119; save New Bern from fire, 58; strong sense of duty of, 144–48; support black suffrage, 171; take retaliatory actions against guerrillas, 138; teach African Americans, 102–3; unscrupulous trade practices of, 151; views of black enlistments, 133–34; views of New Bern, 59; want to leave North Carolina, 171

U.S. Sanitary Commission, 169

U.S. Treasury Department, 64, 67, 68, 70, 151, 153, 165

University of North Carolina, 87

Vance, Zebulon B., 41, 42, 43, 51, 52; comments on Confederate soldiers' depredations, 156; narrowly escapes capture, 56–57

Vance, Mrs. Zebulon B., 49

Verrazano, Giovanni da, 9

Vinson, John Rogers, 16

Walcott, Charles, 141

Walker, David, 14

Walker, William Augustus, 123, 131

Wallace, Robert, 158, 159

Ward, Andrew, 93

Warner, Nathaniel, 211 (n. 49)

Washington, Lewis, 97

Washington, Mary, 91, 97

Washington, N.C., 130

Welles, Gideon, 124

Wellington, Henry, 103

Wesson, Hale, 133, 135, 136

West Newton, Mass., 108

Weston, George H., 139

West Point, 41, 43, 50–51, 60, 87

Wetherington, Riley, 157

Whipple, George, 108, 111, 113, 116

Whitby, Emeline, 89

Whitby, James, 89

White, Henry, 124

White, Moses J., 51, 59, 60, 61

Whitehurst, D. W., 60, 66

Whitehurst, Elijah, 45, 46

Whitehurst, Samuel, 45

Whitford, John D., 20, 188 (n. 38)

Whitford, John N., 31, 43

Whitty, Joseph, 32, 43, 72

Wild, Edward, 99, 134

Williams, James, 138

Williams, Mary S., 108

Williams, Toby, 90

Willis, Charles P., 61

Willis, Martin, 61

Willoughby, William Augustus, 142

Wilmington, N.C., 11, 16, 61, 108

Wilmington-Weldon Railroad, 16

Witherington, Solomon, 66, 153, 154

Wolf, John B., 174

Wood, Josiah, 145

Worcester, Mass., 88

Works Progress Administration, slave interviews of, 100

Yale College, 103

Young Men's Christian Association, 77

975.6192 BRO
Shifting loyalties : the
union occupation of easte
Browning, Judkin.

MAR 2 1 2011

McDowell County Public Library
90 West Court Street
Marion, NC 28752